Personal Groupings, Award Documents and Ephemera of

Rommel's Afrikakorps

Die Wehrmacht

HERAUSGEGEBEN VOM OBERKOMMANDO DER WEHRMAC

6. Jahrgang · Nummer 26 · Berlin, den 16. Dezember
Einzelpreis 25 Rpf und Bestellgeld · Erscheint vierzehnt

Sprung nach Tu

(Seite 3 bis 6 Bild- und Textbe
von Kriegsberichter Gert Habed
über den Kampf in Tunes

Personal Groupings, Award Documents and Ephemera of

Rommel's Afrikakorps

Army • Luftwaffe • Kriegsmarine

Robert Kurtz

Schiffer Military History
Atglen, PA

ACKNOWLEDGEMENTS

The publisher wishes to thank David Bunch and John Keener who generously opened their collections for this book, and who graciously gave of their time, expertise, and hospitality. Their participation and enthusiasm made this book possible.

Thanks to Kristian Anderson, Gary Armitage, Alan Beadle, David E. Bunch, Sr., Monty Cheney, G.R. Egilz, Klaus-Peter Emig, Ken Ettin, Lou Fielack, Daniel Fisher, Malcolm Fisher, D. Göre, *Ing*., Russ Hamilton, Jack Hatter, Ralph Heinz, Charlie Hinz, John Hodgin, Raoul Ingröch, John J.F. Kelly, Dick Lafayette, E.M.B. Landin, Mick Linz, Rich Long, Brian Maederer, Chris Mason, Dal McGuirk, Andy Merkle, Chris Mybro, Tom O'Maley, Len Panneri, Terry Patton, Bernd Peitz, George Petersen, Jim Peterson, Brana Radovic, Robert Ruzzier, Toomas Salazar, Gary Schaefer, Willi Schumacher, Rob Settel, Bill Shea, Roger Sodanowicz, Pat Spayd, Ramsey Speer, Dennis Todd, Gus Villarreal, Helmut Weitze, Gilbert White, Gary Wilkins, Ron Wolin, and Charles Woolley for their much appreciated support. Thanks to David Johnston for translating select documents from the original German, Rod Oakland for translating select documents from the original Indian and Arabic, and to Ann Nybor for translating select documents from the original French.

Book design and photography by Robert Biondi.

Library of Congress Catalog Number: 2004104166.

Printed in China.
ISBN: 0-7643-2113-7

We are always looking for people to write books on new and related subjects. If you have an idea for a book, please contact us at the address below.

Published by Schiffer Publishing Ltd.
4880 Lower Valley Road
Atglen, PA 19310
Phone: (610) 593-1777
FAX: (610) 593-2002
E-mail: Info@schifferbooks.com.
Visit our web site at: www.schifferbooks.com
Please write for a free catalog.
This book may be purchased from the publisher.
Please include $3.95 postage.
Try your bookstore first.

In Europe, Schiffer books are distributed by:
Bushwood Books
6 Marksbury Ave.
Kew Gardens
Surrey TW9 4JF
England
Phone: 44 (0)20 8392-8585
FAX: 44 (0)20 8392-9876
E-mail: Bushwd@aol.com.
Free postage in the UK. Europe: air mail at cost.
Try your bookstore first.

Contents

Introduction

Deutsches Afrikakorps. The name alone conjures up images of soldiers far away from home enduring the greatest hardships of a world at war in a merciless desert terrain. Serving in this renowned force and earning the honor of wearing the AFRIKA cufftitle or tropical uniform was highly coveted by every German soldier. Although the *Afrikakorps* was a small force, its men were seasoned veterans and confident in battle. It eventually took the weight of the British Empire and powerful American war machine to seal their fate in May 1943.

Of course, one cannot speak of the *Afrikakorps* without thinking of its illustrious commander, Erwin Rommel. Indeed, it was "The Desert Fox" that made the *Afrikakorps*. He expected a lot from his men and became the heartbeat of the *Afrikakorps* that earned him both respect on the battlefield and admiration back home. Despite being constantly outnumbered and deprived of even the most basic supplies, the *Afrikakorps* enjoyed the respect of their enemies and in the heat of battle, offered their respect in return. This is how the legend of the *Afrikakorps* was born and is honored today in the annals of history.

Collecting German tropical militaria from World War II helps bring this mystique back to life! Indeed, the unique aura of the *Afrikakorps* survives today with what has been preserved and superbly documented for all to enjoy in this two volume set. As collectors, our interests have evolved into a deep passion as we attempt to preserve the remaining pieces of *Afrikakorps* memorabilia to survive the war.

Because the Germans were involved in several tropical areas during the war, we have gathered a wide array of German tropical items that were used by the three respective German *Wehrmacht* services: *Heer*/Army, *Luftwaffe*, and *Kriegsmarine*. Although the *Waffen-SS* was not engaged in the North African theatre, these units were involved in several other tropical climates such as Italy and Greece so several period examples of typical *Waffen-SS* tropical issue clothing are included.

Most of what you will see in these books are war trophies and battlefield mementos sent home by the conquering Allies in Africa and other parts of the Mediterranean theatre of operations. When the war ended, many German *Afrikaner* veterans simply discarded their old uniforms as they began rebuilding their lives. Therefore, what little German tropical memorabilia remaining today is of great interest to military collectors, hobbyists and historians alike!

Of course, when you think of the *Afrikakorps* you must envision the famous tropical visored field cap. More than anything else, this cap became synonymous with the *Afrikakorps* and was a badge of honor to the men that wore them. In volume one, we've assembled over forty of these exceptional field caps, including eleven extremely rare officer caps. To put into perspective the rarity of tropical officer field caps, only four out of every one-hundred factory made field caps were produced with officer's aluminum piping. Another little known fact about the *Afrikakorps* field cap is that with its extended visor and grommet/ventilation holes, these caps became a model in redesigning the modern American baseball cap after the war!

For German military document collectors this volume has a treasure trove of rare *Afrikakorps* related award documents, propaganda leaflets, *Soldbuchs*, *Wehrpass* and Remembrance/Death cards. This book is quite interesting in that it vividly reminds us of the realities of war through the faces, names, places and events identified. Among the many rare documents you will see both Allied and German/Italian propaganda leaflets, *Afrikakorps* field newspapers, and two field-made newsletters associated with the *Sonderverband 288* unit. We have also assembled several complete *Afrikakorps* veteran groupings and every known document variant of the AFRIKA cuffband and Italian-German Medal.

A primary focus of this endeavor is to share with you some of the rarest original *Afrikakorps* and German tropical militaria known to exist in private collections today. Practically anything "German tropical" is rare and highly sought after by militaria collectors and enthusiasts alike. Unfortunately, with the advent of exceptionally well made reproductions hitting the internet and trade shows every year, a second goal is to offer you high quality photographs of these German tropical war relics to help you make informed decisions when evaluating German tropical militaria.

It is our hope that you will enjoy these books as much as we did putting them together. Every tunic, cap, document, helmet, insignia and piece of equipment has been carefully photographed and described. For example, *Afrikakorps* enthusiasts, militaria collectors and modelers will see in vivid color the material factory variations that were inherent in the making of tropical uniforms, as well as the dramatic impact the harsh sun and constant washing had on most tropical attire. We have also gathered a breathtaking collection of *Luftwaffe* blue-gray tropical issue clothing and equipment. All of these artifacts survived the war to tell a tale expressed in this body of photographs.

The *Afrikakorps* and its commander have earned a respectable place in military history. The evolution of tropical attire worn by these ground troops, aviators and sailors is well documented herein. By focusing on the uniforms, equipment and men of the *Afrikakorps*, these books bring history closer to life as we carefully study the military garments and items they used. We hope this serves as an ongoing tribute to these valiant men as we strive to guard these remaining keepsakes for future generations to relish and remember.

David Bunch
April 2004

CHAPTER ONE

Personal Groupings

Any *Soldbuch* (pay book) or *Wehrpass* (military identification book) belonging to *Afrikakorps* soldiers and collected as souvenirs by Allied soldiers on North African battlefields are rarer today than pay books for the *Waffen-SS*, or for that matter any other branch of the *Wehrmacht*.

• • •

Extremely rare *Wehrpass* issued to *Oberpionier* Alois Opfolter. This soldier was assigned to the *3 Kompanie/Pionier Bataillon 200* of the *21st Panzer Division*. (David Bunch)

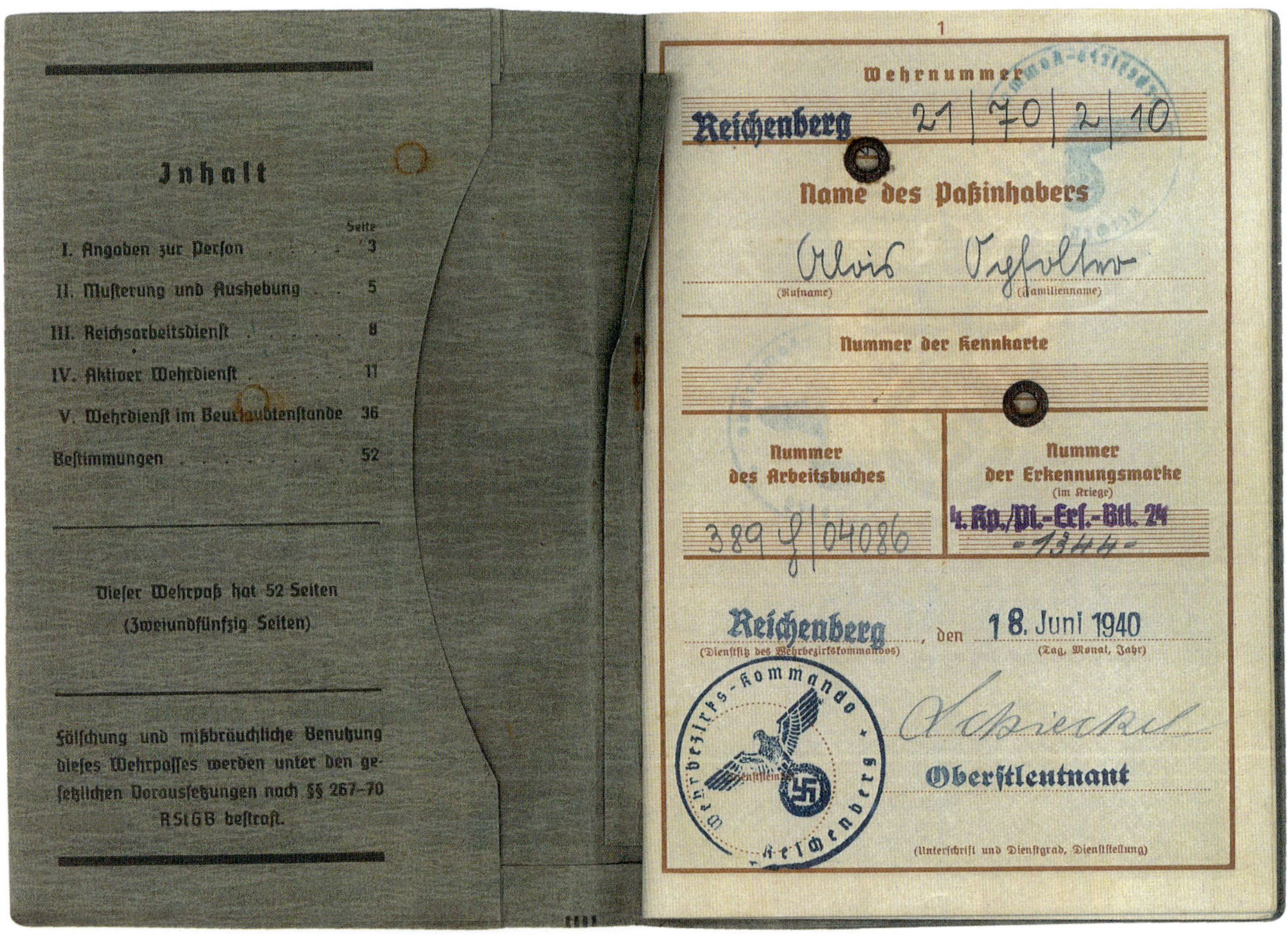

First page of *Wehrpass* indicating it was issued on June 18, 1940.

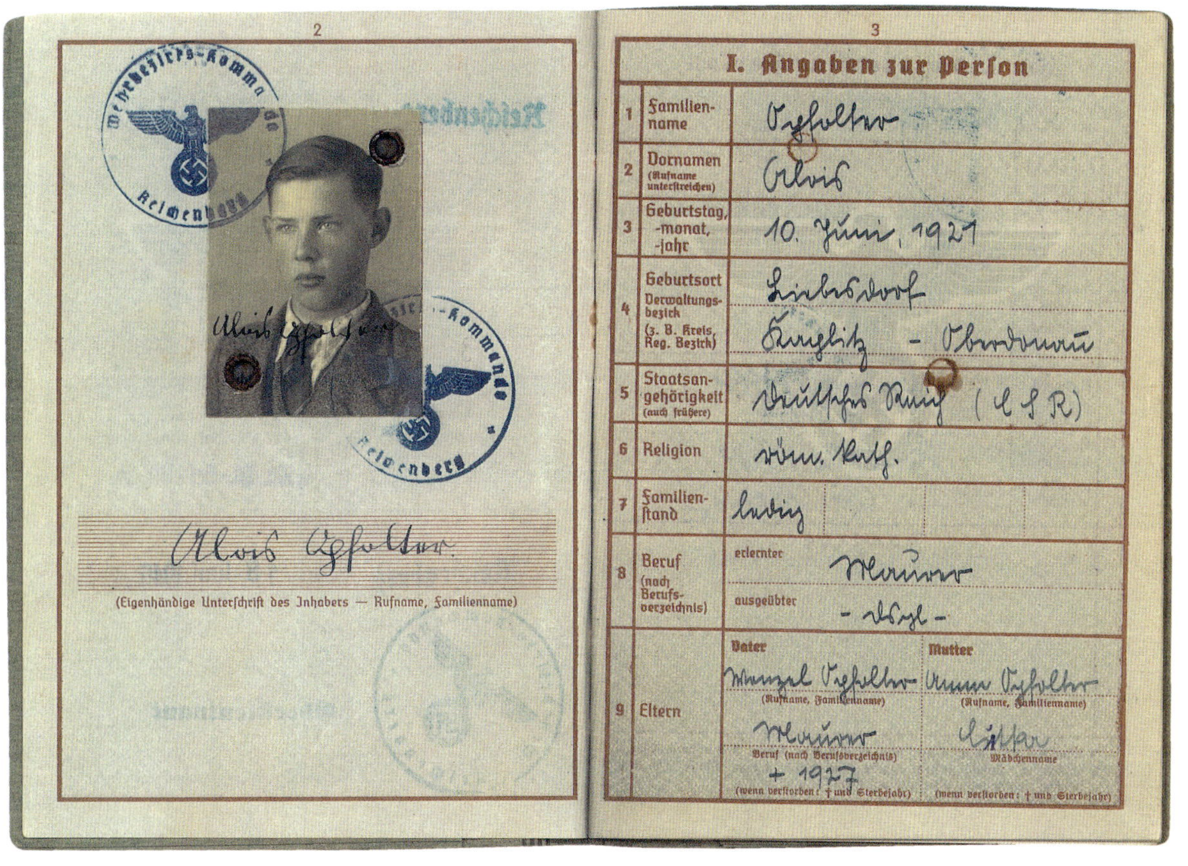

Riveted photo of Alois Opfolter in civilian clothing as he entered service. Born on June 10, 1921, Opfolter had just turned nineteen years old when he was activated for military service.

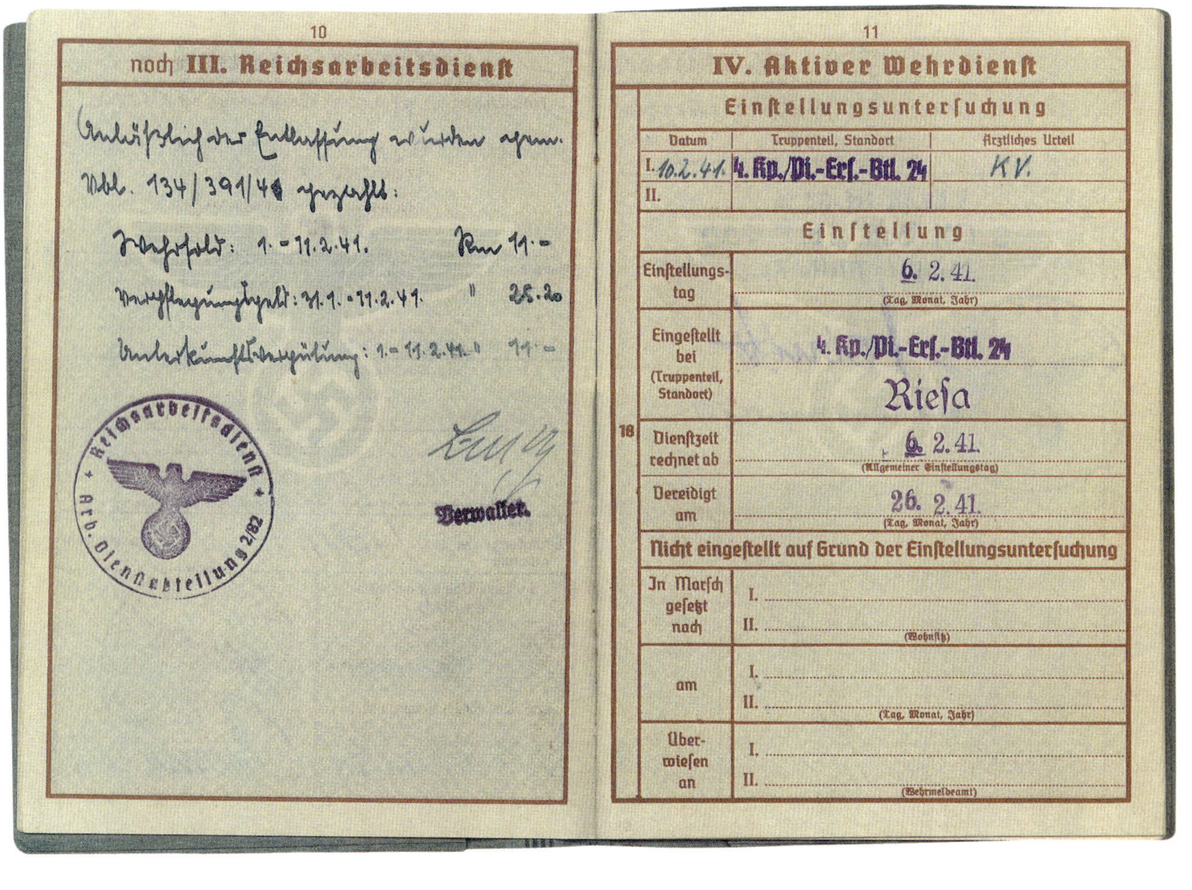

Page 10 reflects his duty in the National Labor Service. On page 11, you can see his official service entry date was February 6, 1941 and Opfolter swore his oath of allegiance to the *Führer* on February 26, 1941.

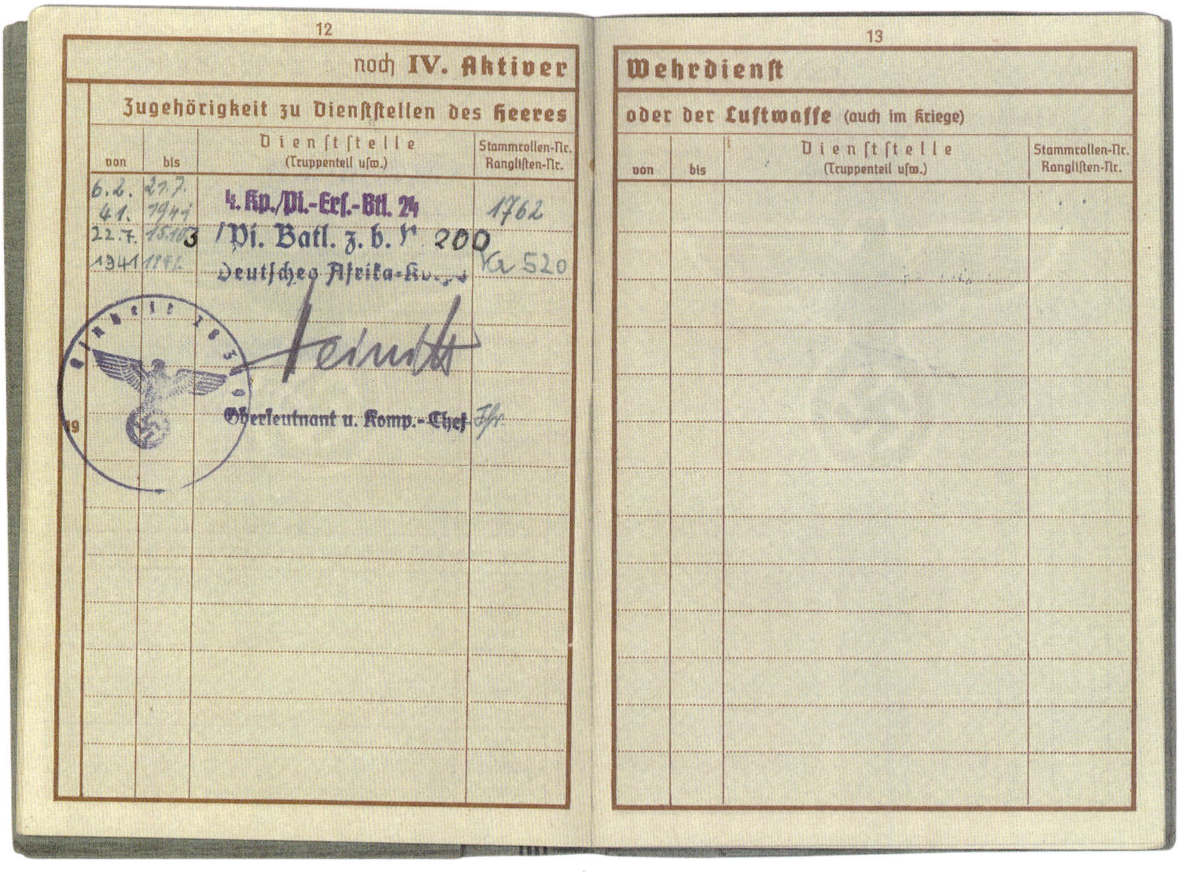

Originally assigned to the 4th Company of the *24th Pionier Battalion*, on July 22, 1941 Opfolter was transferred to the 3rd Company of the *200th Pionier Battalion*. Note the unique company unit stamp signed by its commander.

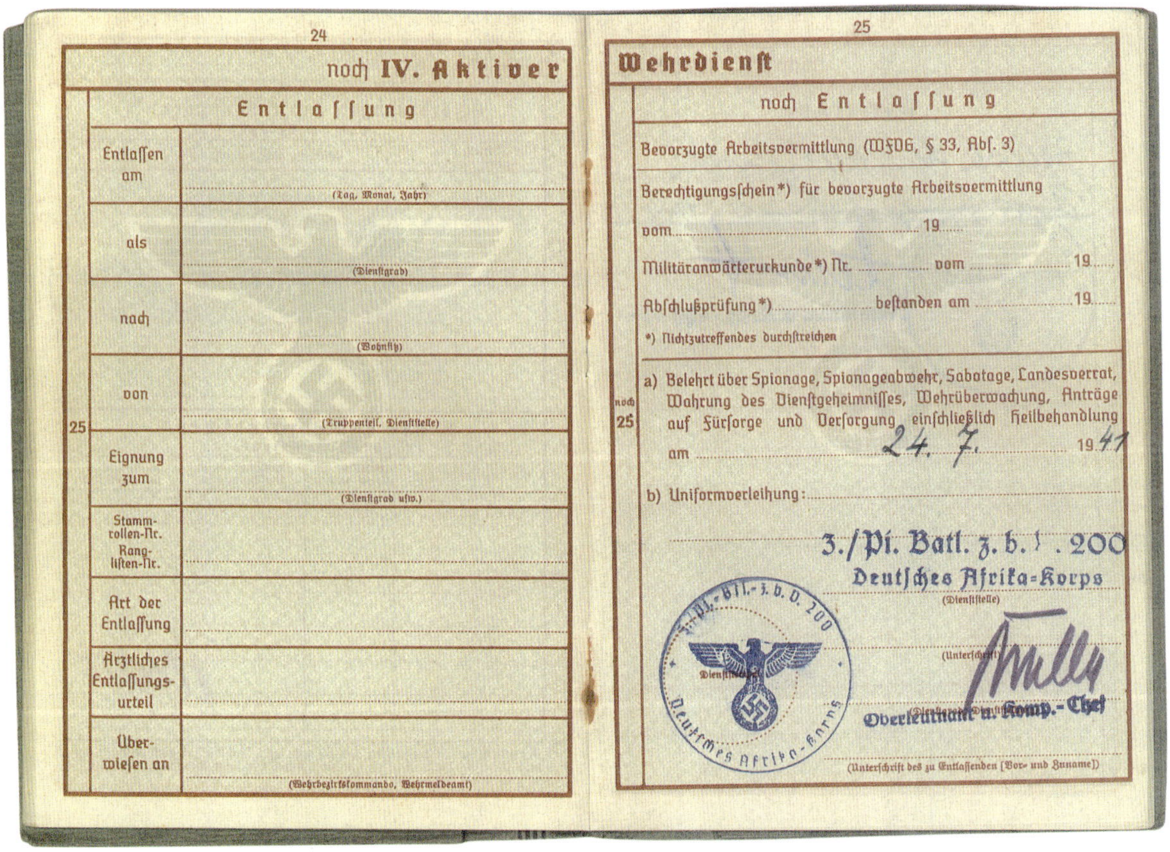

On July 24, 1941 the 3rd Pioneer Company commander again noted the transfer assignment. It's very unusual to see a company unit stamp include a reference to the "*Deutsches Afrika-korps*." Part of the *21st Panzer Division*, this Company was clearly proud to be associated with the much celebrated *Afrikakorps*.

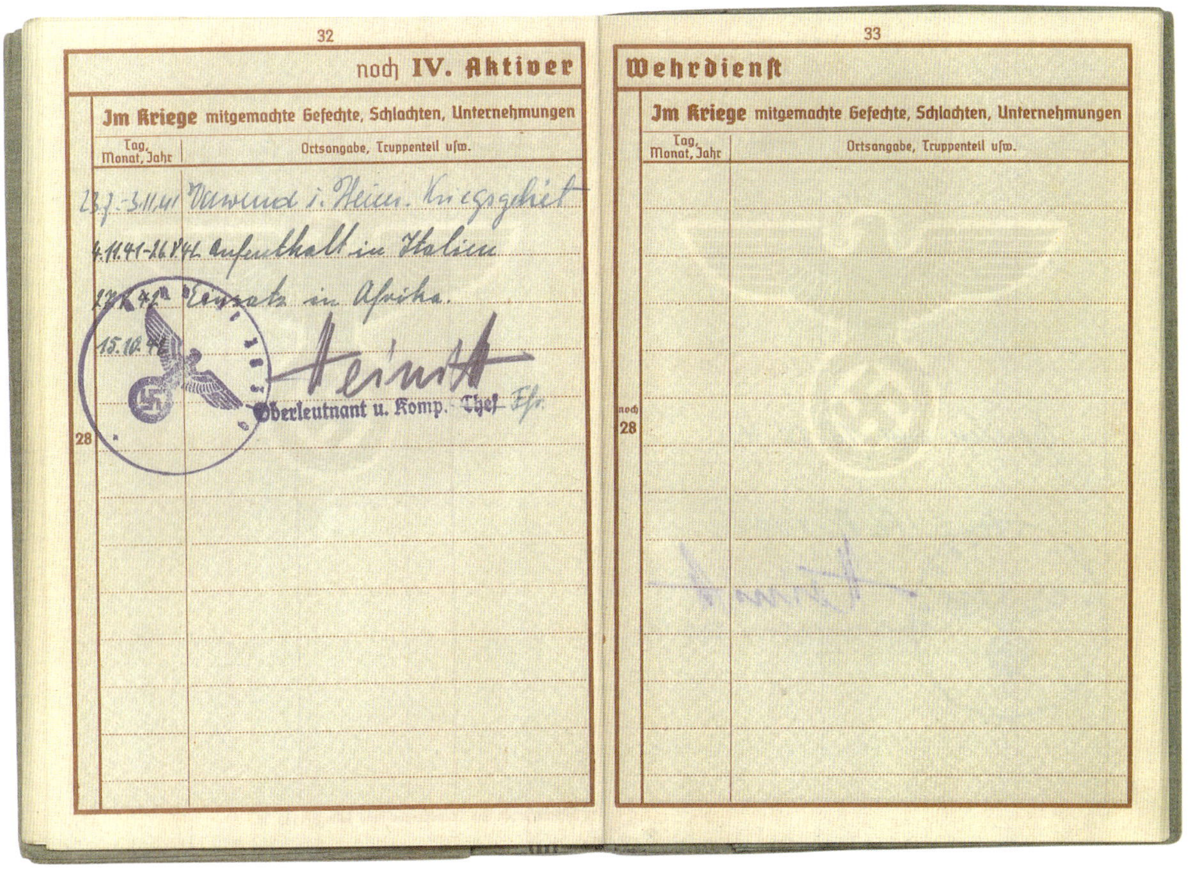

Page 32 indicates a reference to Italy and his July 27, 1941 arrival in Africa. The final entry is the date he was killed. Top to bottom entries read: wounded in combat zone; period in Italy; action in Africa.

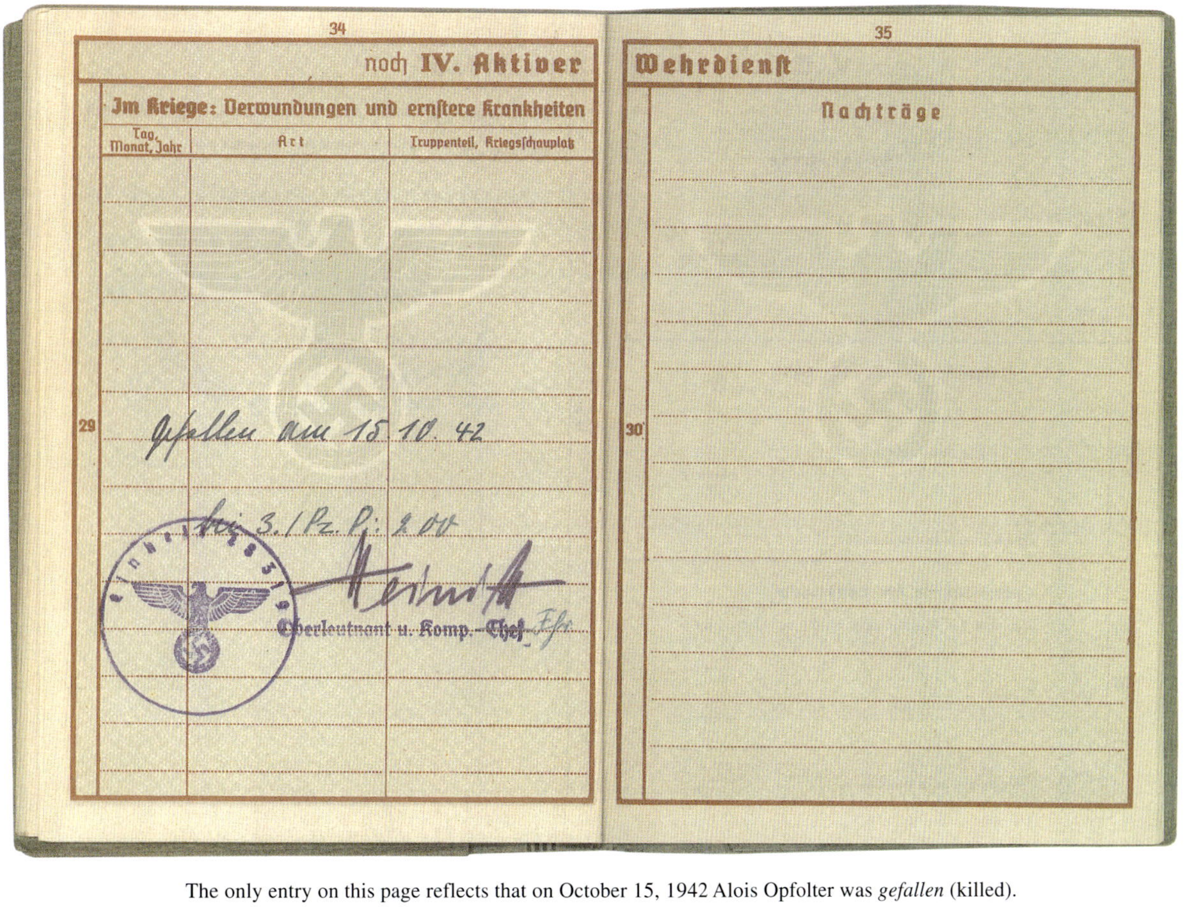

The only entry on this page reflects that on October 15, 1942 Alois Opfolter was *gefallen* (killed).

Personal photographs taken by and of Alois Opfolter in Africa.

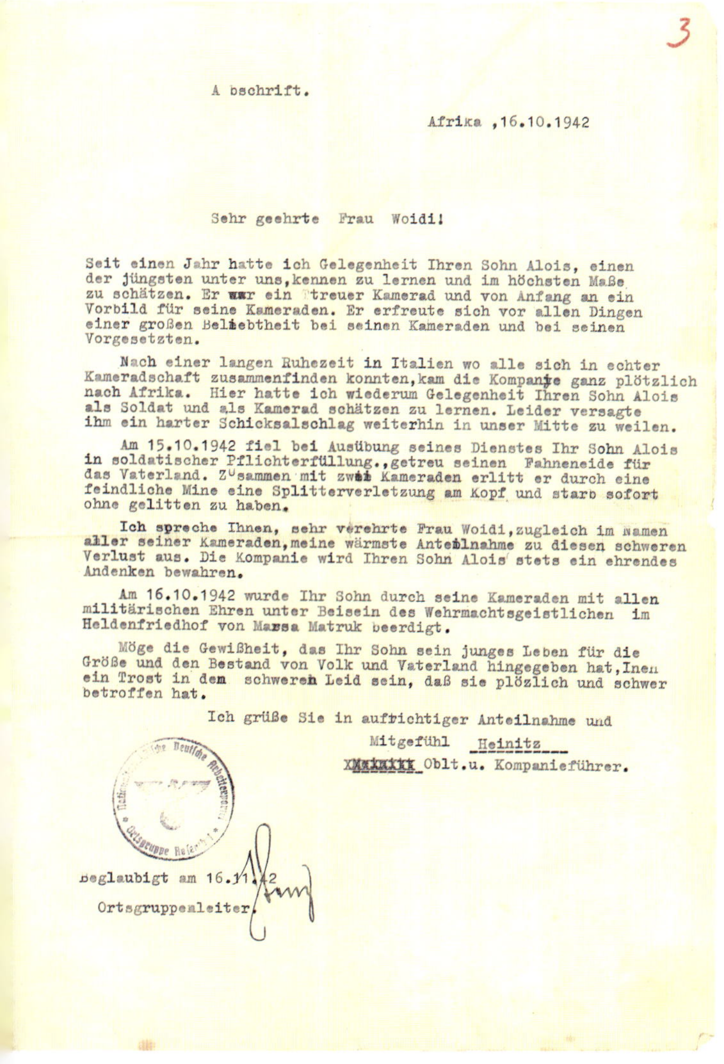

3

Abschrift.

Afrika ,16.10.1942

Sehr geehrte Frau Woidi!

Seit einen Jahr hatte ich Gelegenheit Ihren Sohn Alois, einen der jüngsten unter uns, kennen zu lernen und im höchsten Maße zu schätzen. Er war ein treuer Kamerad und von Anfang an ein Vorbild für seine Kameraden. Er erfreute sich vor allen Dingen einer großen Beliebtheit bei seinen Kameraden und bei seinen Vorgesetzten.

Nach einer langen Ruhezeit in Italien wo alle sich in echter Kameradschaft zusammenfinden konnten, kam die Kompanie ganz plötzlich nach Afrika. Hier hatte ich wiederum Gelegenheit Ihren Sohn Alois als Soldat und als Kamerad schätzen zu lernen. Leider versagte ihm ein harter Schicksalschlag weiterhin in unser Mitte zu weilen.

Am 15.10.1942 fiel bei Ausübung seines Dienstes Ihr Sohn Alois in soldatischer Pflichterfüllung., getreu seinen Fahneneide für das Vaterland. Zusammen mit zwei Kameraden erlitt er durch eine feindliche Mine eine Splitterverletzung am Kopf und starb sofort ohne gelitten zu haben.

Ich spreche Ihnen, sehr verehrte Frau Woidi, zugleich im Namen aller seiner Kameraden, meine wärmste Anteilnahme zu diesen schweren Verlust aus. Die Kompanie wird Ihren Sohn Alois stets ein ehrendes Andenken bewahren.

Am 16.10.1942 wurde Ihr Sohn durch seine Kameraden mit allen militärischen Ehren unter Beisein des Wehrmachtsgeistlichen im Heldenfriedhof von Marsa Matruk beerdigt.

Möge die Gewißheit, das Ihr Sohn sein junges Leben für die Größe und den Bestand von Volk und Vaterland hingegeben hat, Inen ein Trost in dem schweren Leid sein, daß sie plözlich und schwer betroffen hat.

Ich grüße Sie in aufrichtiger Anteilnahme und Mitgefühl Heinitz

Oblt.u. Kompanieführer.

Beglaubigt am 16.11.42

Ortsgruppenleiter

Christliches Andenken an unseren lieben Sohn und Bruder

Alois Opfolter

aus Rosenthal 8

welcher am 15. Oktober als Oberpionier in Afrika im Alter von 22 Jahren sein Leben für Führer und Heimat gab.

Im Kampf für Vaterland und Ehre,
Den Tod geholt vom Schlachtenfeld,
Ein selig Leben ging mir auf,
O hemmet Euren Tränenlauf.
Ich bin Euch nicht gestorben,
Hab mir den Heldenkranz erworben.
Hat man begraben mich als Held.
Der Heimat fern, in fremder Erde,
Drum weinet, meine Lieben, nicht,
Ich tat es ja als meine Pflicht.

Leichenbestg. A. Windhager Hohenfurth

Franz Marchal, Buchdruckerei, Krummau a. M.

Remembrance Card of Alois Opfolter prepared and distributed by the parents to honor the death of their son.

A personal condolence letter dated October 16, 1942 from *Oberleutnant und Kompanieführer* (Company Commander) Heinitz to the mother of Alois Opfolter. Note that Heinitz signature is repeated several times in the *Wehrpass*. This touching letter indicates Alois Opfolter was killed in action at Mersa Matruh (Egypt) and reads:

Dear Mrs. Woidi,

In the past year I got to know your son, the youngest man in the unit, and became very fond of him. He was a loyal comrade and from the very beginning an example to his comrades. He was very well liked by his fellow soldiers, and superiors alike.

After a lengthy rest period in Italy, where we comrades had a good time together, the company was quite suddenly sent to Africa. There I once again had the opportunity to come to value your son Alois as a soldier and comrade. Unfortunately, a cruel turn of fate prevented him from remaining with us.

Your son was killed in action on 15 Oct. 1942 while doing his duty as a soldier, faithful to his oath. He and two other soldiers set off a land mine. He was hit in the head and died immediately, without suffering.

My dearest Mrs. Woidi, I wish to tell you that my comrades and I were deeply affected by this terrible loss. The company will always honor the memory of your son Alois.

On 16 Oct. 1942 your son was buried with full military honors in the military cemetery in Marsa Matruk in the presence of the military chaplain.

May the knowledge that your son gave his young life for the greatness and good of our people and nation be of comfort to you as you deal with this sudden and difficult loss.

With all sympathy and regret,

Heinitz, Oblt. and Acting Company Commander

Extremely rare and complete "*Afrikakampfer*" document grouping to *Obergefreiter* Herbert Franke of the *164th leichte Afrika-Division.* (David Bunch)

Outside front cover of his *Soldbuch* (Paybook)

An extremely rare combination, this officer's aluminum *Erkennungsmarke* is still with his original *Soldbuch*. His tag is marked to the *Inf. Ers. Battalion 476* with his *Erkennungsmarke* and blood type confirmed in the *Soldbuch*.

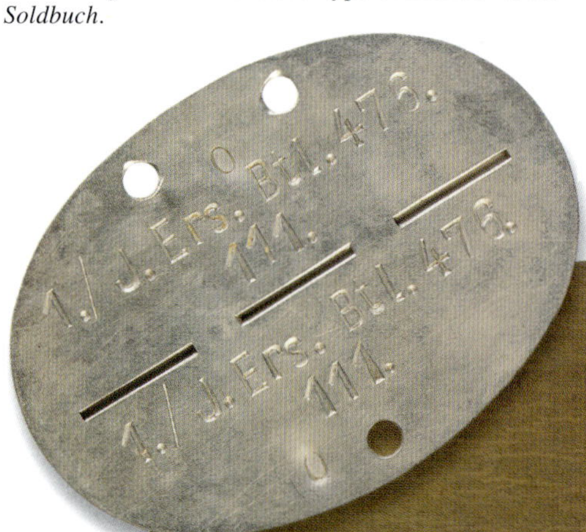

Inside cover with photograph and basic information indicating his progression of rank (ultimately becoming an *Unteroffizier* in 1944), full name, "dog tag" number (*Erkennungsmarke*), blood type O, gas mask size and lineal number.

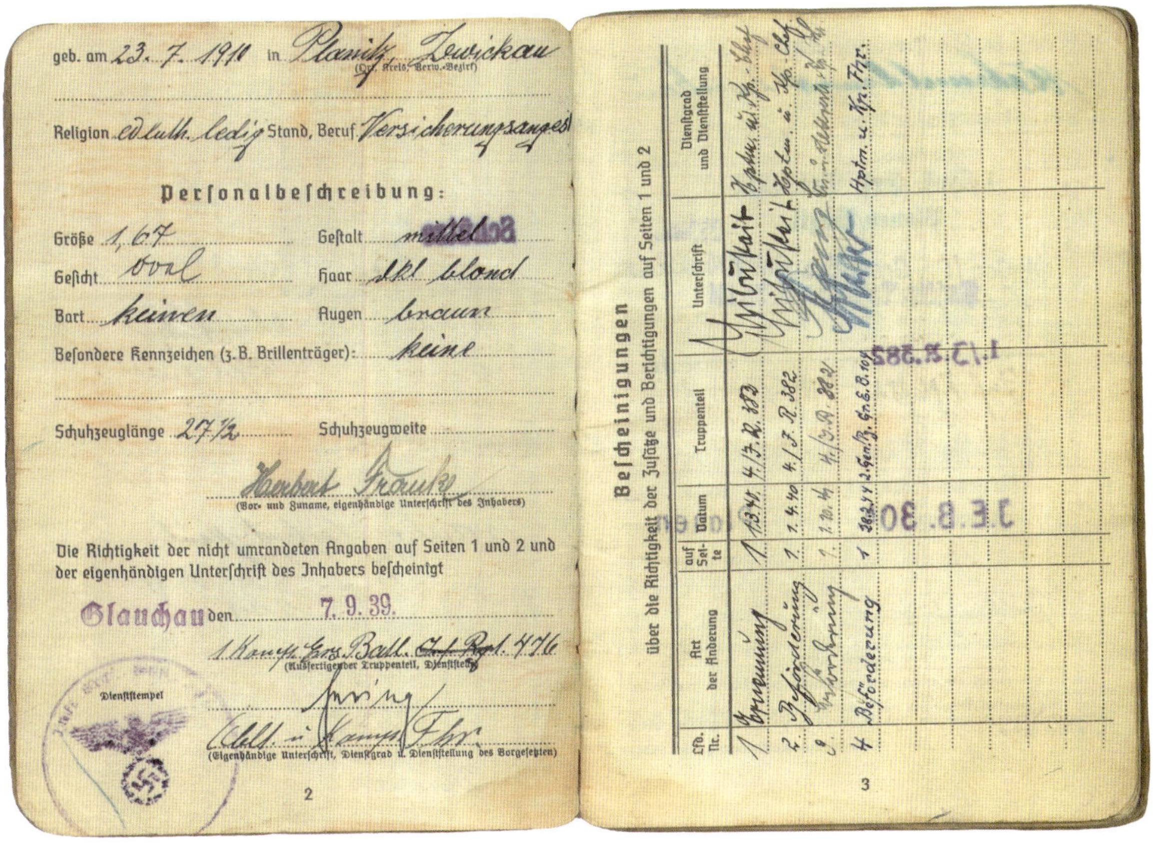

Personal information such as birth date, birthplace, religion and "*Personalbeschreibung*" or physical characteristics is described on page 2. The issuing officer of the *Soldbuch* witnessed Franke's signature and signed the document with the appropriate unit stamps to attest to its validity. Page 3 reflects appointments and promotions and was used to further validate the basic information on the first page.

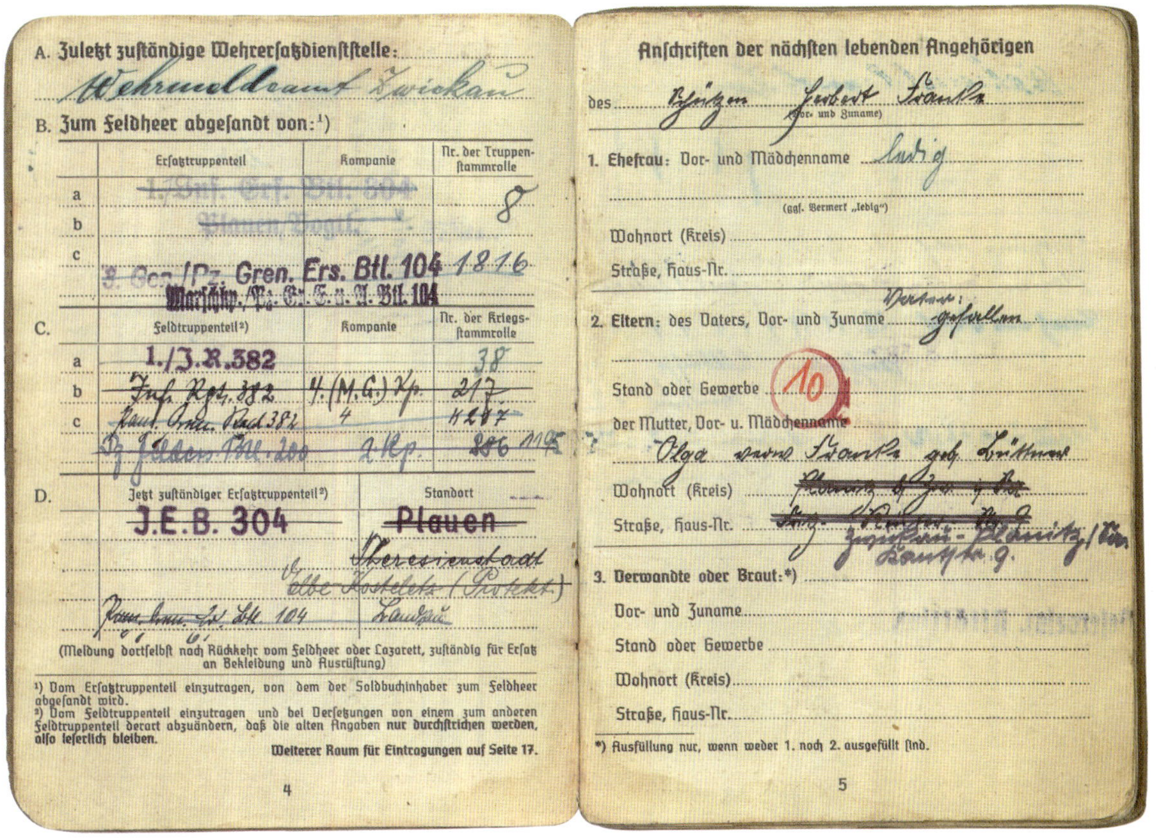

Page four consists of sections A through D. Section A listed the unit responsible for holding Franke's records. Section B shows the reserve units he was assigned before being sent to a field unit. Section C identified his field unit assignments and section D reflected his unit when returning from the field or hospital. All unit changes had a line drawn through them, but were to remain legible. Names and addresses of next of kin are written on page 5.

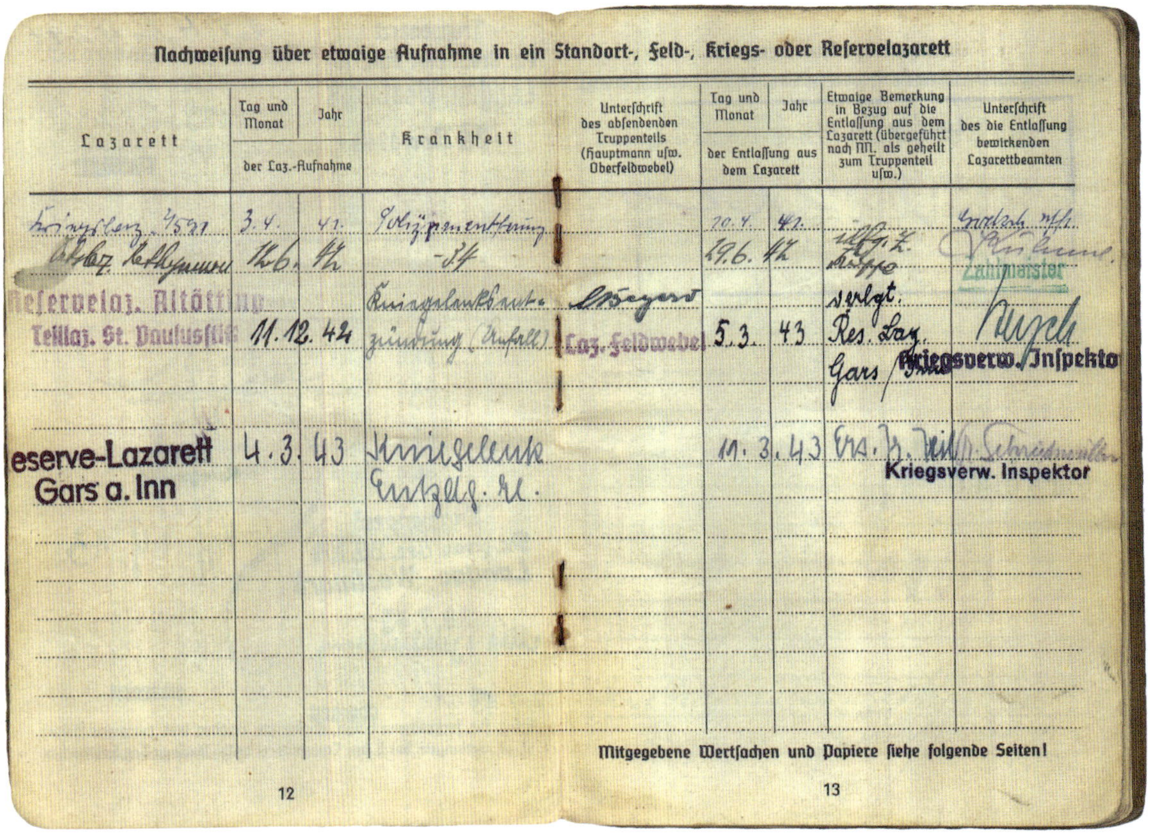

Page 12 lists his three hospital admissions while page 13 reflects hospital discharges.

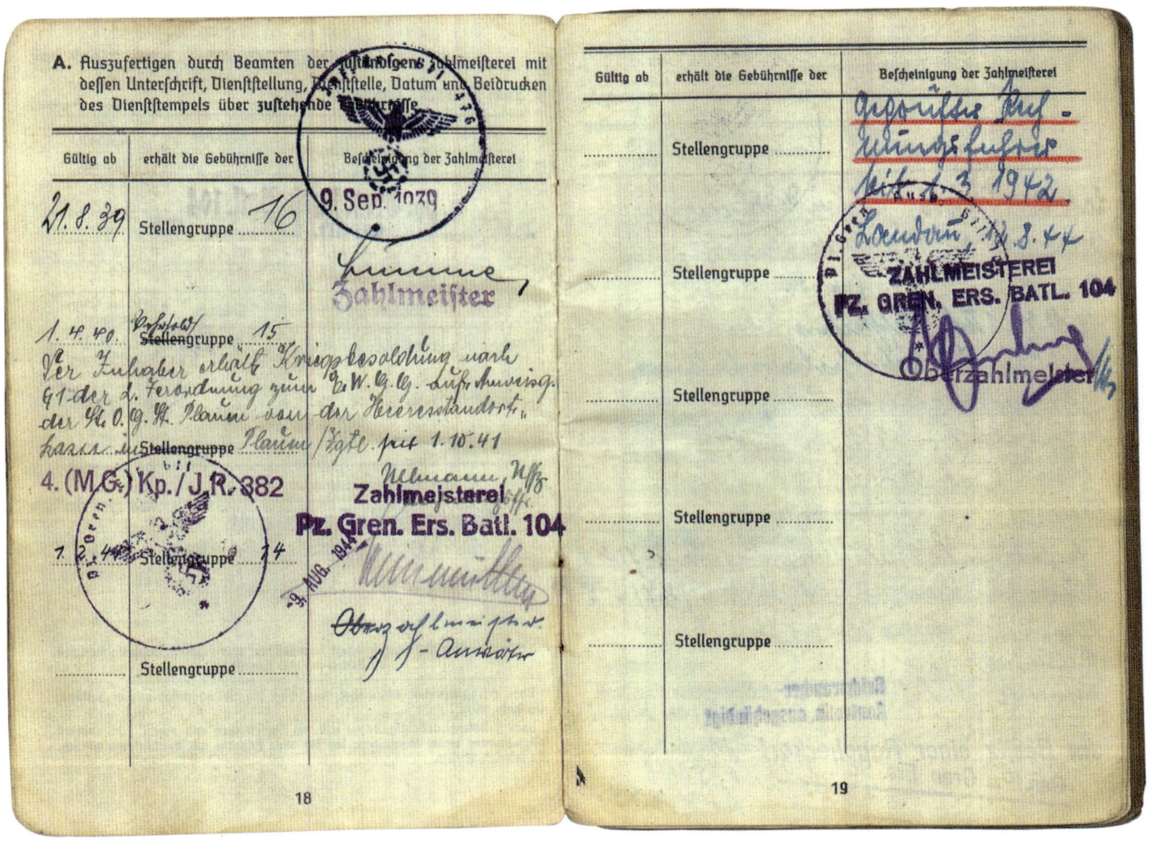

Pages 18 and 19 reflect entries made by paymasters of the units to which Franke was assigned.

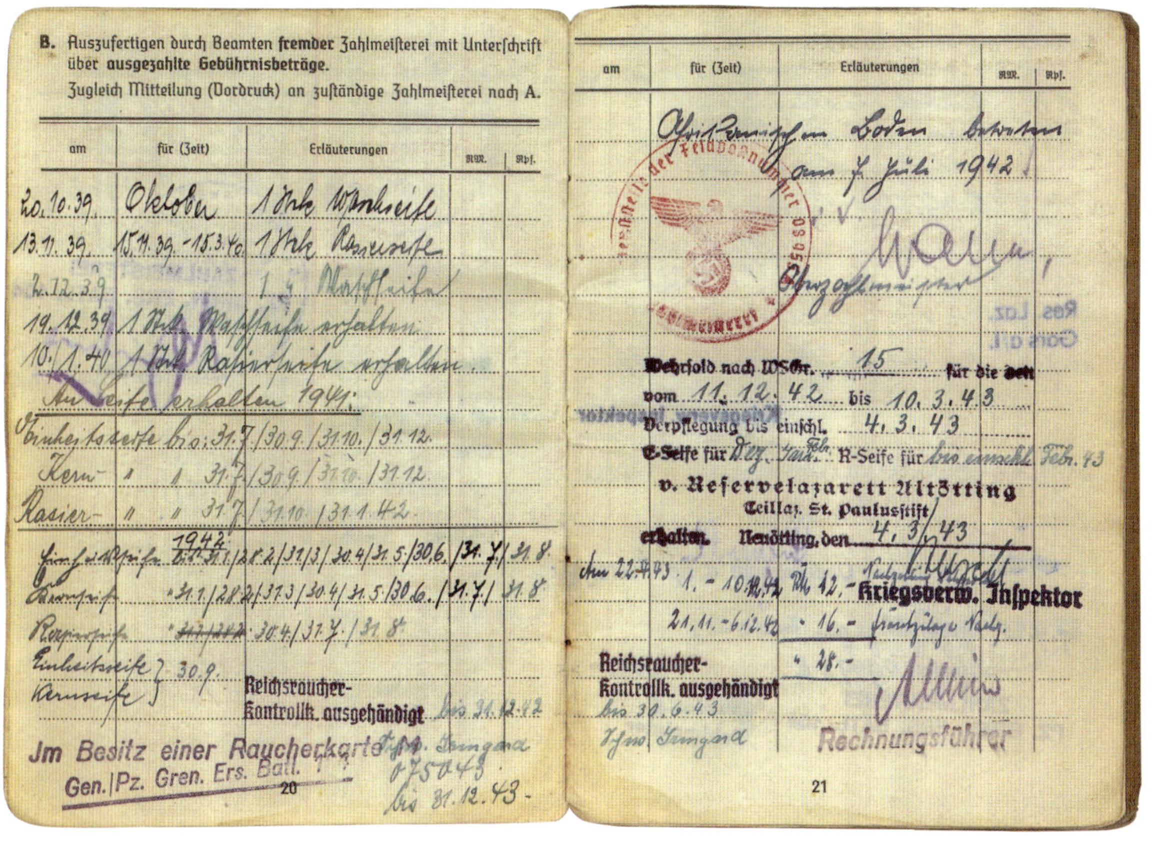

Pages 20 and 21 reflect additional pay entries in hospitals and notations for decoration awards.

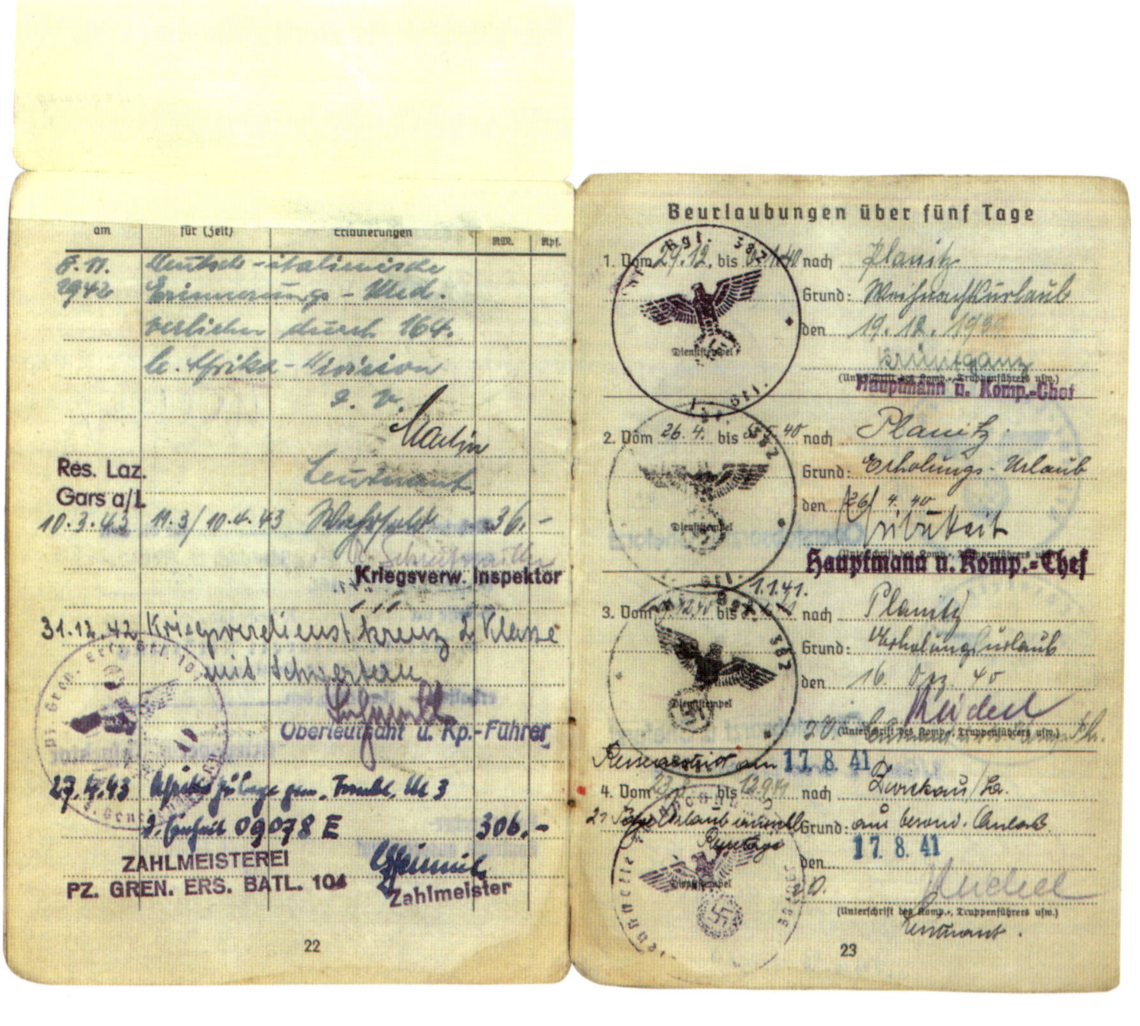

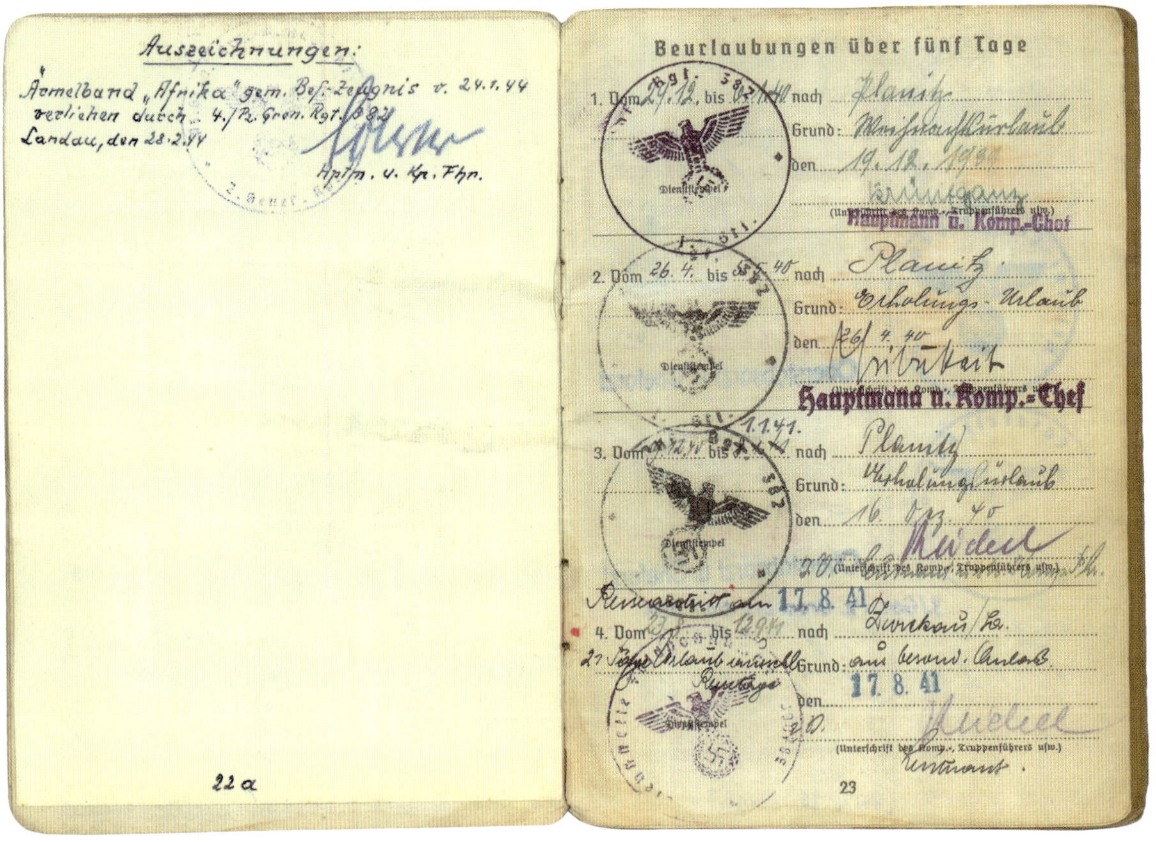

Page 22 reflects Franke receiving the Italian-German Award on November 8, 1942 and War Service Cross (Second Class) with Swords on December 31, 1942. A paper insert was glued as page "22a" and reflects Franke receiving the AFRIKA cufftitle award on February 28, 1944. Page 23 reflects his authorized leave record.

Pages 24 and 25 indicate further authorized leave through July 1944.

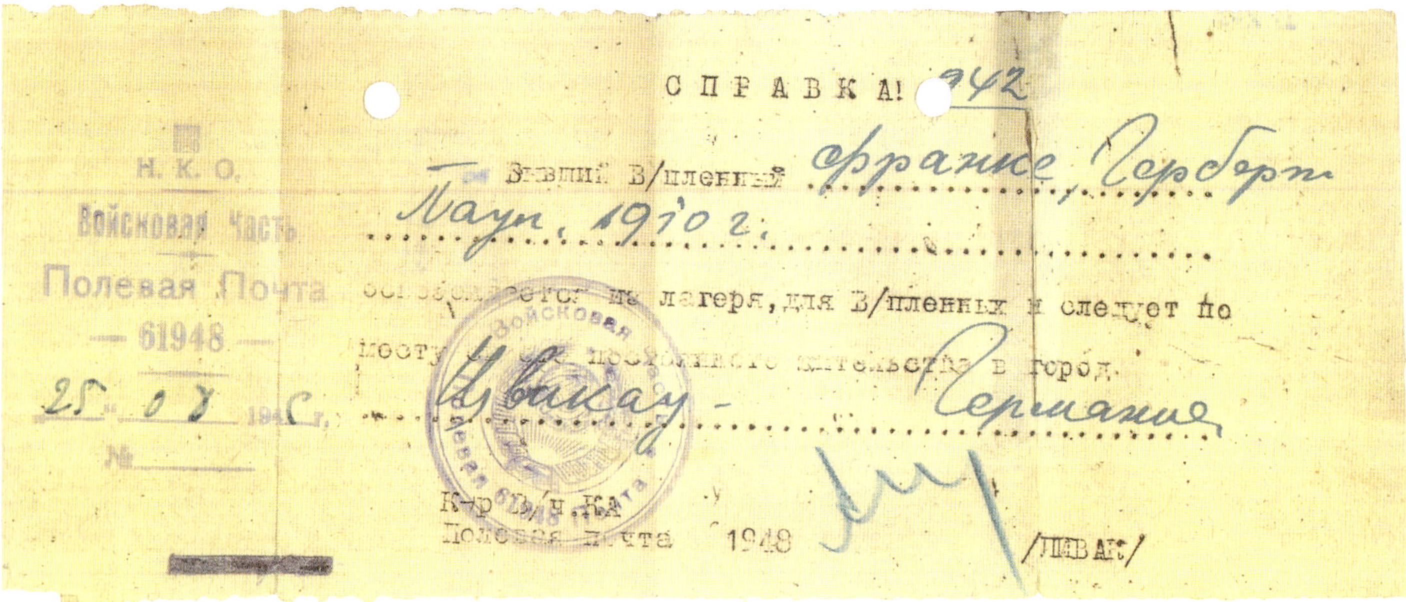

Н. К. О.
Войсковая Часть
Полевая Почта
— 61948 —
25 07 194С г.
№

СПРАВКА № 942

Бывший в/пленный Франке, Герберт Паул, 1910 г.

освобождается из лагеря для в/пленных и следует по месту постоянного жительства в город Цвикау - Германия.

К-р в/ч КА
Полевая почта 61948

/...../

Unteroffizier Franke survived the war as indicated by this Russian pass issued in Dresden in 1948.

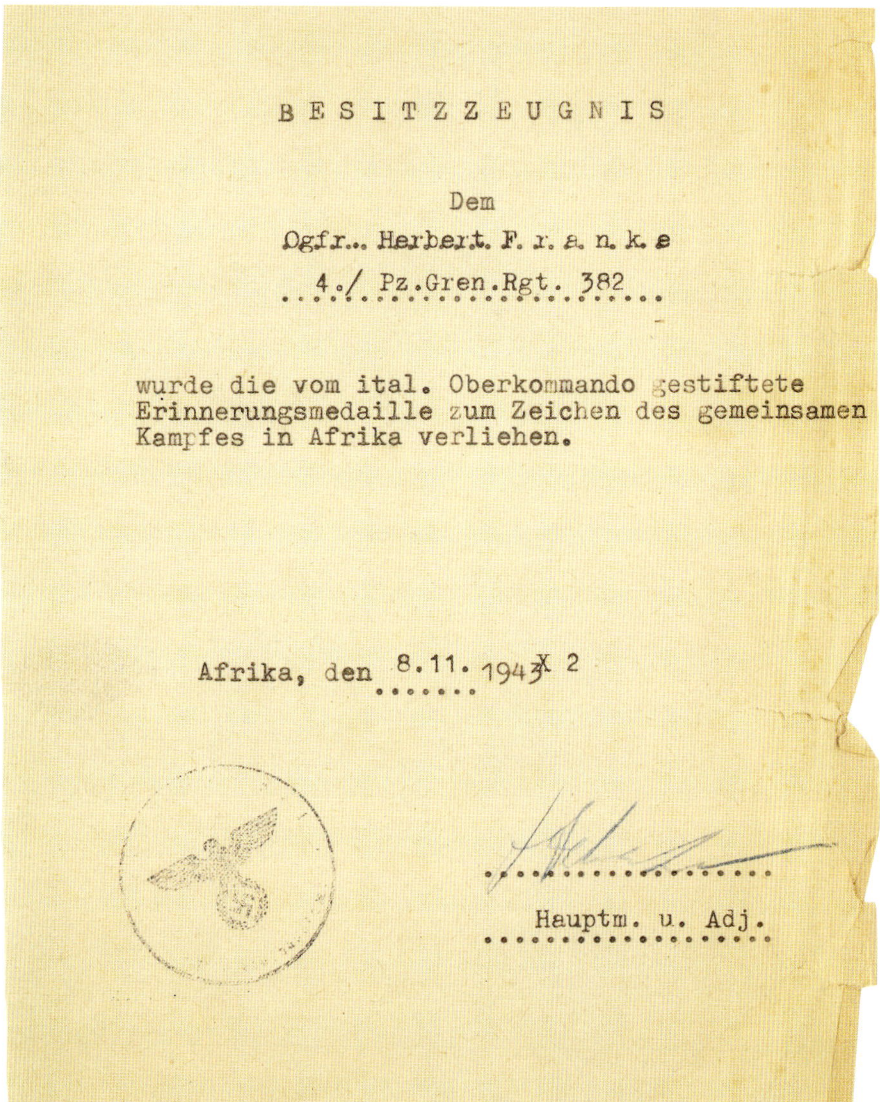

B E S I T Z Z E U G N I S

Dem

Ogfr.. Herbert F r a n k e

4./ Pz.Gren.Rgt. 382

wurde die vom ital. Oberkommando gestiftete Erinnerungsmedaille zum Zeichen des gemeinsamen Kampfes in Afrika verliehen.

Afrika, den 8.11. 1942

Hauptm. u. Adj.

Field made Italian-German *Afrika* Medal award document given to *Obergefreiter* Franke when he was assigned to the *4th Companie* of *Panzergrenadier Regiment 382*. Dated November 8, 1942, this document was prepared in Africa with a unit rubber stamp and a *Hauptmann* adjutant's signature.

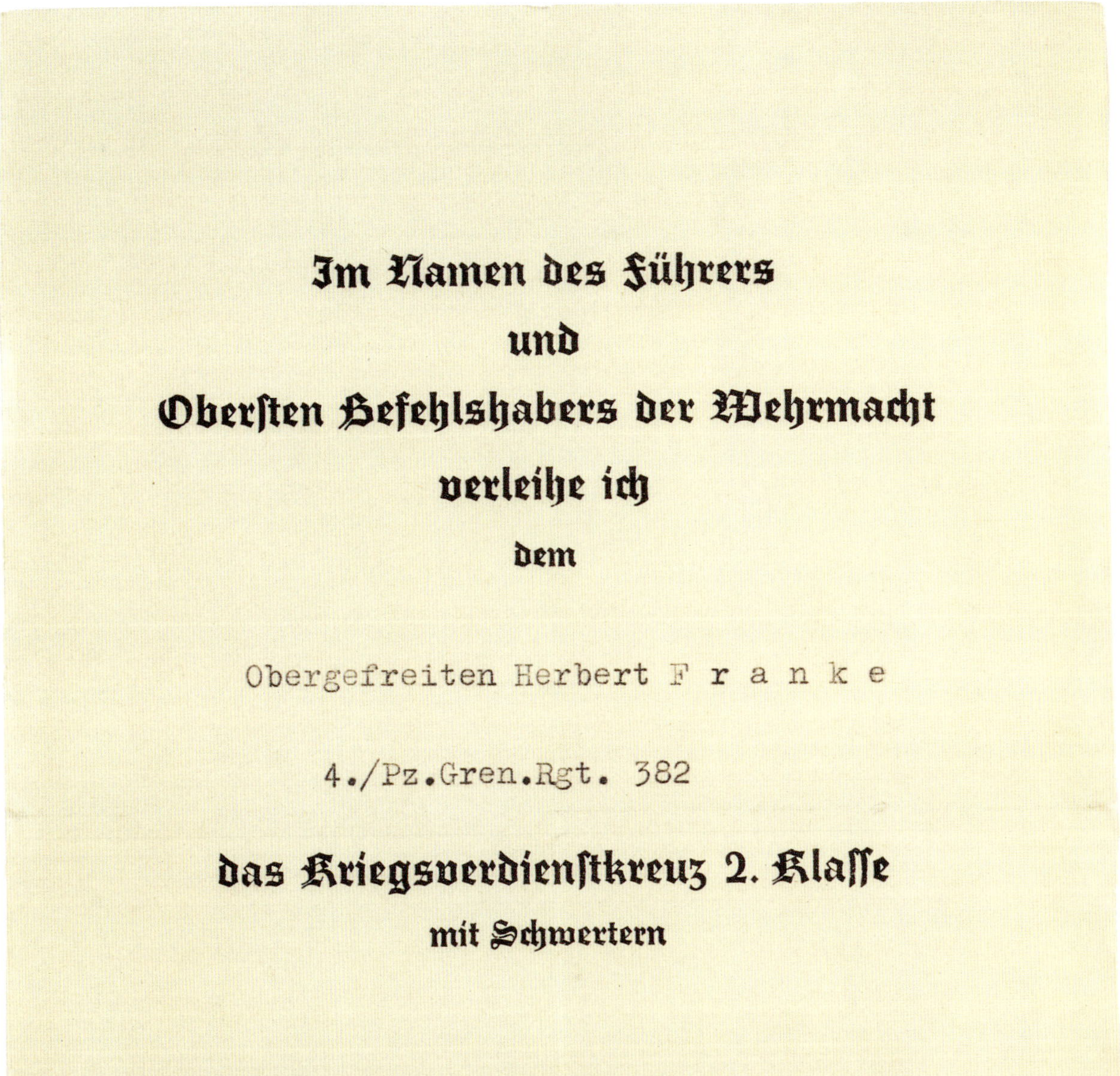

Im Namen des Führers

und

Obersten Befehlshabers der Wehrmacht

verleihe ich

dem

Obergefreiten Herbert F r a n k e

4./Pz.Gren.Rgt. 382

das Kriegsverdienstkreuz 2. Klasse

mit Schwertern

Div.Gef.Stand, den 31.Dezember 19 42

Kdo. 164. le Afrika Division

(Dienstsiegel)

Oberst und Führer
der 164.le.Afrika-Division

(Dienstgrad und Dienststellung)

War Service Cross Second Class with Swords Award Document to *Obergefreiter* Franke. Dated December 31, 1942, this document has the rare "*164th le Afrika Division*" rubber stamp and commanding officer signature of *Oberst* von Liebenstein.

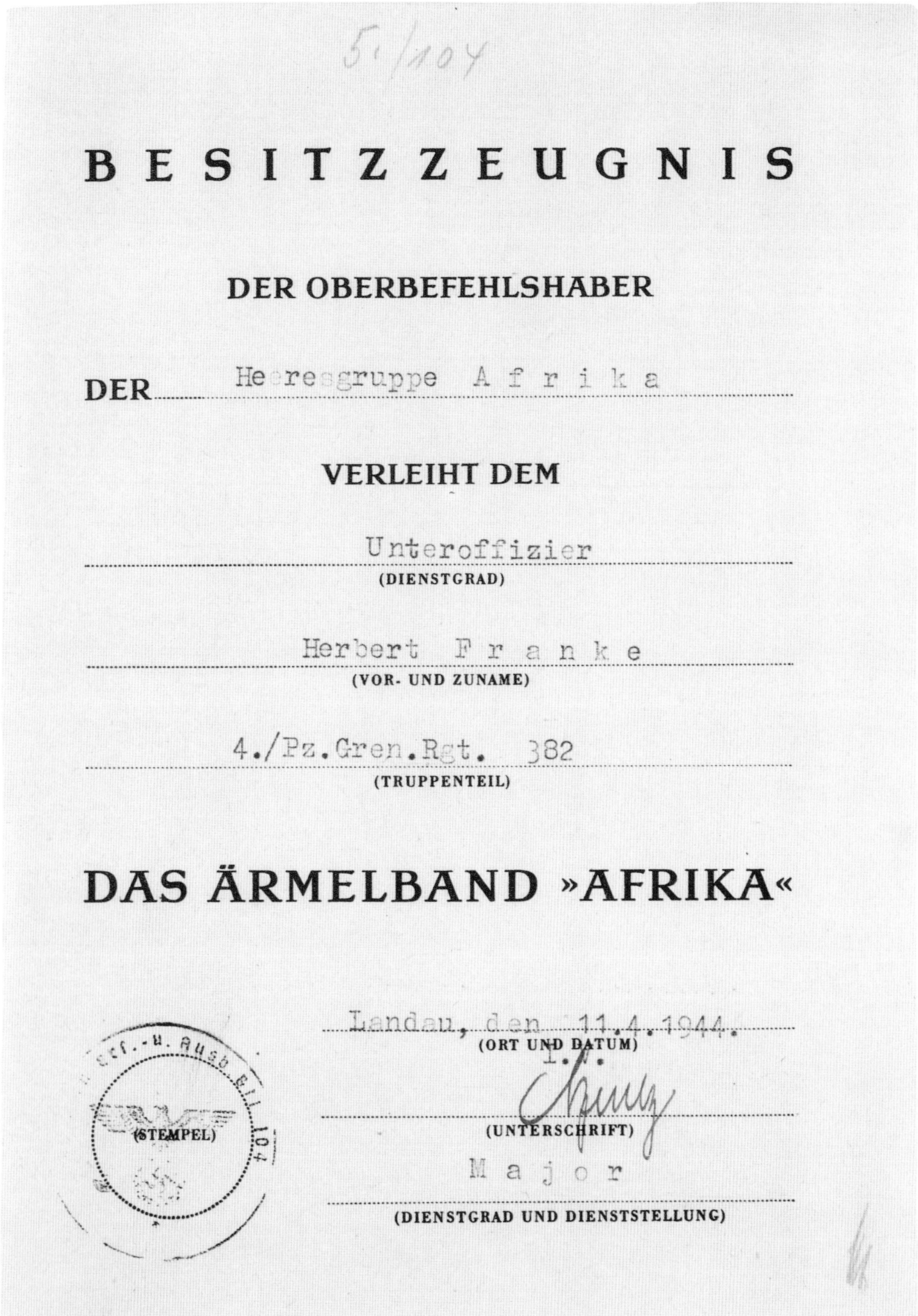

5¹/104

BESITZZEUGNIS

DER OBERBEFEHLSHABER

DER Heeresgruppe Afrika

VERLEIHT DEM

Unteroffizier
(DIENSTGRAD)

Herbert Franke
(VOR- UND ZUNAME)

4./Pz.Gren.Rgt. 382
(TRUPPENTEIL)

DAS ÄRMELBAND »AFRIKA«

Landau, den 11.4.1944.
(ORT UND DATUM)

(STEMPEL)

I.V.

(UNTERSCHRIFT)

Major
(DIENSTGRAD UND DIENSTSTELLUNG)

Franke's AFRIKA cufftitle award document dated April 11, 1944. At the time of this award, Franke had been promoted to *Unteroffizier*.

Extremely rare and intriguing *Luftwaffe Soldbuch*, *Erkennungsmarke* (identification disk) and documents for *Unteroffizier* Ernst Weidermann of the Flak Regiment of the *Hermann Göring Division*. (David Bunch)

Front cover of blue *Luftwaffe Soldbuch*. Weidemann's *Luftwaffe Soldbuch* is in good condition with a clean cover and very few wrinkles.

The *Erkennungsmarke* or "dog tag" is unbroken and very legible. It is clearly marked "93 A, 6./Flak - Rgt. H.G." and matches the information provided on page 1 of Weidermann's *Soldbuch*. The disk has taken on a very dark patina over most of the surface, though there are some lighter areas still remaining.

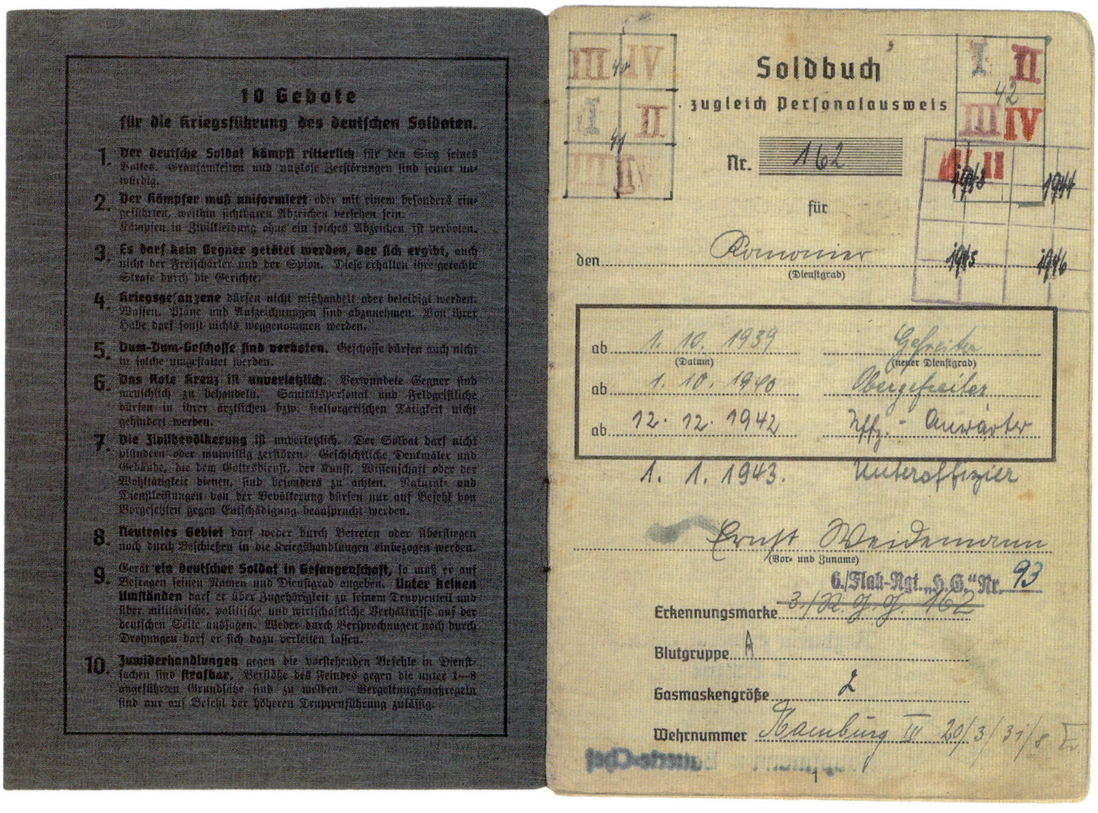

Unlike the Army *Soldbuch*, the *Luftwaffe* had the "Zehn Gebote" ("Ten Commandments") inside their front cover. This was designed to be a military code of conduct and included such matters as not revealing information if taken prisoner and respecting neutral territories. Ernst Weidermann was first assigned with the rank of *Kanonier* to the 3rd *Regiment General Göring*. This entry was later crossed out and replaced with "6th FlaK-Rgt.". He was promoted four times with his last promotion to *Unteroffizier* on January 1, 1943. Weidermann surrendered in North Africa with most of the original units of the elite *Hermann Göring Division*.

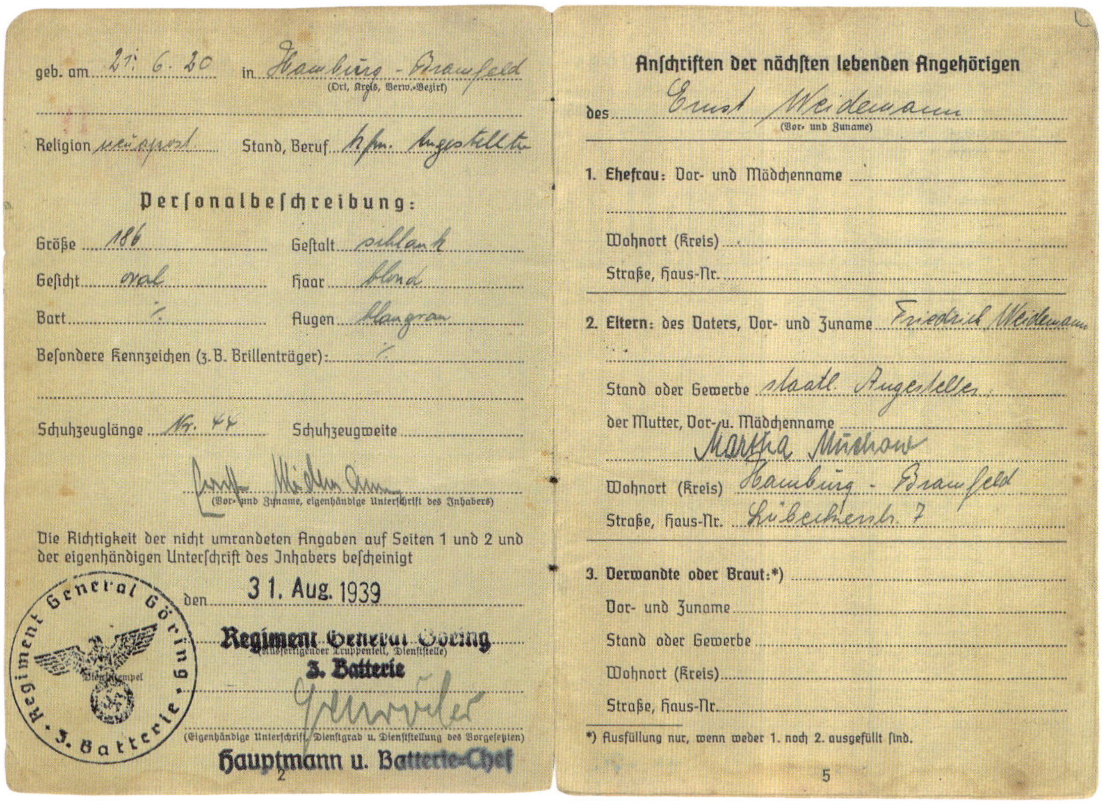

Page 4 reveals that Weidermann was born in Hamburg in 1920 and completed these first entries in his new *Soldbuch* on August 31, 1939 (the eve of World War II). Note the unique *Regiment General Göring* (*R.G.G.*) 3rd Batterie unit stamp to witness the information provided by the *Soldbuch* holder.

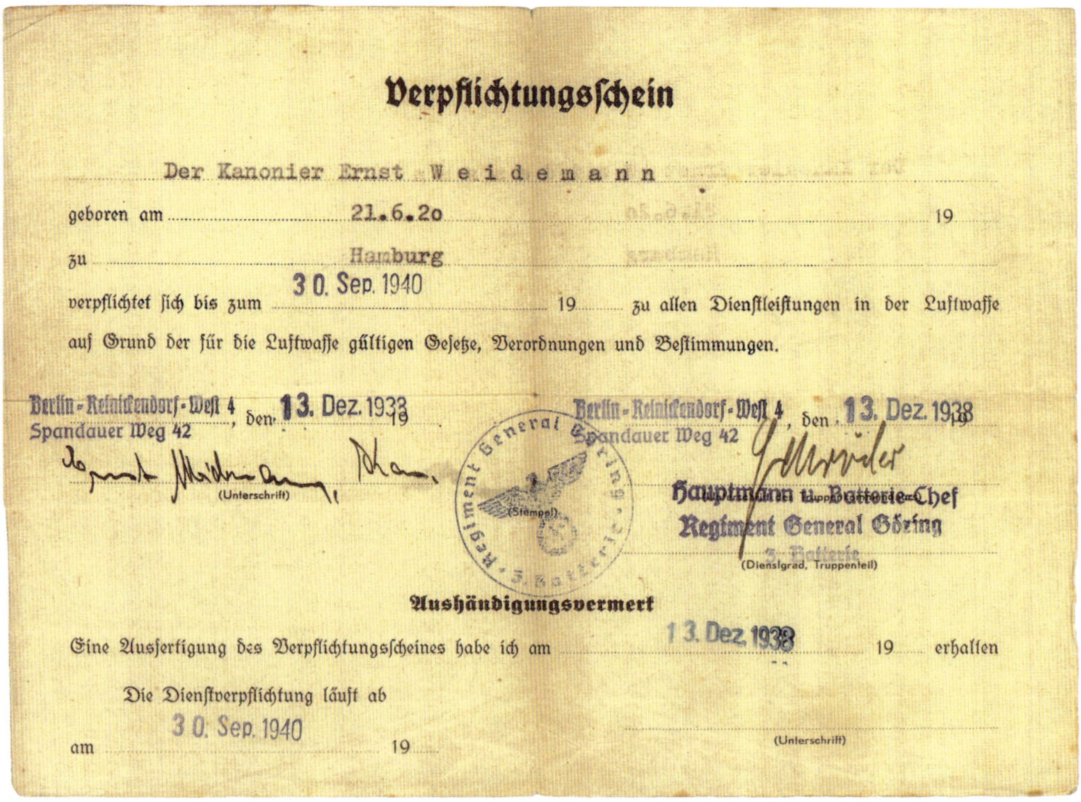

Verpflichtungsschein

Der Kanonier Ernst Weidemann

geboren am 21.6.2o 19

zu Hamburg

verpflichtet sich bis zum 30. Sep. 1940 19 zu allen Dienstleistungen in der Luftwaffe auf Grund der für die Luftwaffe gültigen Gesetze, Verordnungen und Bestimmungen.

Berlin-Reinickendorf-West 4 Spandauer Weg 42, den 13. Dez. 1938

(Unterschrift)

Berlin-Reinickendorf-West 4 Spandauer Weg 42, den 13. Dez. 1938

(Stempel)

Hauptmann u. Batterie-Chef
Regiment General Göring
3. Batterie
(Dienstgrad, Truppenteil)

Aushändigungsvermerk

Eine Ausfertigung des Verpflichtungsscheines habe ich am 13. Dez. 1938 19 erhalten

Die Dienstverpflichtung läuft ab

am 30. Sep. 1940 19

(Unterschrift)

Weidermann's original service obligation. He was apparently a volunteer (his enlistment was for a period of nearly two years, ending on 30 September 1940). The document bears a clear *Regiment General Göring* certification stamp with Weidermann's signature and that of a "Captain and 3rd Battery Commander."

Im Namen des Führers
und
Obersten Befehlshabers der Wehrmacht
verleihe ich

dem Kanonier Ernst Weidemann

die Medaille zur Erinnerung an den 1. Oktober 1938

Berlin, den 23. August 1939

Für die Richtigkeit:

Oberst u. Rgt.-Kommandeur

Der Kommandeur im Luftgau III
gez. Weise
Generalleutnant

Nr. I./730 /39
(des Verzeichnisses der Verleihungsbehörde)

Award certificate for the Austrian Annexation Medal, issued on August 23, 1939 by the Commander of *Luftgau* III and signed by a Colonel of *R.G.G.*

***Soldbuch*, extremely rare *Sardinienschild* (Sardinian Shield) citation and award documents to a member of 20th Motorized Infantry Regiment of the *90th leichte Afrika-Division*. *Obergefreiter* Xaver Zistler returned to Germany before fighting ended in Africa and was transferred to the newly formed *90th Panzergrenadier Division* that replaced his former unit in Africa. As noted in his *Soldbuch*, Zistler went on to fight with his division on Corsica and Sardinia.** (David Bunch)

Front cover and first page of Xaver Zistler's *Soldbuch*. His *Soldbuch* is quite worn after five years of war! As reflected on the first page, Zistler was promoted to *Obergefreiter* after his service in Africa. His *Soldbuch* photo became detached and is now missing.

This *Soldbuch* was issued to Zistler on June 20, 1940 and his promotion to *Obergefreiter* in June 1943 is confirmed on page 3.

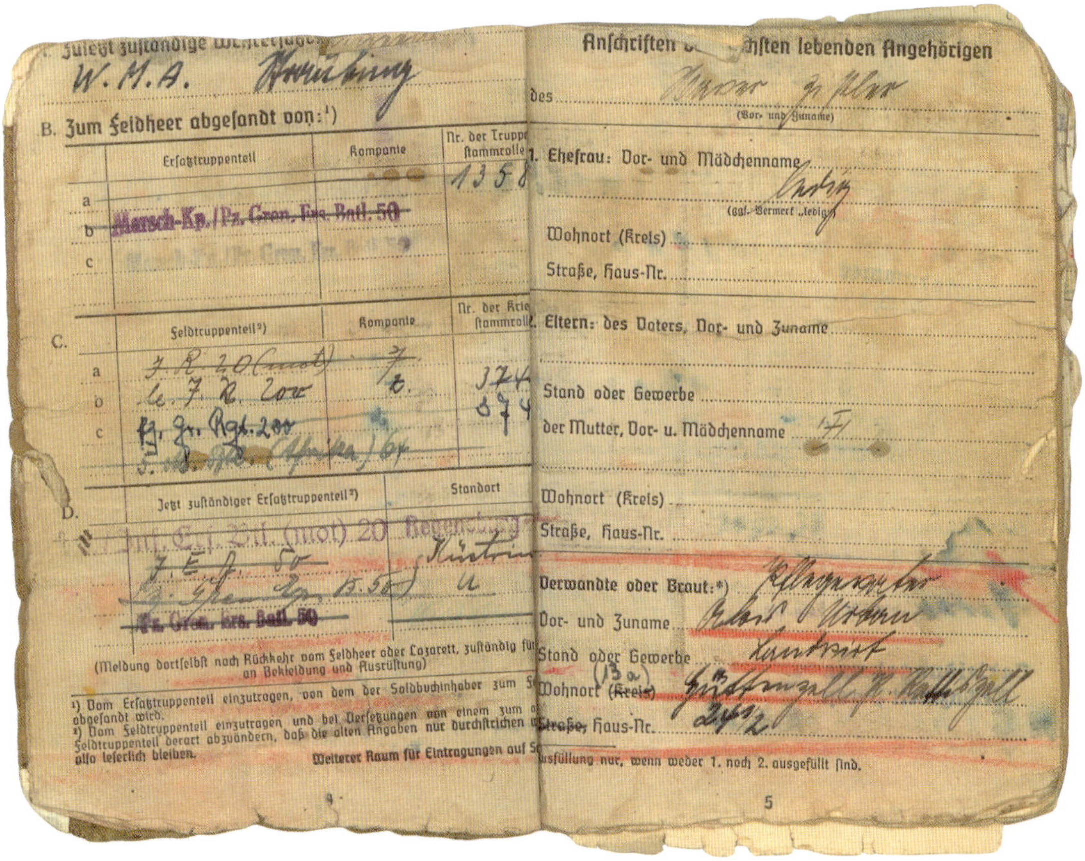

Page 4 reflects his field unit assignments (and transfers) in Africa and Italy. Prior unit changes had a line drawn through them but were suppose to remain legible. Additional field unit changes are indicated on page 17 of this *Soldbuch*. Page 5 denotes his relatives.

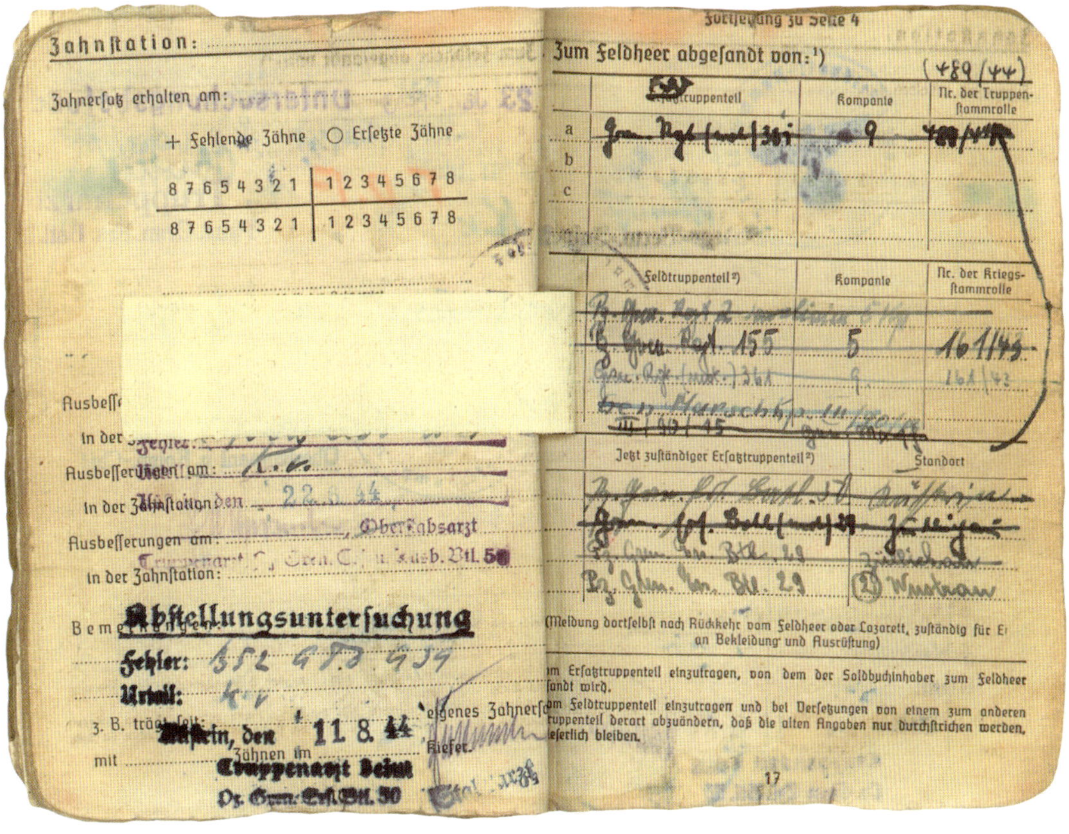

Additional field unit changes are documented as Zistler is wounded and transferred to/from hospital units and reserve units during the war.

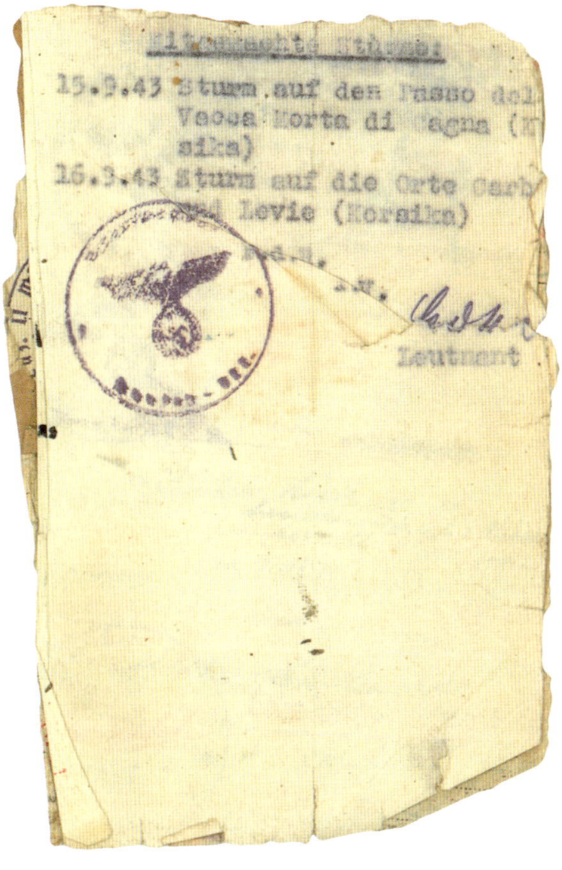

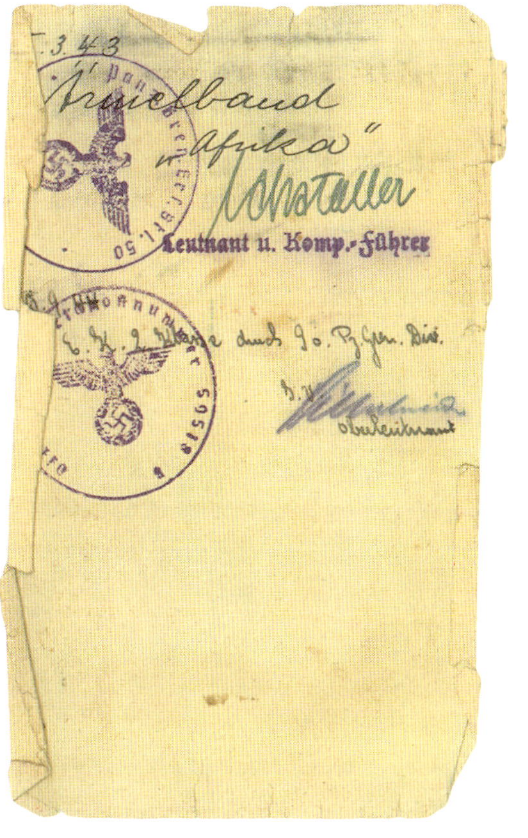

… of several *Soldbuch* inserts denoting two days of close combat fighting on Korsika …rsica).

Another *Soldbuch* insert documenting Zistler earning the AFRIKA cufftitle and Iron Cross (Second Class) while fighting with the *90th Panzergrenadier Division*.

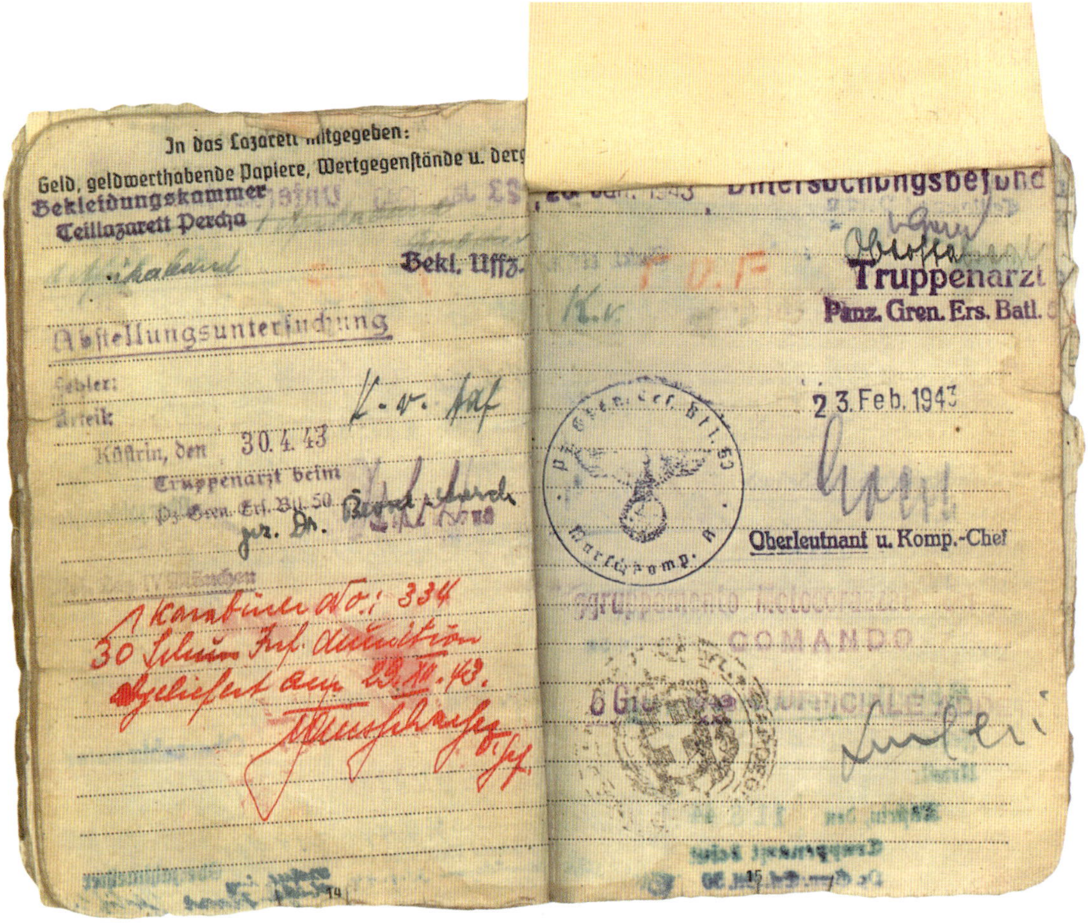

Security checks and administrative notes were typically written on these pages. Note the Italian unit stamp on the bottom of page 15.

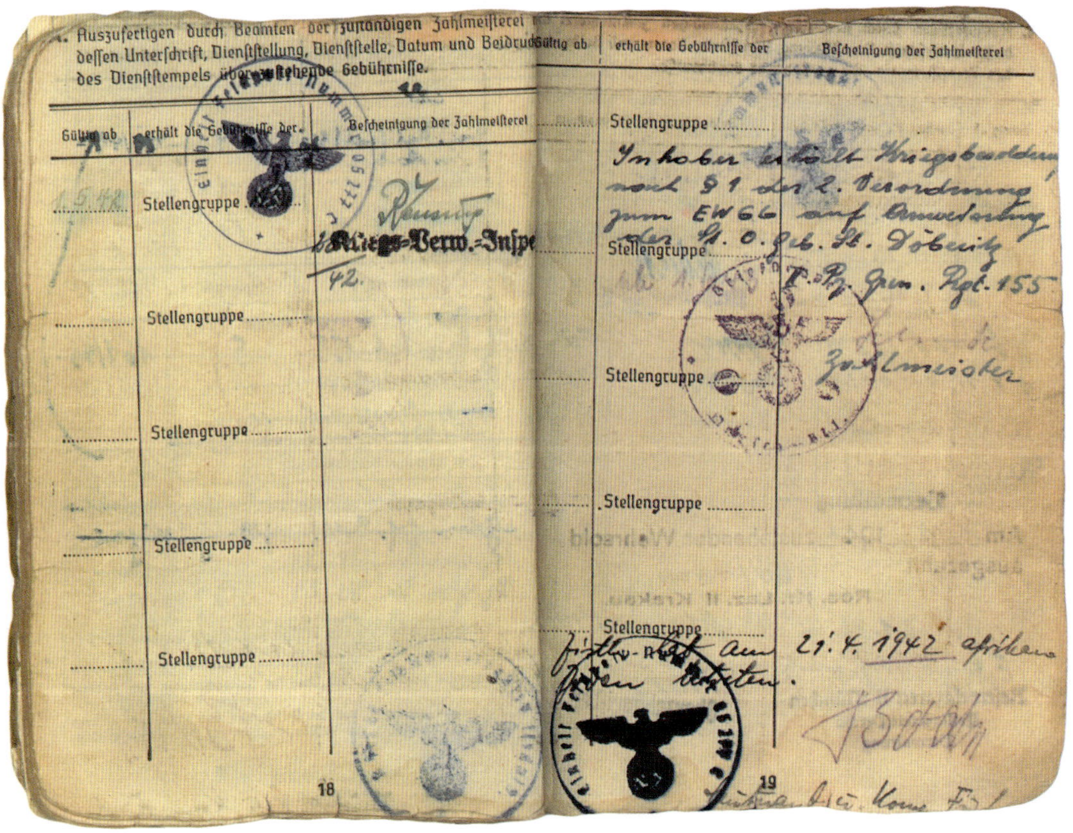

These two pages were typically reserved for paymaster entries. The bottom of page 19 reflects Zistler's arrival to Africa in April 1942.

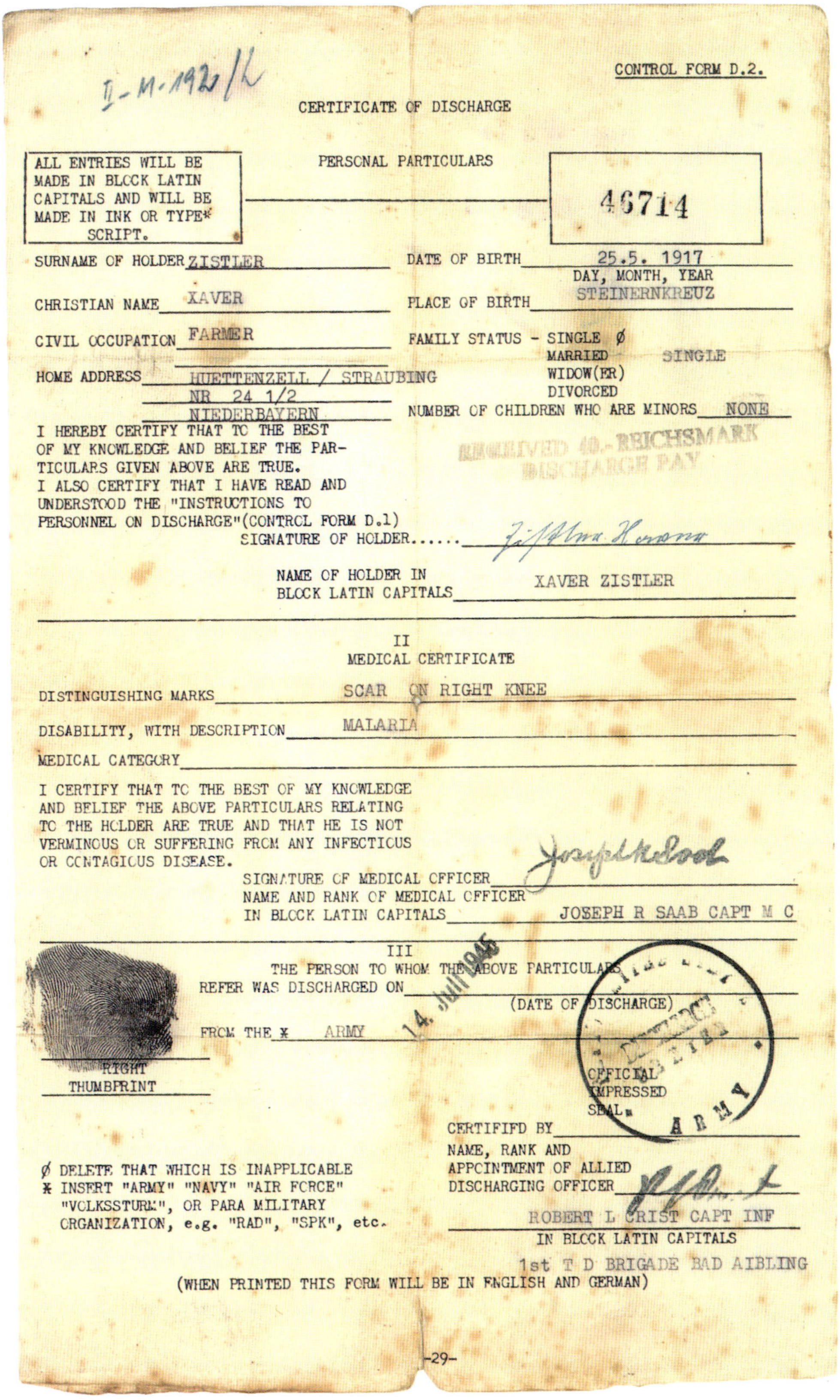

II-M.192/K

CONTROL FORM D.2.

CERTIFICATE OF DISCHARGE

ALL ENTRIES WILL BE MADE IN BLOCK LATIN CAPITALS AND WILL BE MADE IN INK OR TYPE* SCRIPT.

PERSONAL PARTICULARS

46714

SURNAME OF HOLDER ZISTLER — DATE OF BIRTH 25.5. 1917 (DAY, MONTH, YEAR)

CHRISTIAN NAME XAVER — PLACE OF BIRTH STEINERNKREUZ

CIVIL OCCUPATION FARMER — FAMILY STATUS - SINGLE Ø MARRIED WIDOW(ER) DIVORCED — SINGLE

HOME ADDRESS HUETTENZELL / STRAUBING NR 24 1/2 NIEDERBAYERN

NUMBER OF CHILDREN WHO ARE MINORS NONE

I HEREBY CERTIFY THAT TO THE BEST OF MY KNOWLEDGE AND BELIEF THE PARTICULARS GIVEN ABOVE ARE TRUE. I ALSO CERTIFY THAT I HAVE READ AND UNDERSTOOD THE "INSTRUCTIONS TO PERSONNEL ON DISCHARGE"(CONTROL FORM D.1)

RECEIVED 40.- REICHSMARK DISCHARGE PAY

SIGNATURE OF HOLDER......

NAME OF HOLDER IN BLOCK LATIN CAPITALS XAVER ZISTLER

II

MEDICAL CERTIFICATE

DISTINGUISHING MARKS SCAR ON RIGHT KNEE

DISABILITY, WITH DESCRIPTION MALARIA

MEDICAL CATEGORY

I CERTIFY THAT TO THE BEST OF MY KNOWLEDGE AND BELIEF THE ABOVE PARTICULARS RELATING TO THE HOLDER ARE TRUE AND THAT HE IS NOT VERMINOUS OR SUFFERING FROM ANY INFECTIOUS OR CONTAGIOUS DISEASE.

SIGNATURE OF MEDICAL OFFICER

NAME AND RANK OF MEDICAL OFFICER IN BLOCK LATIN CAPITALS JOSEPH R SAAB CAPT M C

III

THE PERSON TO WHOM THE ABOVE PARTICULARS REFER WAS DISCHARGED ON 14. Juli 1945 (DATE OF DISCHARGE)

FROM THE * ARMY

RIGHT THUMBPRINT

OFFICIAL IMPRESSED SEAL.

ARMY

CERTIFIED BY

NAME, RANK AND APPOINTMENT OF ALLIED DISCHARGING OFFICER

ROBERT L CRIST CAPT INF

IN BLOCK LATIN CAPITALS

1st T D BRIGADE BAD AIBLING

Ø DELETE THAT WHICH IS INAPPLICABLE

* INSERT "ARMY" "NAVY" "AIR FORCE" "VOLKSSTURM", OR PARA MILITARY ORGANIZATION, e.g. "RAD", "SPK", etc.

(WHEN PRINTED THIS FORM WILL BE IN ENGLISH AND GERMAN)

-29-

On April 22, 1945, Xaver Zistler was captured by the Americans and discharged to return home on July 14, 1945.

After the war, a commercial effort was made to honor and document the actions those that had survived the war. This is the "Chronik" (Chronicle) folder and bri history of Xaver Zistler that was stored for many years along with his *Soldbuch* a award documents photographed for this book. From his own accord, *Obergefreiter* Xav Zistler began his training on 7th June 1940 in Thüringia and at Hildesheim. On 22 June 1941 he took part in the invasion of Russia and was wounded on August 10th. I returned to Regensburg in Germany and on 22nd April 1942 was sent to Africa. Wound again on 31st September 1943, he was returned to Germany again, and then returned action in Corsica and Sardinia. On 22nd April 1945, he was captured by the America and returned home on 22nd July 1945. He lists his awards as the Wound Badge Silver, German/Italian War Medal, Infantry Assault Badge, Iron Cross II, AFRIK cufftitle and Sardinian Shield.

Zistler Xaver

Obergefreiter

Er rückte am 1. Juni 1940 nach Regensburg zur Ausbildung ein. Nach deren Absolvierung kam er nach Thüringen u. Hildesheim. Am 22. Juni 1941 wurde er in Rußland Mittelabschnitt eingesetzt. Am 10. Aug. 1941 wurde er verwundet. Nach Genesung z. Ers. Baon nach Regensburg. Am 22. April 1942 kam er nach Afrika, wo er am 31. Sept. 1943 verwundet wurde u. kam nach Deutschland ins Lazarett. Nach Genesung Einsatz in Sardinien-Korsika Italien. Am 22. April 1945 geriet er in amerik. KG. Heimkehr am 22. Juli 1945

Ausz.: Verw. Abz. i. Silb., Deutsch. Ital. Er. Med., Inf. Sturmabz., EK II, Afrika-Ärmelband, Sardinenschild,

Postcard studio portrait of *Obergefreiter* Zistler in his field gray greatcoat proudly wearing a green and silver AFRIKAKORPS cufftitle on the right sleeve.

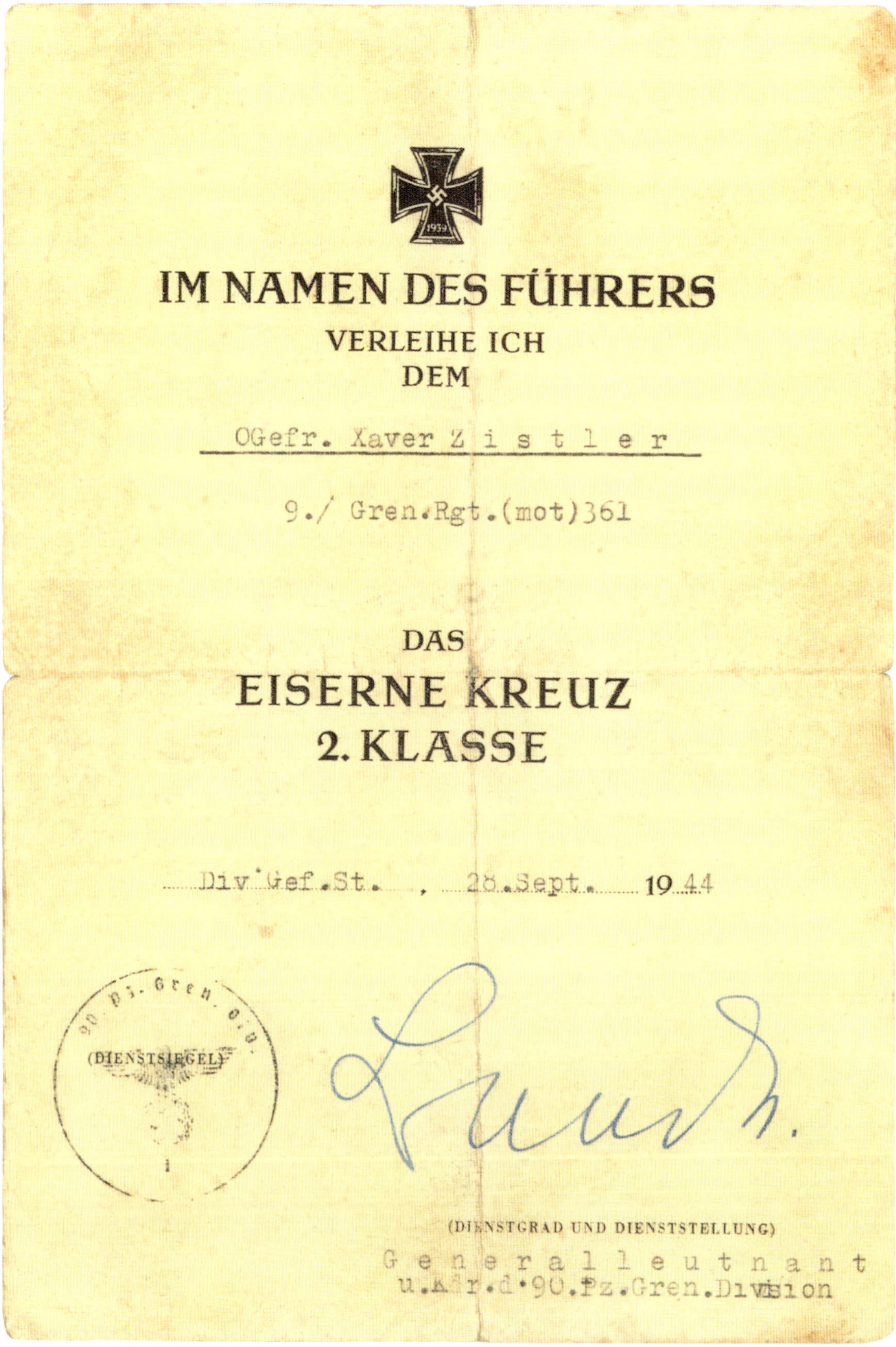

IM NAMEN DES FÜHRERS
VERLEIHE ICH
DEM

OGefr. Xaver Z i s t l e r

9./ Gren.Rgt.(mot)361

DAS
EISERNE KREUZ
2. KLASSE

Div.Gef.St., 28.Sept. 1944

(DIENSTSIEGEL)

(DIENSTGRAD UND DIENSTSTELLUNG)
G e n e r a l l e u t n a n t
u.Kdr.d.90.Pz.Gren.Division

Iron Cross (Second Class) award document to Xaver Zistler dated September 28, 1944 and signed by *Generalleutnant* Fritz Polack, commanding officer of the *90th Panzergrenadier Division* and Knight's Cross with Oak Leaves winner.

BESITZZEUGNIS

DER OBERBEFEHLSHABER

DER Heeresgruppe Afrika

VERLEIHT DEM

Obergefreiten

(DIENSTGRAD)

Xaver Zistler

(VOR- UND ZUNAME)

9./ Gren. Rgt. (mot.) 361

(TRUPPENTEIL)

DAS ÄRMELBAND »AFRIKA«

Rgt. Gef. Std., 18.8.44

(ORT UND DATUM)

(STEMPEL)

(UNTERSCHRIFT)

Oberstlt. u. stellvertr. Rgt.-Kdr.

(DIENSTGRAD UND DIENSTSTELLUNG)

AFRIKA cufftitle document awarded to *Obergefreiter* Zistler on August 18, 1944 and signed by the acting commander of *Grenadier Regiment 361*.

In die Tasche des Soldbuchs einlegen!

Inhaber ist Angehöriger der

90. Pz.-Gren.-Division

und trägt an der Mütze den

Sardinienschild

(Dienststempel)

Extremely rare "*Sardinienschild*" citation that was inserted into Zistler's *Soldbuch*. Note the *Panzergrenadier Regiment 361* unit stamp.

Top
The original "*Sardinienschild*" pin representing the island of Sardinia crossed by a sword. These pins were locally made in brass and typically worn on the left side of the cap.

Rare *Afrikakorps* Penal Battalion *Soldbuch* to Marc Wittkowski of *Afrika Schützen Regiment 961*. This soldier was assigned to this special penal battalion in November 1942 (page 2) and arrived in Africa on March 23, 1943 (page 19) as part of the *999th Afrika-Brigade, 961 Infantry Regiment* (page 4). His *Soldbuch* includes a rare insert indicating full issuance of tropical clothing and field gear on February 12, 1943. He survived the final combat days in Africa and became a POW. (David Bunch)

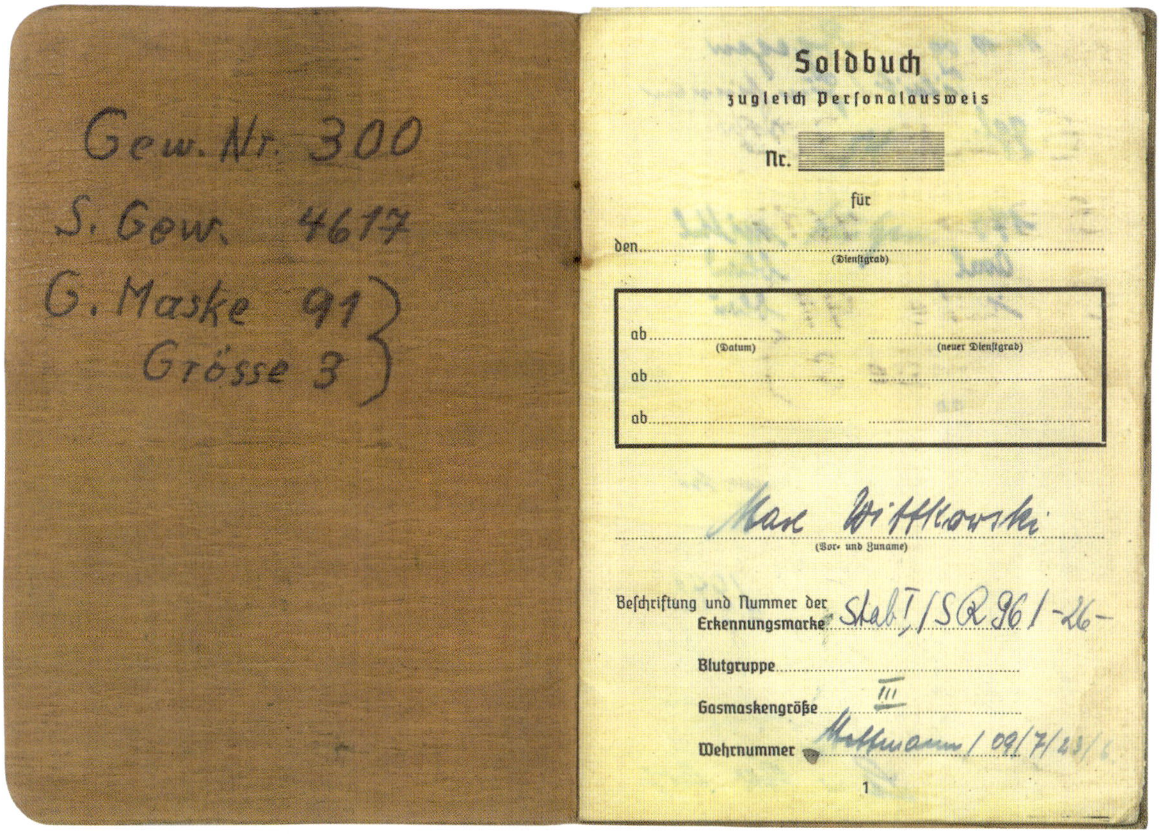

Gew. Nr. 300
S. Gew. 4617
G. Maske 91
Grösse 3

Soldbuch
zugleich Personalausweis
Nr.
für
den
(Dienstgrad)
ab (Datum) (neuer Dienstgrad)
ab
ab
Max Wittkowski
(Vor- und Zuname)
Beschriftung und Nummer der Erkennungsmarke Stab I/SR 961-26-
Blutgruppe
Gasmaskengröße III
Wehrnummer
1

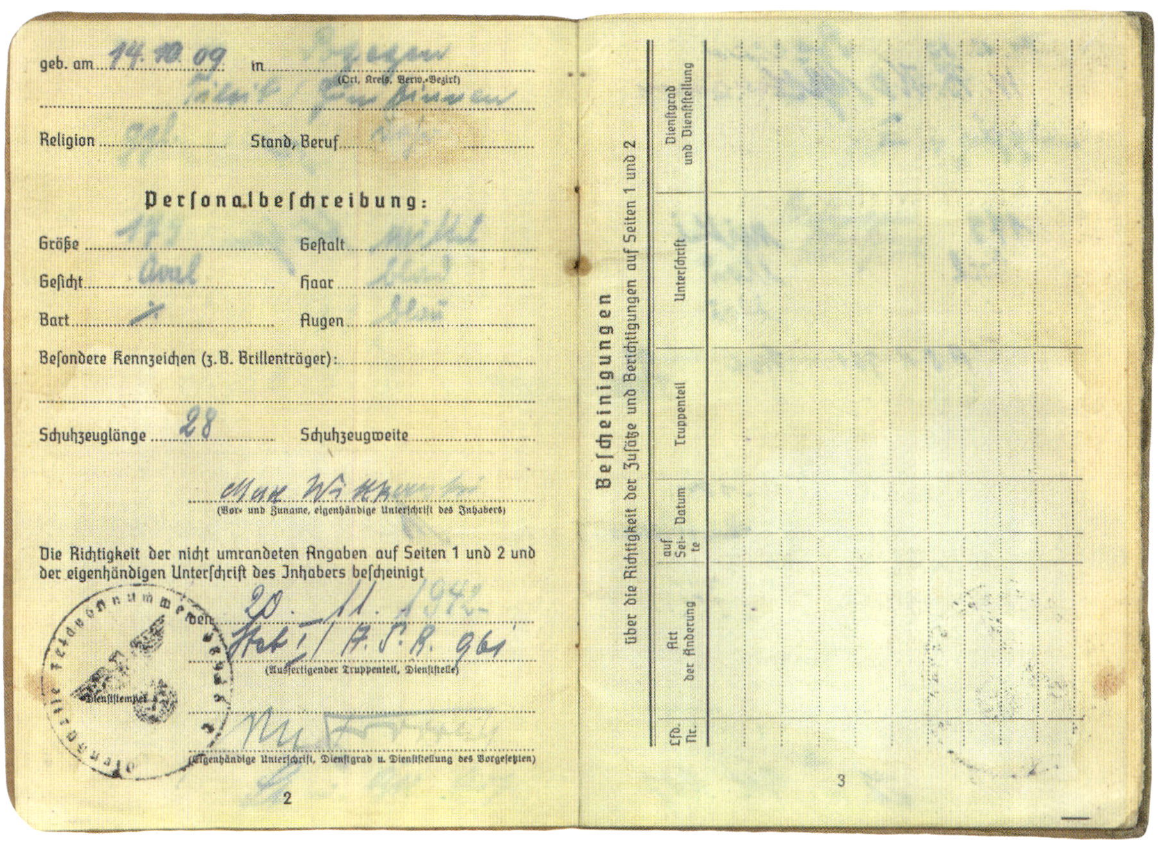

geb. am 14.10.09 in
(Ort, Kreis, Verw.-Bezirk)
Religion
Stand, Beruf
Personalbeschreibung:
Größe
Gestalt
Gesicht
Haar
Bart
Augen
Besondere Kennzeichen (z.B. Brillenträger):
Schuhzeuglänge 28
Schuhzeugweite
(Vor- und Zuname, eigenhändige Unterschrift des Inhabers)
Die Richtigkeit der nicht umrandeten Angaben auf Seiten 1 und 2 und der eigenhändigen Unterschrift des Inhabers bescheinigt
den 20. 11. 1942
Stab I/A.S.R. 961
(Ausfertigender Truppenteil, Dienststelle)
Dienststempel
(Eigenhändige Unterschrift, Dienstgrad u. Dienststellung des Vorgesetzten)
2

Bescheinigungen
über die Richtigkeit der Zusätze und Berichtigungen auf Seiten 1 und 2

Lfd. Nr.	Art der Änderung	auf Seite	Datum	Truppenteil	Unterschrift	Dienstgrad und Dienststellung

3

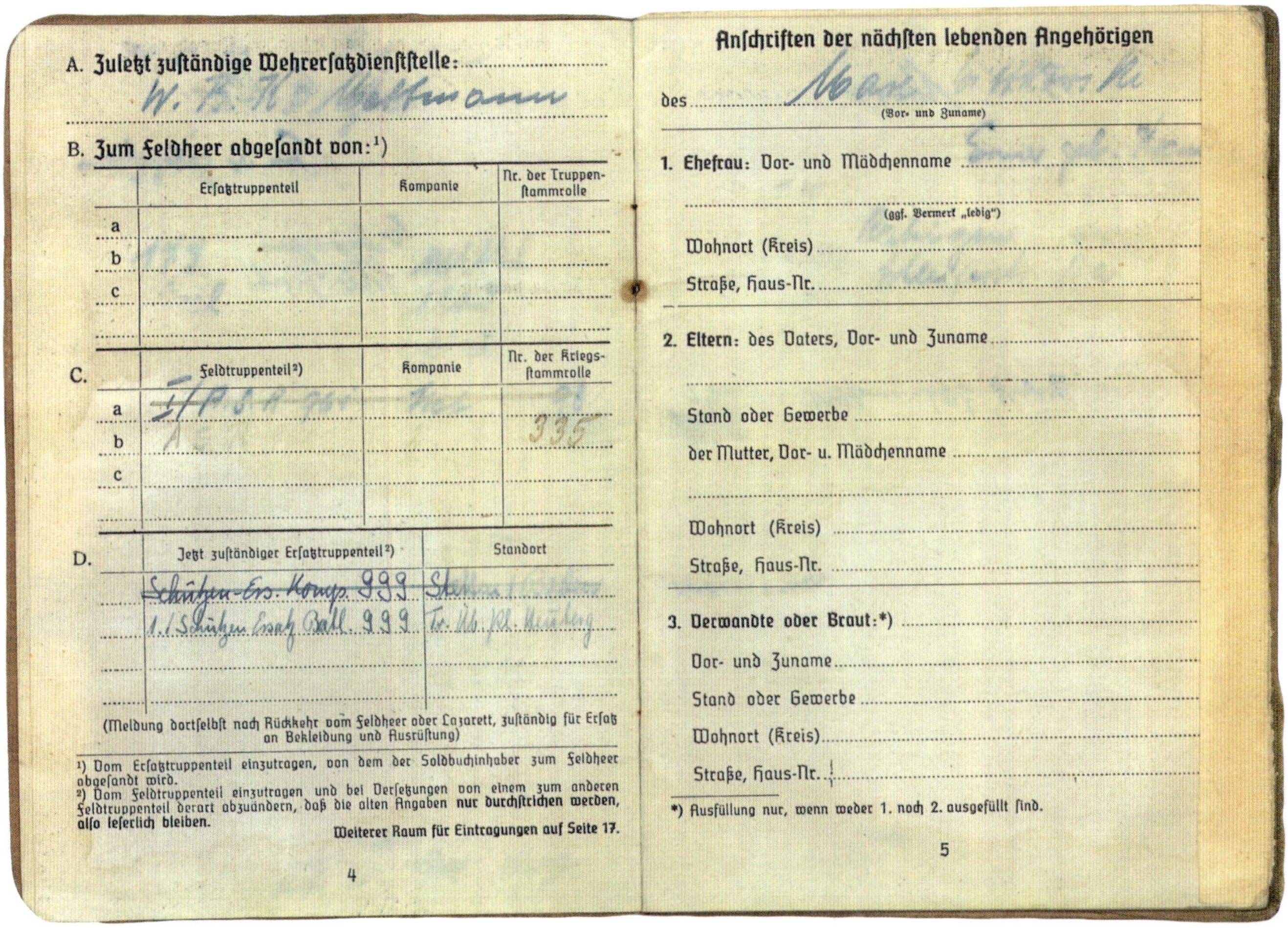

A. **Zuletzt zuständige Wehrersatzdienststelle:**

B. **Zum Feldheer abgesandt von:**[1])

	Ersatztruppenteil	Kompanie	Nr. der Truppen-stammrolle
a			
b			
c			

C.

	Feldtruppenteil[2])	Kompanie	Nr. der Kriegs-stammrolle
a			
b			335
c			

D.

Jetzt zuständiger Ersatztruppenteil[2])	Standort
~~Schützen-Ers. Komp. 999~~	
1./Schützen Ersatz Batl. 999	

(Meldung dortselbst nach Rückkehr vom Feldheer oder Lazarett, zuständig für Ersatz an Bekleidung und Ausrüstung)

1) Vom Ersatztruppenteil einzutragen, von dem der Soldbuchinhaber zum Feldheer abgesandt wird.
2) Vom Feldtruppenteil einzutragen und bei Versetzungen von einem zum anderen Feldtruppenteil derart abzuändern, daß die alten Angaben **nur durchstrichen werden, also leserlich bleiben.**

Weiterer Raum für Eintragungen auf Seite 17.

4

Anschriften der nächsten lebenden Angehörigen

des .... (Vor- und Zuname)

1. **Ehefrau:** Vor- und Mädchenname .... (ggf. Vermerk „ledig")
Wohnort (Kreis) ....
Straße, Haus-Nr. ....

2. **Eltern:** des Vaters, Vor- und Zuname ....
Stand oder Gewerbe ....
der Mutter, Vor- u. Mädchenname ....
Wohnort (Kreis) ....
Straße, Haus-Nr. ....

3. **Verwandte oder Braut:***)
Vor- und Zuname ....
Stand oder Gewerbe ....
Wohnort (Kreis) ....
Straße, Haus-Nr. ....

*) Ausfüllung nur, wenn weder 1. noch 2. ausgefüllt sind.

5

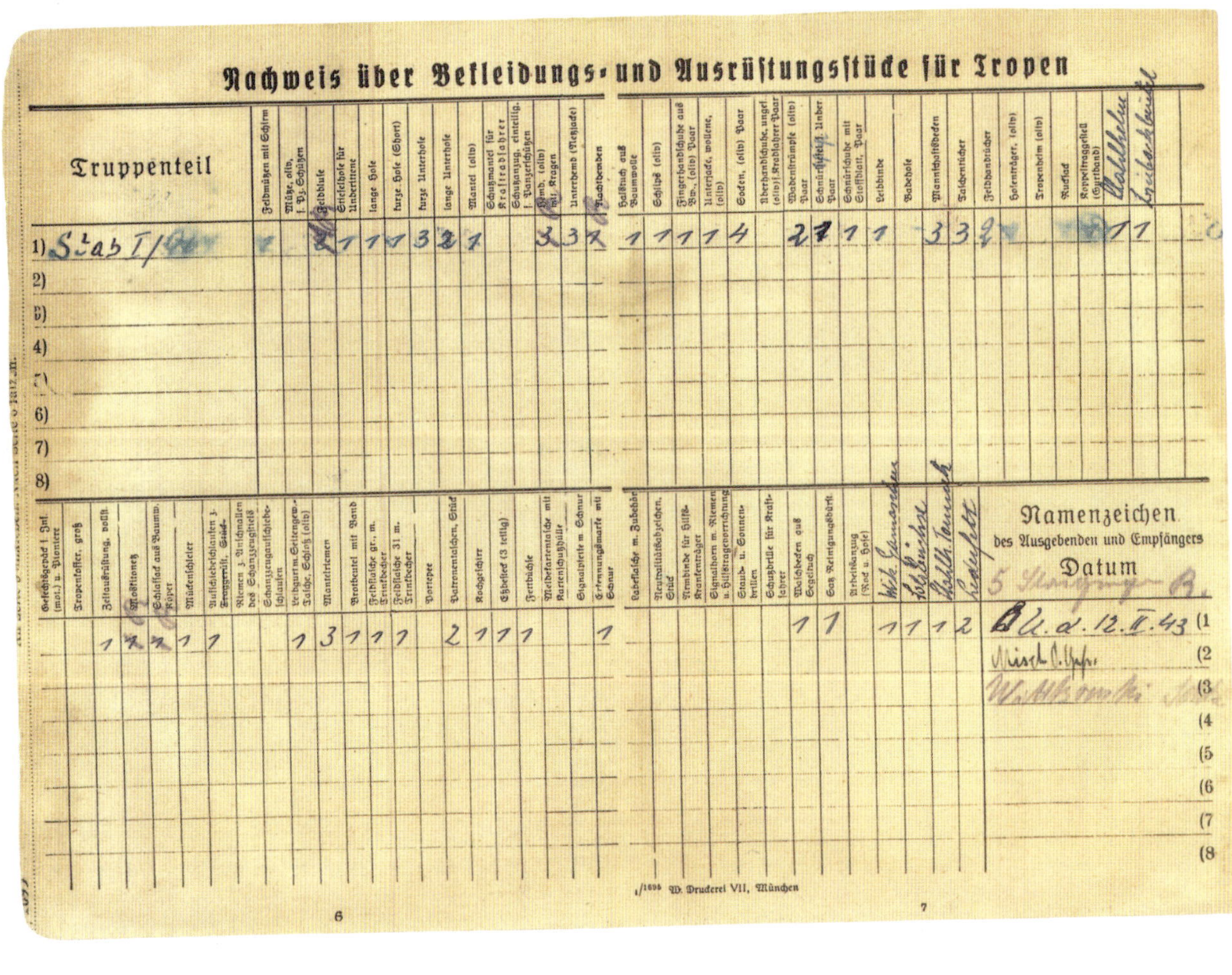

Nachweis über Bekleidungs- und Ausrüstungsstücke für Tropen

Truppenteil

1) Stab I/...
2)
3)
4)
5)
6)
7)
8)

Namenzeichen des Ausgebenden und Empfängers Datum

(1 Bl. d. 12. II. 43
(2
(3
(4
(5
(6
(7
(8

6

7

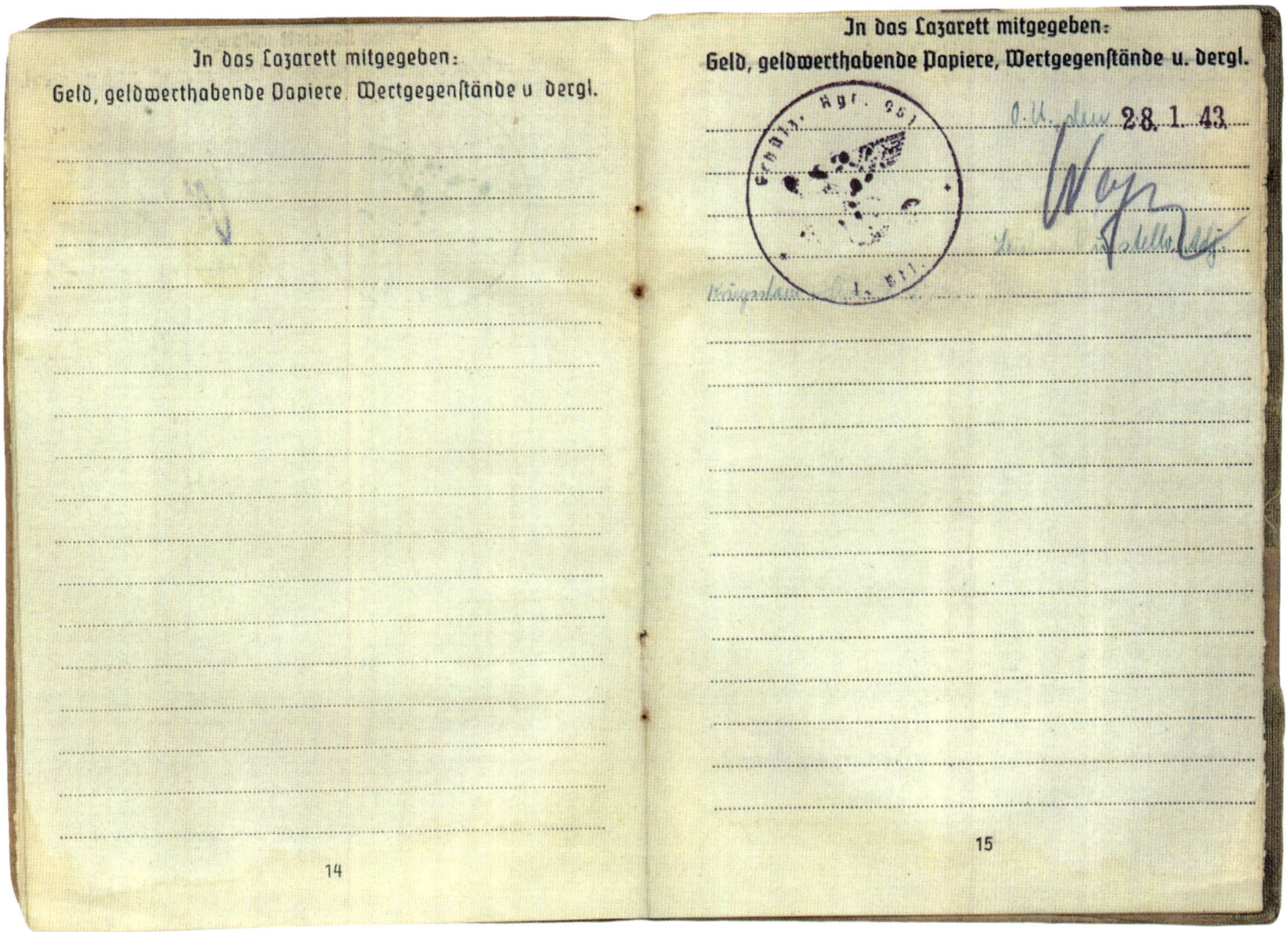

In das Lazarett mitgegeben:
Geld, geldwerthabende Papiere, Wertgegenstände u. dergl.

14

In das Lazarett mitgegeben:
Geld, geldwerthabende Papiere, Wertgegenstände u. dergl.

O.U., den 28. 1. 43

15

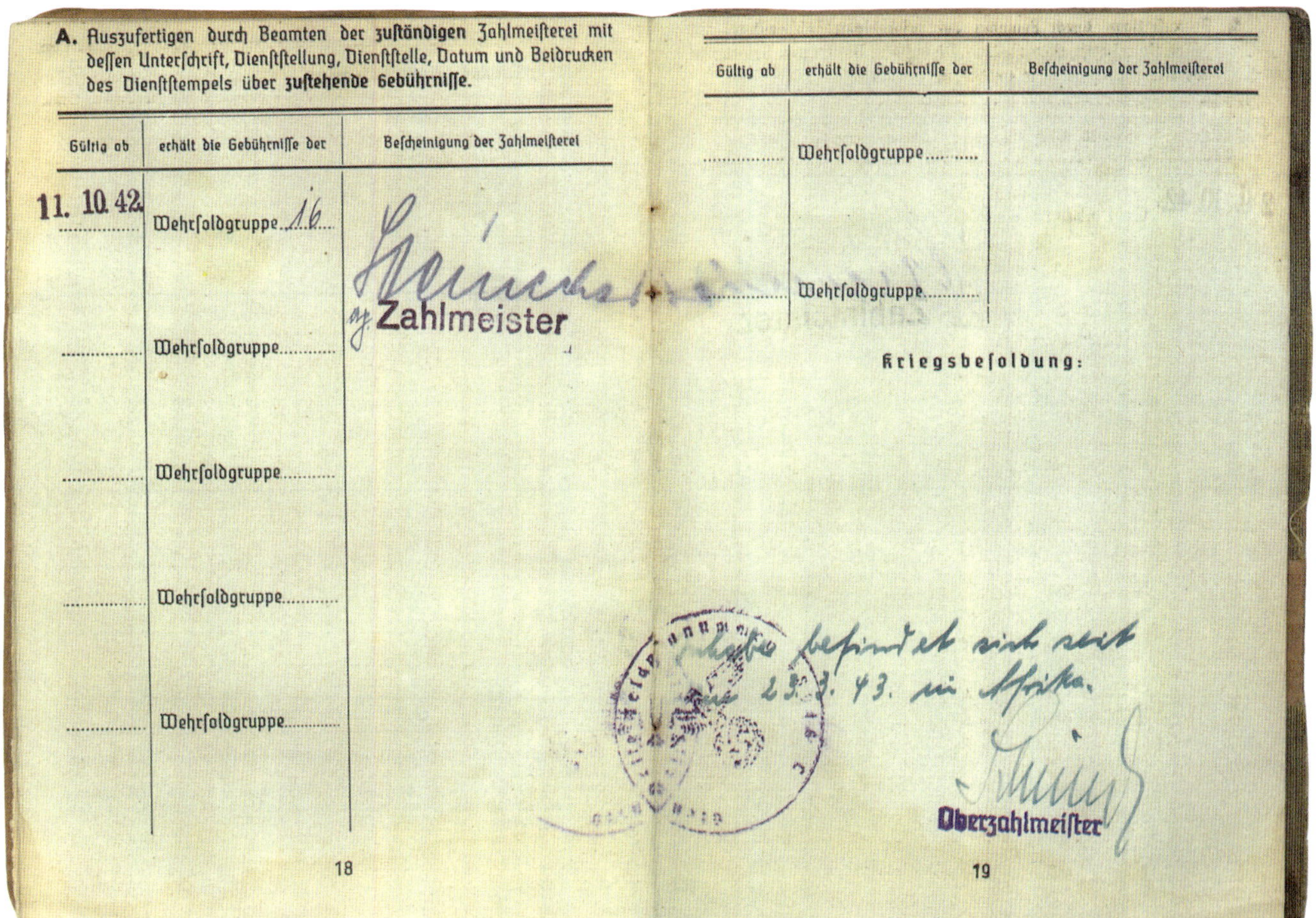

A. Auszufertigen durch Beamten der **zuständigen** Zahlmeisterei mit dessen Unterschrift, Dienststellung, Dienststelle, Datum und Beidrucken des Dienststempels über **zustehende Gebührnisse**.

Gültig ab	erhält die Gebührnisse der	Bescheinigung der Zahlmeisterei
11. 10. 42	Wehrsoldgruppe 16	Zahlmeister
	Wehrsoldgruppe	
	Wehrsoldgruppe	
	Wehrsoldgruppe	
	Wehrsoldgruppe	

18

Gültig ab	erhält die Gebührnisse der	Bescheinigung der Zahlmeisterei
	Wehrsoldgruppe	
	Wehrsoldgruppe	

Kriegsbesoldung:

befindet sich seit 23. 3. 43. in Afrika.

Oberzahlmeister

19

Exceptionally rare *Afrikakorps* personal identification disk (*Erkennungsmarke*) for a soldier of the *Afrika Schützen Regiment 962*. This was the second penal battalion sent to Africa in early 1943 to form the greater part of the *999th Afrika-Brigade*.

A rare AFRIKA cufftitle award document belonging to Kurt Bruckner from the third companie of *Afrika-Schützen-Regiment 962*. Many soldiers from this penal battalion were wounded (see his black wound badge document) or killed in the final weeks of the African campaign. *Schützen* Bruckner was fortunate to survive and was later recognized for his service in Africa.

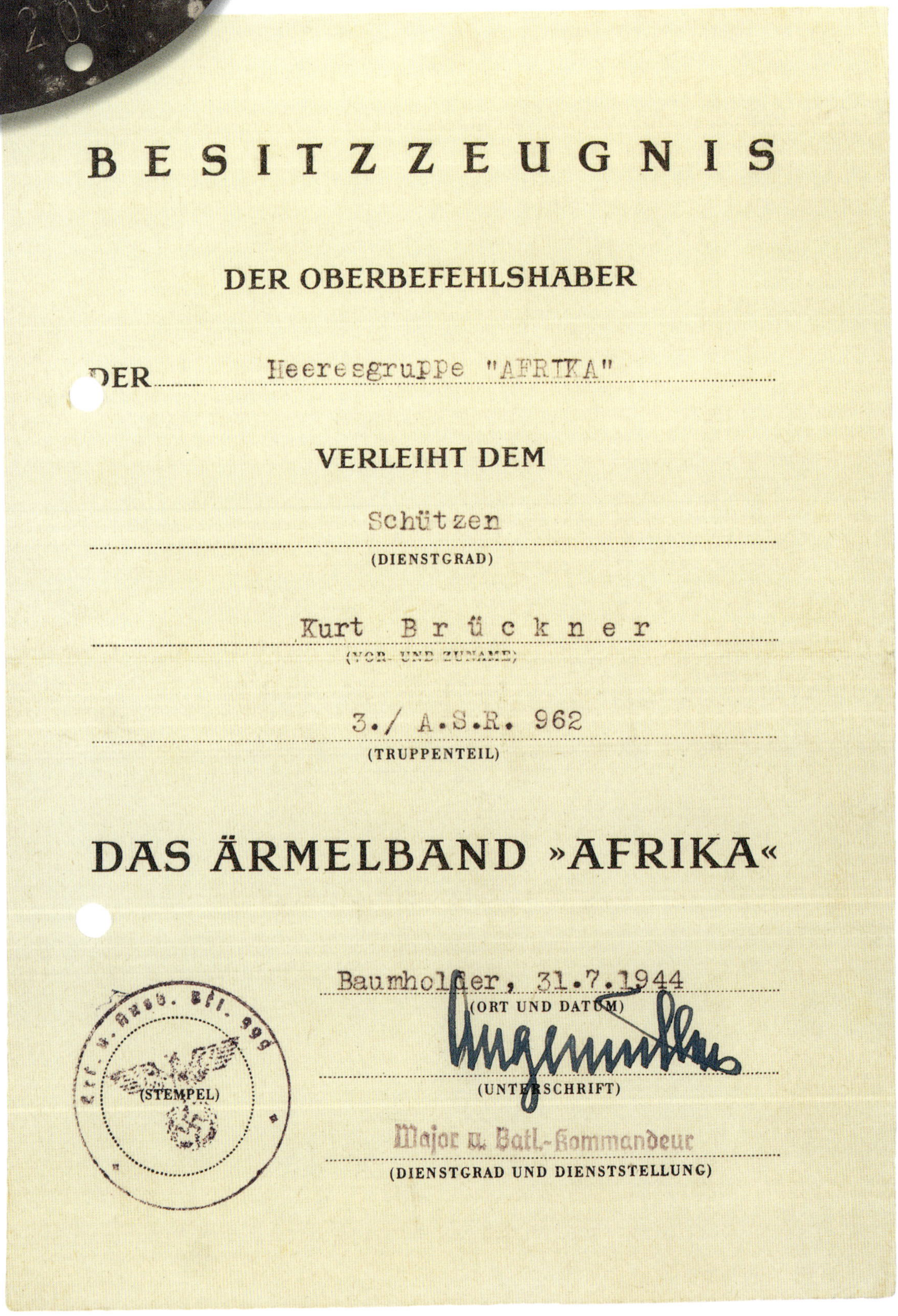

BESITZZEUGNIS

DER OBERBEFEHLSHABER

DER Heeresgruppe "AFRIKA"

VERLEIHT DEM

Schützen

(DIENSTGRAD)

Kurt Brückner

(VOR- UND ZUNAME)

3./ A.S.R. 962

(TRUPPENTEIL)

DAS ÄRMELBAND »AFRIKA«

Baumholder, 31.7.1944

(ORT UND DATUM)

(STEMPEL)

(UNTERSCHRIFT)

Major u. Batl.-Kommandeur

(DIENSTGRAD UND DIENSTSTELLUNG)

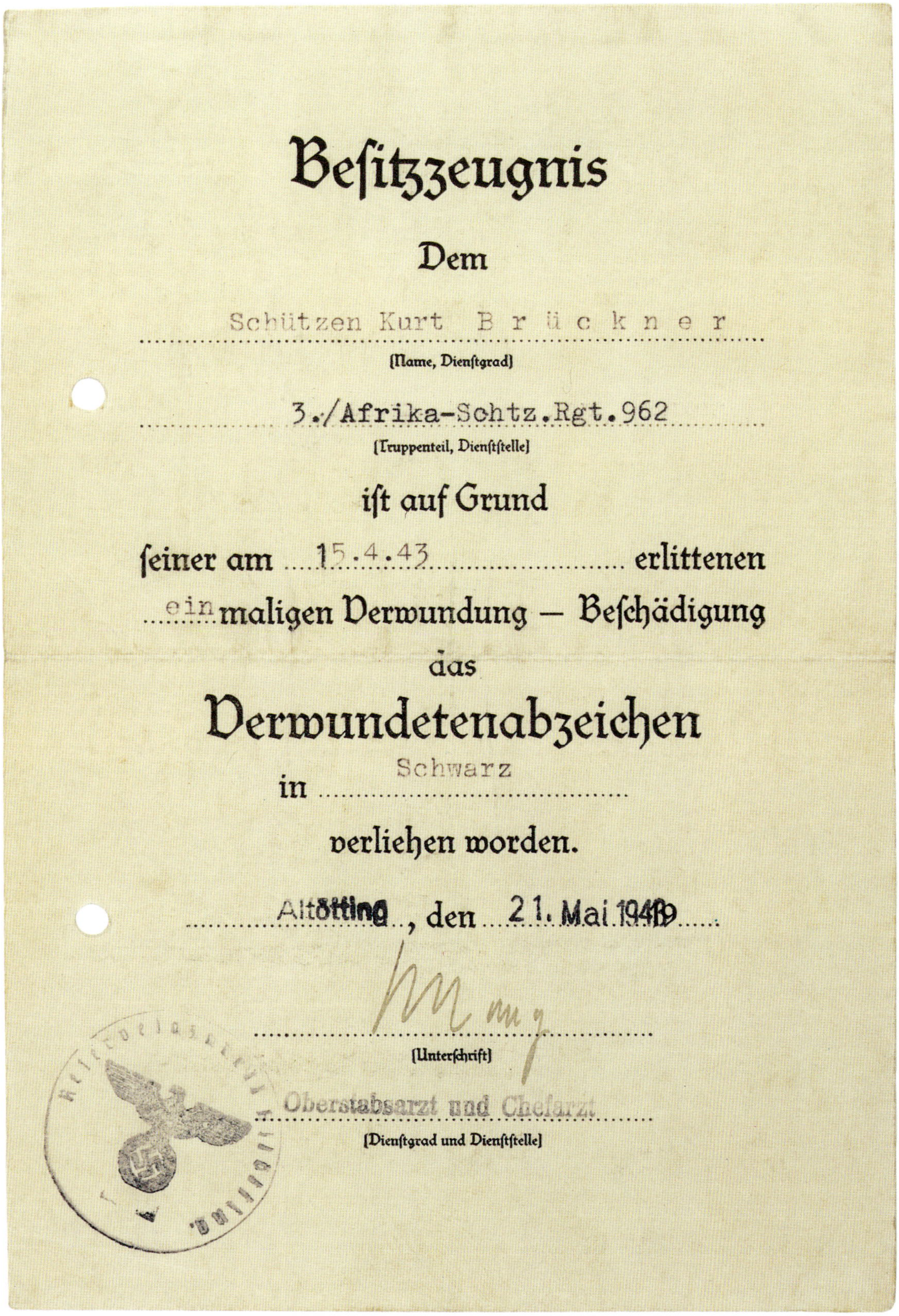

Besitzzeugnis

Dem

Schützen Kurt Brückner

(Name, Dienstgrad)

3./Afrika-Schtz.Rgt.962

(Truppenteil, Dienststelle)

ist auf Grund

seiner am 15.4.43 erlittenen

einmaligen Verwundung — Beschädigung

das

Verwundetenabzeichen

in Schwarz

verliehen worden.

Altötting, den 21. Mai 1943

(Unterschrift)

Oberstabsarzt und Chefarzt

(Dienstgrad und Dienststelle)

On April 15, 1943, Kurt Bruckner was wounded in action in Africa and awarded the Black Wound badge on May 21, 1943.

Another exceptional *Afrikakorps* Penal Battalion *Soldbuch* to *Obergefreiter* Johann Rotter of the Medical Company of the *999 leichte Afrika-Division (San.Komp.999).* (David Bunch)

Soldbuch
zugleich Personalausweis
Nr. 9755
für
den Krankenträger (Dienstgrad)
ab 24.12.1943 Obersoldat (Datum) (neuer Dienstgrad)
ab 1.3.1944 Gefreiter
ab 1.4.1945 Obergefreiter
Johann Rotter (Vor- und Zuname)
Beschriftung und Nummer der Erkennungsmarke 9755
Blutgruppe 0
Gasmaskengröße 3
Wehrnummer Freudenthal 04/11/2/8
1

Front inside cover includes a photo of Johann Rotter in a tropical shirt. He was promoted three times during the war with his last promotion to *Obergefreiter* on April 1, 1945.

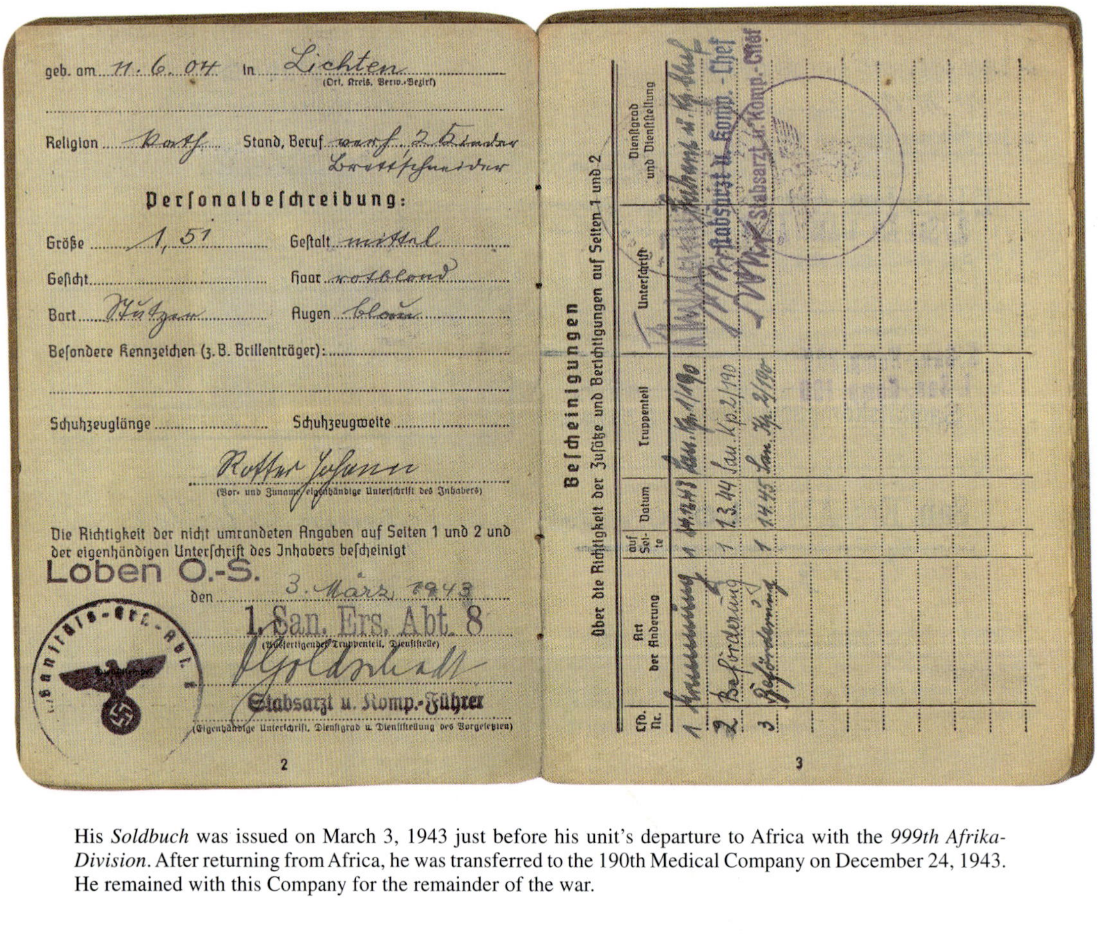

geb. am 11.6.04 in Lichten (Ort, Kreis, Verw.-Bezirk)
Religion Kath. Stand, Beruf
Personalbeschreibung:
Größe 1,57 Gestalt mittel
Gesicht Haar
Bart Augen blau
Besondere Kennzeichen (z.B. Brillenträger):
Schuhzeuglänge Schuhzeugweite
Rotter Johann (Vor- und Zuname, eigenhändige Unterschrift des Inhabers)
Die Richtigkeit der nicht umrandeten Angaben auf Seiten 1 und 2 und der eigenhändigen Unterschrift des Inhabers bescheinigt
Loben O.-S. den 3. März 1943
1. San. Ers. Abt. 8 (Ausfertigende Truppenteil, Dienststelle)
Stabsarzt u. Komp.-Führer
(Eigenhändige Unterschrift, Dienstgrad u. Dienststellung des Vorgesetzten)
2

Bescheinigungen
über die Richtigkeit der Zusätze und Berichtigungen auf Seiten 1 und 2

Lfd. Nr.	Art der Änderung	auf Seite	Datum	Truppenteil	Unterschrift	Dienstgrad und Dienststellung
1	Versetzung	1	24.12.43	San. Kp. 1/190		
2	Beförderung	1	1.3.44	San. Kp. 2/190		Stabsarzt u. Komp.-Chef
3	Beförderung	1	1.4.45	San. Kp. 2/190		Stabsarzt u. Komp.-Chef

3

His *Soldbuch* was issued on March 3, 1943 just before his unit's departure to Africa with the *999th Afrika-Division*. After returning from Africa, he was transferred to the 190th Medical Company on December 24, 1943. He remained with this Company for the remainder of the war.

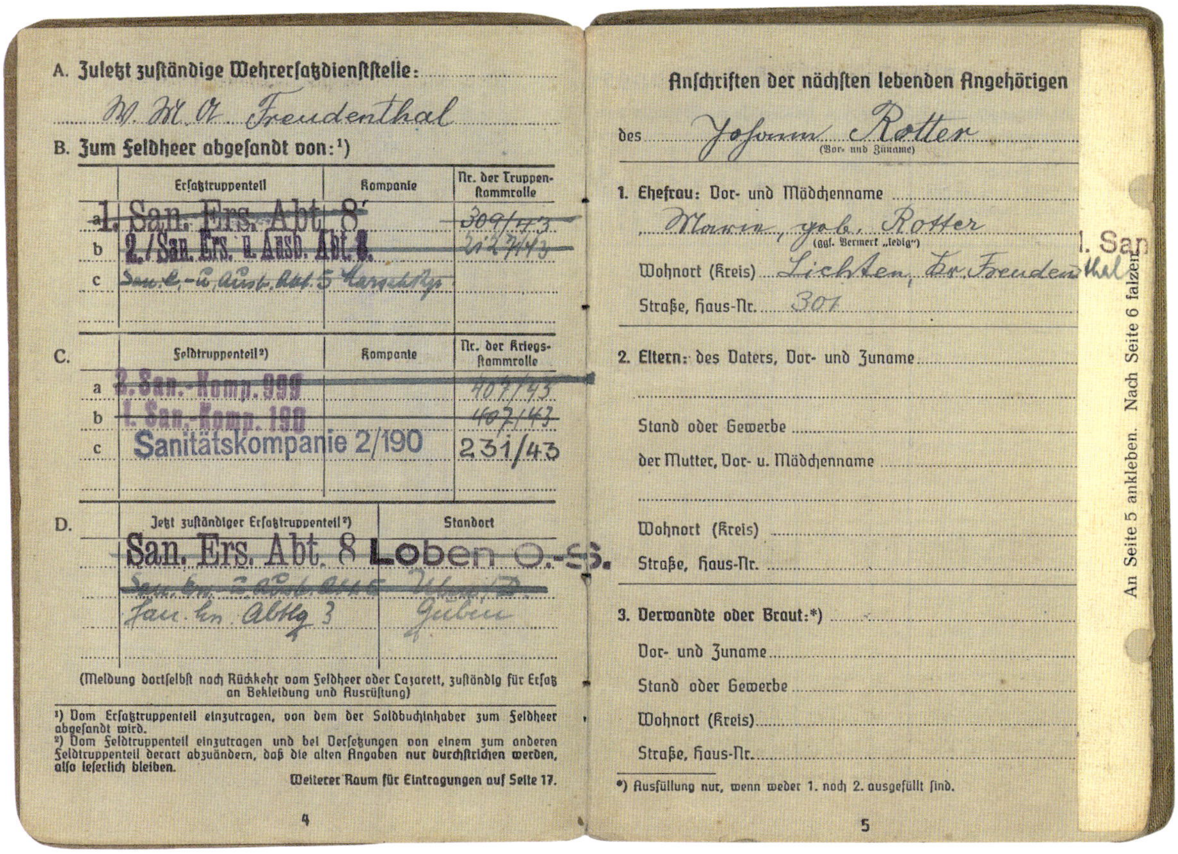

A. Zuletzt zuständige Wehrersatzdienststelle:
W. M. A. Freudenthal

B. Zum Feldheer abgesandt von:[1])

	Ersatztruppenteil	Kompanie	Nr. der Truppenstammrolle
a	~~1. San. Ers. Abt. 8~~		~~309/43~~
b	~~2./San. Ers. u. Ausb. Abt. 8~~		~~212/43~~
c	San. Ers. u. Ausb. Abt. 5 ...		

C.

	Feldtruppenteil[2])	Kompanie	Nr. der Kriegsstammrolle
a	~~2. San.-Komp. 999~~		~~407/43~~
b	~~1. San.-Komp. 190~~		~~407/43~~
c	Sanitätskompanie 2/190		231/43

D.

Jetzt zuständiger Ersatztruppenteil[2])	Standort
~~San. Ers. Abt. 8~~	~~Loben O.-S.~~
~~San. Ers. ...~~	~~...~~
San. Ers. Abtlg. 3	Guben

(Meldung dortselbst nach Rückkehr vom Feldheer oder Lazarett, zuständig für Ersatz an Bekleidung und Ausrüstung)

[1]) Vom Ersatztruppenteil einzutragen, von dem der Soldbuchinhaber zum Feldheer abgesandt wird.
[2]) Vom Feldtruppenteil einzutragen und bei Versetzungen von einem zum anderen Feldtruppenteil derart abzuändern, daß die alten Angaben nur durchstrichen werden, also leserlich bleiben.

Weiterer Raum für Eintragungen auf Seite 17.

4

Anschriften der nächsten lebenden Angehörigen

des Johann Rotter (Vor- und Zuname)

1. Ehefrau: Vor- und Mädchenname Maria, geb. Rotter (ggf. Vermerk „ledig")
Wohnort (Kreis) Lichten, Kr. Freudenthal
Straße, Haus-Nr. 301

2. Eltern: des Vaters, Vor- und Zuname
Stand oder Gewerbe
der Mutter, Vor- u. Mädchenname
Wohnort (Kreis)
Straße, Haus-Nr.

3. Verwandte oder Braut:*)
Vor- und Zuname
Stand oder Gewerbe
Wohnort (Kreis)
Straße, Haus-Nr.

*) Ausfüllung nur, wenn weder 1. noch 2. ausgefüllt sind.

5

An Seite 5 ankleben. Nach Seite 6 falzen

Page 4 reflects his initial field unit assignment to the "*2.San.-Komp.999*" (2nd Medical Company of *999th Afrika Division*) in Section C. This entry was later crossed out when he was transferred to a reserve unit and eventually to the 1st Medical Company of the 190th Regiment attached to the *90th Panzergrenadier Division*.

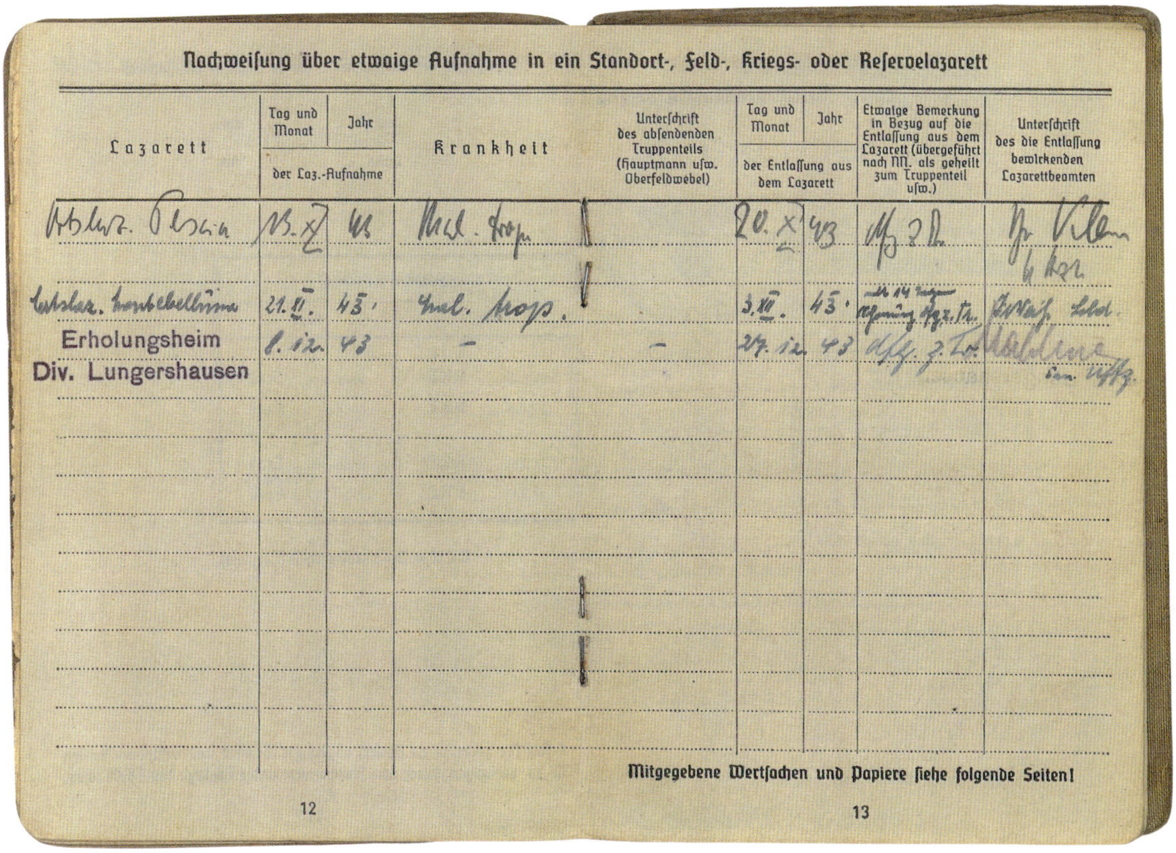

Nachweisung über etwaige Aufnahme in ein Standort-, Feld-, Kriegs- oder Reservelazarett

Lazarett	Tag und Monat (der Laz.-Aufnahme)	Jahr	Krankheit	Unterschrift des absendenden Truppenteils (Hauptmann usw. Oberfeldwebel)	Tag und Monat (der Entlassung aus dem Lazarett)	Jahr	Etwaige Bemerkung in Bezug auf die Entlassung aus dem Lazarett (übergeführt nach Nr. als geheilt zum Truppenteil usw.)	Unterschrift des die Entlassung bewirkenden Lazarettbeamten
Kr. Lz. ...	15. X.	43	Mal. trop.		20. X	43	...	...
...	21. XI.	43	Mal. trop.		3. XII.	43	...	...
Erholungsheim Div. Lungershausen	8. 12.	43	–	–	24. 12.	43	...	...

Mitgegebene Wertsachen und Papiere siehe folgende Seiten!

12 13

Page 12 indicates he was admitted to a hospital on October 15, 1943 with Malaria and discharged on October 20. However, he apparently had two relapses shortly after his initial release.

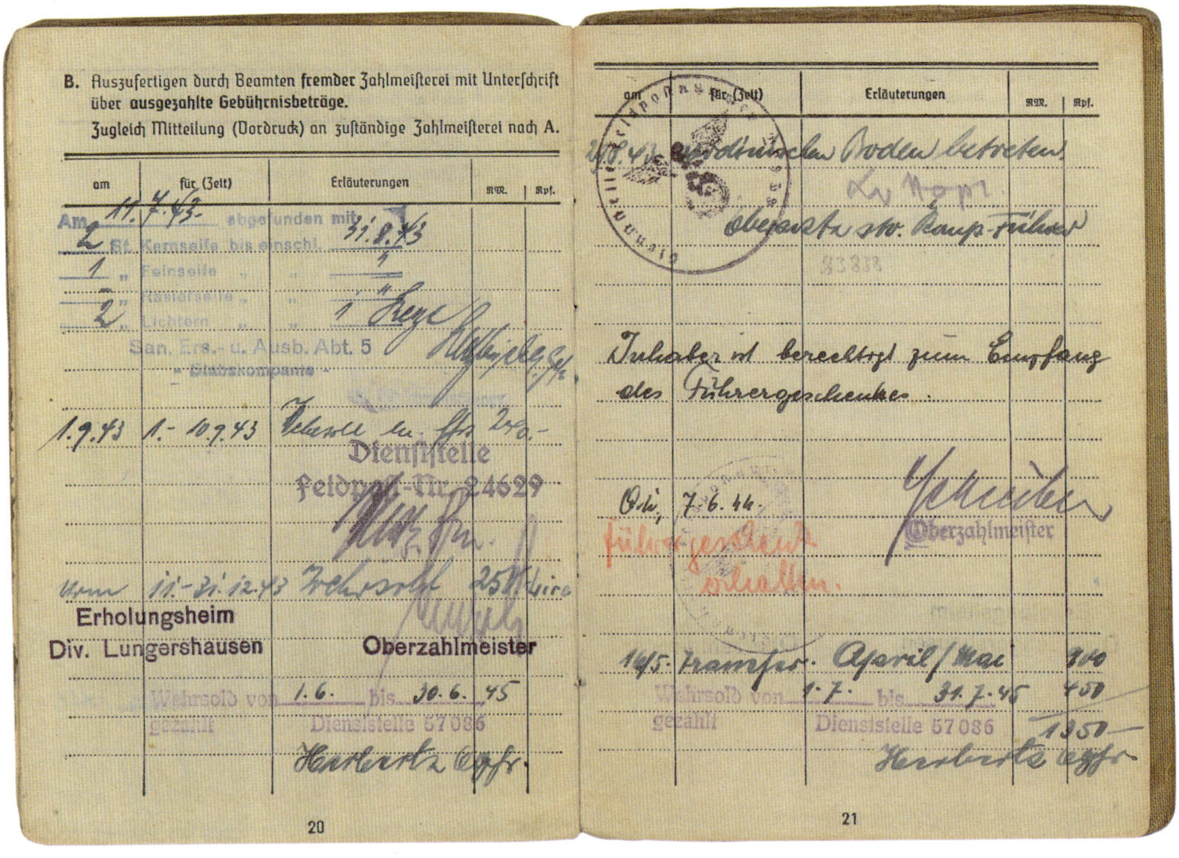
B. Auszufertigen durch Beamten fremder Zahlmeisterei mit Unterschrift über ausgezahlte Gebührnisbeträge.
Zugleich Mitteilung (Vordruck) an zuständige Zahlmeisterei nach A.

am	für (Zeit)	Erläuterungen	RM.	Rpf.
Am 11.7.43	abgefunden mit	2 St. Kernseife bis einschl. 31.8.43		
		1 „ Feinseife		
		2 „ Rasierseife		
		Lichtern		
		San. Ers.- u. Ausb. Abt. 5 – Stabskompanie		
1.9.43	1.–10.9.43	Dienststelle Feldpost-Nr. 24629		
vom	11.–31.12.43	Wehrsold 25 Lire – Erholungsheim Div. Lungershausen – Oberzahlmeister		
		Wehrsold von 1.6. bis 30.6.45 gezahlt – Dienststelle 57086		

20

am	für (Zeit)	Erläuterungen	RM.	Rpf.
28.4.43		nordafrikanischen Boden betreten – Oberarzt u. stv. Komp.-Führer		
		Inhaber ist berechtigt zum Empfang des Führergeschenkes.		
Ort, 7.6.44.		Oberzahlmeister – führergeschenk erhalten.		
1.4.5.		Wehrsold von 1.7. bis 31.7.45 gezahlt – Dienststelle 57086		

21

Pages 20 and 21 reflect various administrative and pay matters while in service in Africa and Italy.

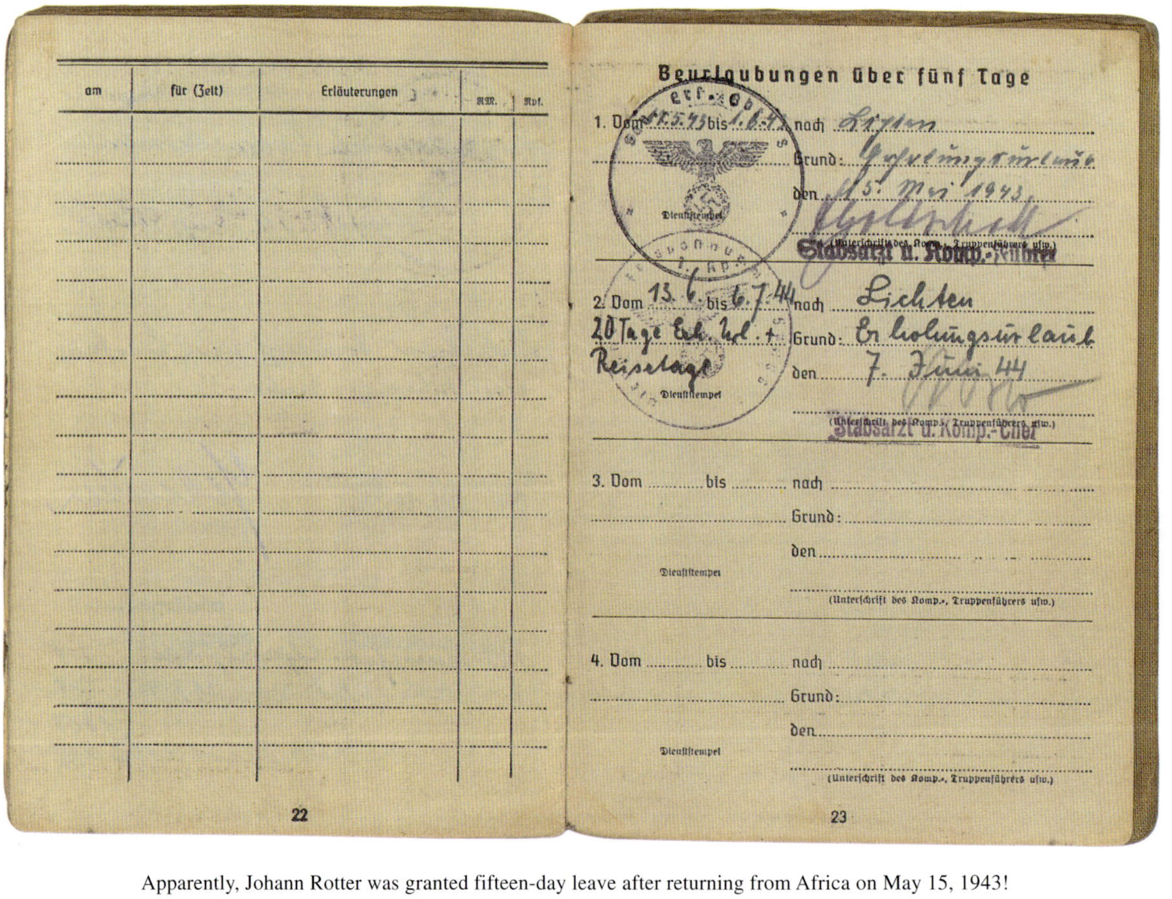
am	für (Zeit)	Erläuterungen	RM.	Rpf.

22

Beurlaubungen über fünf Tage

1. Vom 15.5.43 bis 1.6.43 nach Lichten
Grund: Erholungsurlaub
den 15. Mai 1943
Dienststempel
(Unterschrift des Komp.-, Truppenführers usw.)
Stabsarzt u. Komp.-Führer

2. Vom 13.6. bis 6.7.44 nach Lichten
20 Tage Erh. Url. + Reisetage
Grund: Erholungsurlaub
den 7. Juni 44
Dienststempel
(Unterschrift des Komp.-, Truppenführers usw.)
Stabsarzt u. Komp.-Chef

3. Vom ...... bis ...... nach ......
Grund: ......
den ......
Dienststempel
(Unterschrift des Komp.-, Truppenführers usw.)

4. Vom ...... bis ...... nach ......
Grund: ......
den ......
Dienststempel
(Unterschrift des Komp.-, Truppenführers usw.)

23

Apparently, Johann Rotter was granted fifteen-day leave after returning from Africa on May 15, 1943!

Very rare *Soldbuch*, and five award document grouping to Willi Radtke, an *Oberfeldwebel* of 1.*Komanie*, Grenadier Regiment 47. (John Keener)

Radtke's *Soldbuch* with photograph showing him in tropical uniform.

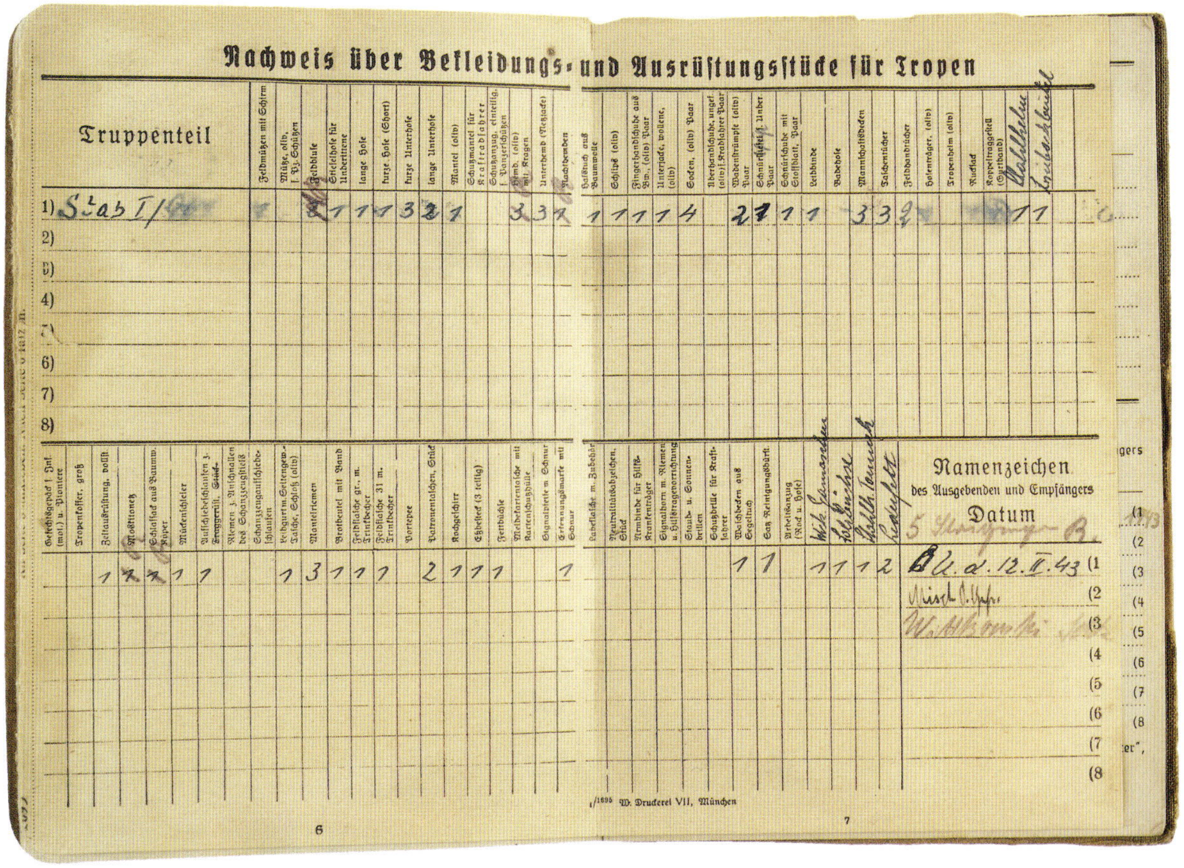

Radtke's *Soldbuch* insert showing issuance of tropical clothing and equipment.

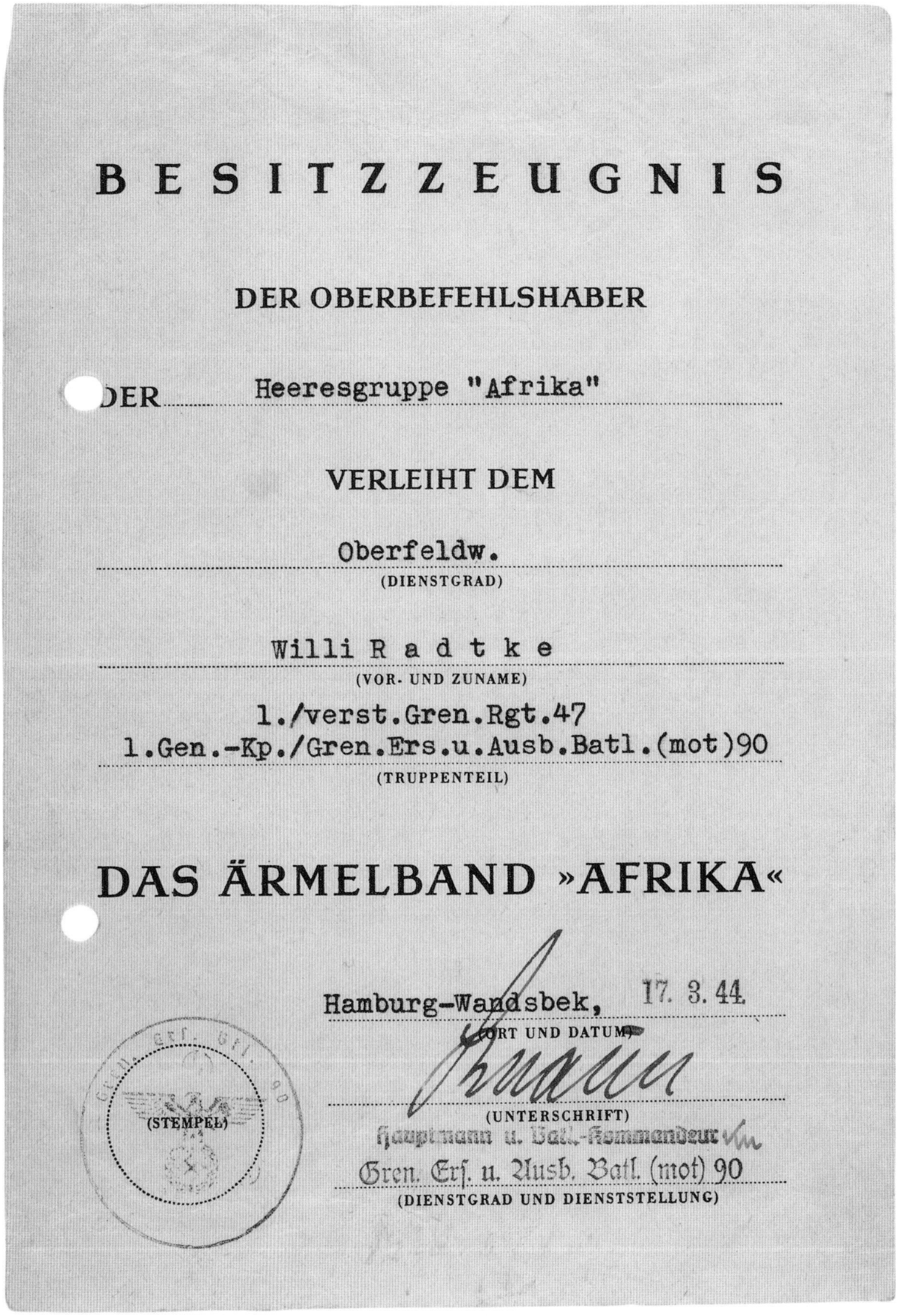

BESITZZEUGNIS

DER OBERBEFEHLSHABER

DER Heeresgruppe "Afrika"

VERLEIHT DEM

Oberfeldw.
(DIENSTGRAD)

Willi Radtke
(VOR- UND ZUNAME)

1./verst.Gren.Rgt.47
1.Gen.-Kp./Gren.Ers.u.Ausb.Batl.(mot)90
(TRUPPENTEIL)

DAS ÄRMELBAND »AFRIKA«

Hamburg-Wandsbek, 17. 3. 44
(ORT UND DATUM)

(STEMPEL)

(UNTERSCHRIFT)

Hauptmann u. Batl.-Kommandeur
Gren. Ers. u. Ausb. Batl. (mot) 90
(DIENSTGRAD UND DIENSTSTELLUNG)

Radtke's AFRIKA cufftitle award document.

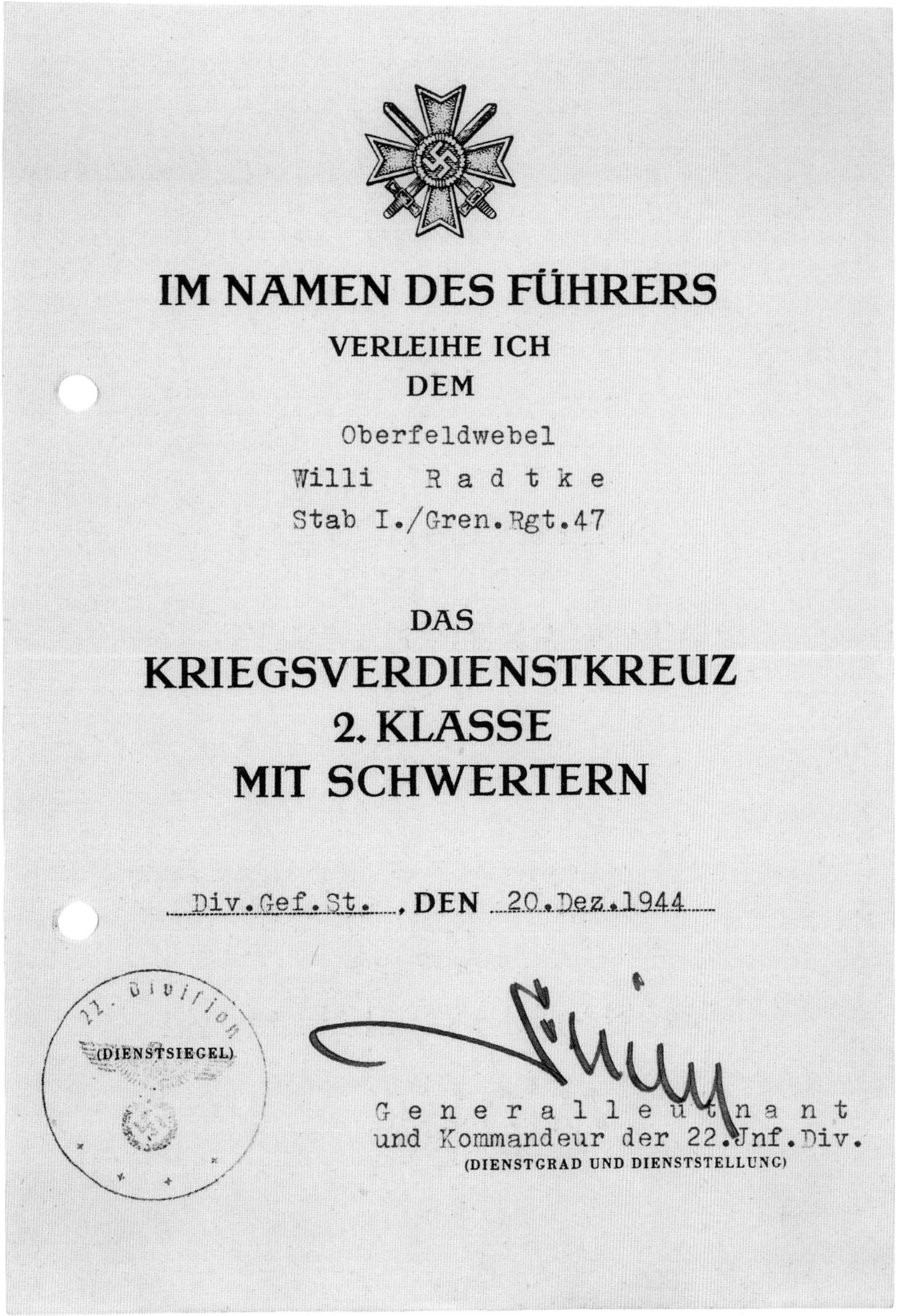

IM NAMEN DES FÜHRERS

VERLEIHE ICH

DEM

Oberfeldwebel

Willi R a d t k e

Stab I./Gren.Rgt.47

DAS

KRIEGSVERDIENSTKREUZ

2. KLASSE

MIT SCHWERTERN

Div.Gef.St. , DEN 20.Dez.1944

22. Division

(DIENSTSIEGEL)

G e n e r a l l e u t n a n t

und Kommandeur der 22.Jnf.Div.

(DIENSTGRAD UND DIENSTSTELLUNG)

Radtke's War Service Cross 2nd Class with Swords award document.

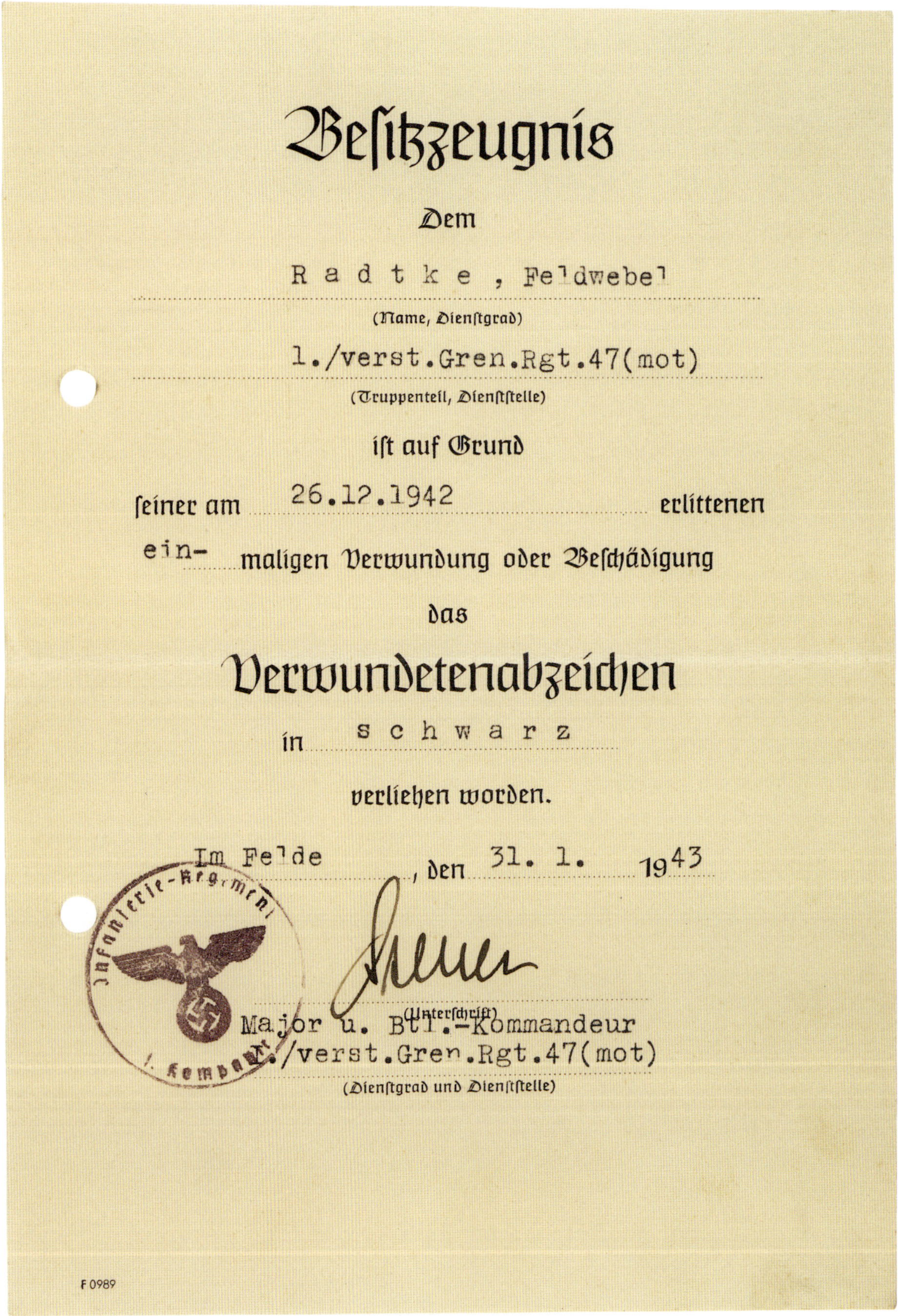

Besitzzeugnis

Dem

R a d t k e , Feldwebel

(Name, Dienstgrad)

1./verst.Gren.Rgt.47(mot)

(Truppenteil, Dienststelle)

ist auf Grund

seiner am 26.12.1942 erlittenen

ein- maligen Verwundung oder Beschädigung

das

Verwundetenabzeichen

in s c h w a r z

verliehen worden.

Im Felde, den 31. 1. 1943

(Unterschrift)

Major u. Btl.-Kommandeur
I./verst.Gren.Rgt.47(mot)

(Dienstgrad und Dienststelle)

F 0989

Radtke's Black Wound Badge award document.

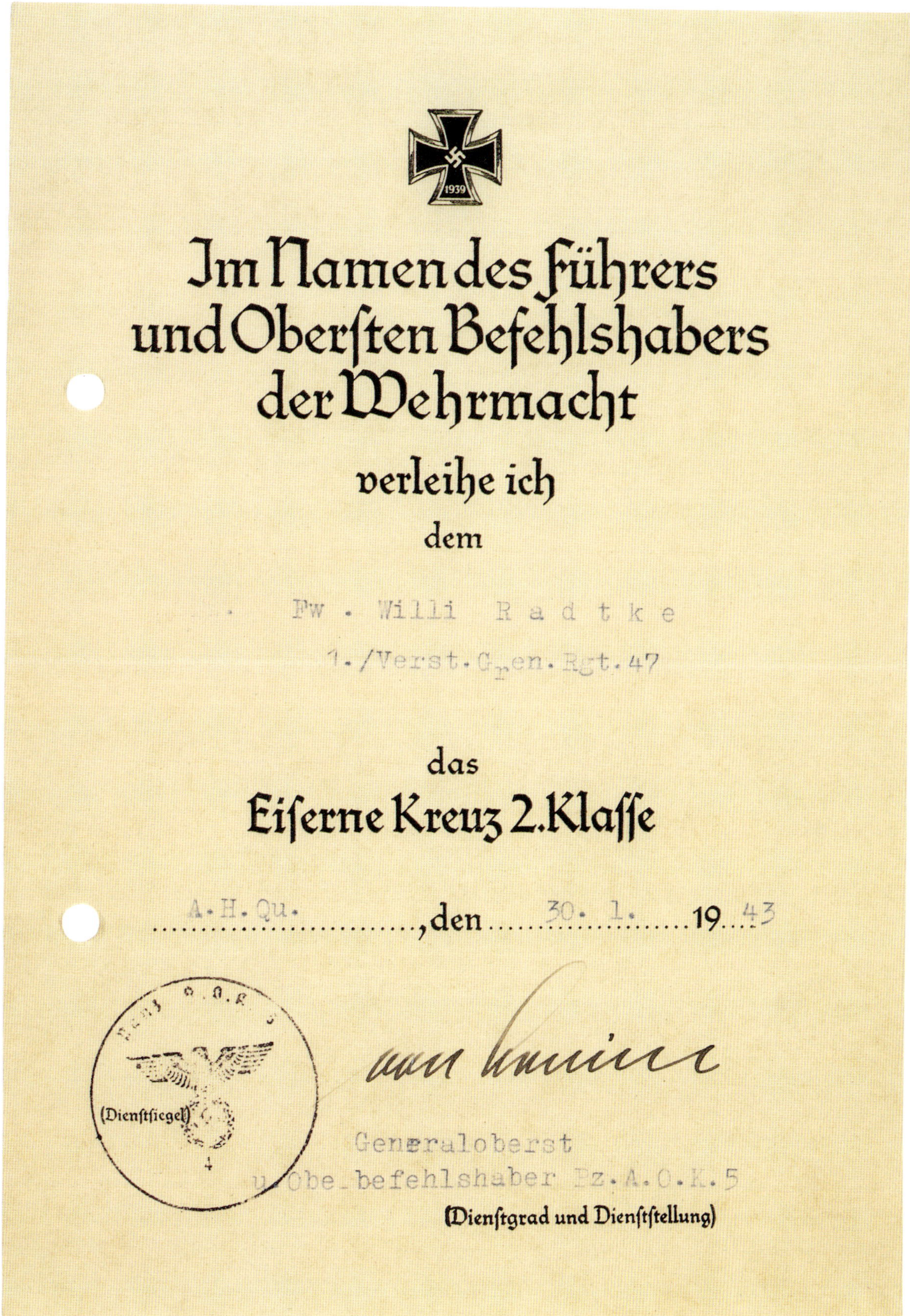

Im Namen des Führers
und Obersten Befehlshabers
der Wehrmacht

verleihe ich

dem

Fw. Willi Radtke
1./Verst.Gren.Rgt.47

das

Eiserne Kreuz 2. Klasse

A.H.Qu., den 30. 1. 1943

(Dienstsiegel)

von Arnim

Generaloberst
u. Oberbefehlshaber Pz.A.O.K.5
(Dienstgrad und Dienststellung)

Radtke's Iron Cross 2nd Class award document. This document is signed by *Generaloberst* von Arnim and would have been presented to Radtke in North Africa.

Im Namen des Führers und Reichskanzlers

verleihe ich

dem Unteroffizier Willi Radtke
(Dienstgrad, Vor- und Zuname)

7. Kompanie-Infanterie-Regiment 69.
(Truppenteil)

für 4 jährige treue Dienste in der Wehrmacht die

Dienstauszeichnung IV. Klasse.

Hamburg, den 1. Nov. 1938.

Schwandner
Generalleutnant
und Divisionskommandeur

Für die Richtigkeit:

Oberst und Rgts. Kdeur.

Wehrkreisdruckerei X, Hamburg

Radtke's Army 4-Year Service Medal award document. This document is signed by *Oberst* Wolfgang Fischer, later to become a *Generalleutnant* and commander of the 10th *Panzer* Division.

A fantastic *Afrikakorps* document grouping to Kuno Wegener, a heroic motor driver who served in Africa and went on to fight in Europe through the remainder of the war. This document set includes his complete *Soldbuch* first issued in 1940 and listing all the awards he earned during the war. Along with the *Soldbuch* are his award documents (including the rarest of all AFRIKA cuffftitle award documents), authorized leave passes and photo albums. (David Bunch)

Kuno Wegener's *Soldbuch* with photograph. Basic information is reflected on page 1 along with field promotions through January 1945. His *Soldbuch* was issued on September 18, 1940 as reflected on page 2 while his rank promotions are validated on page 3.

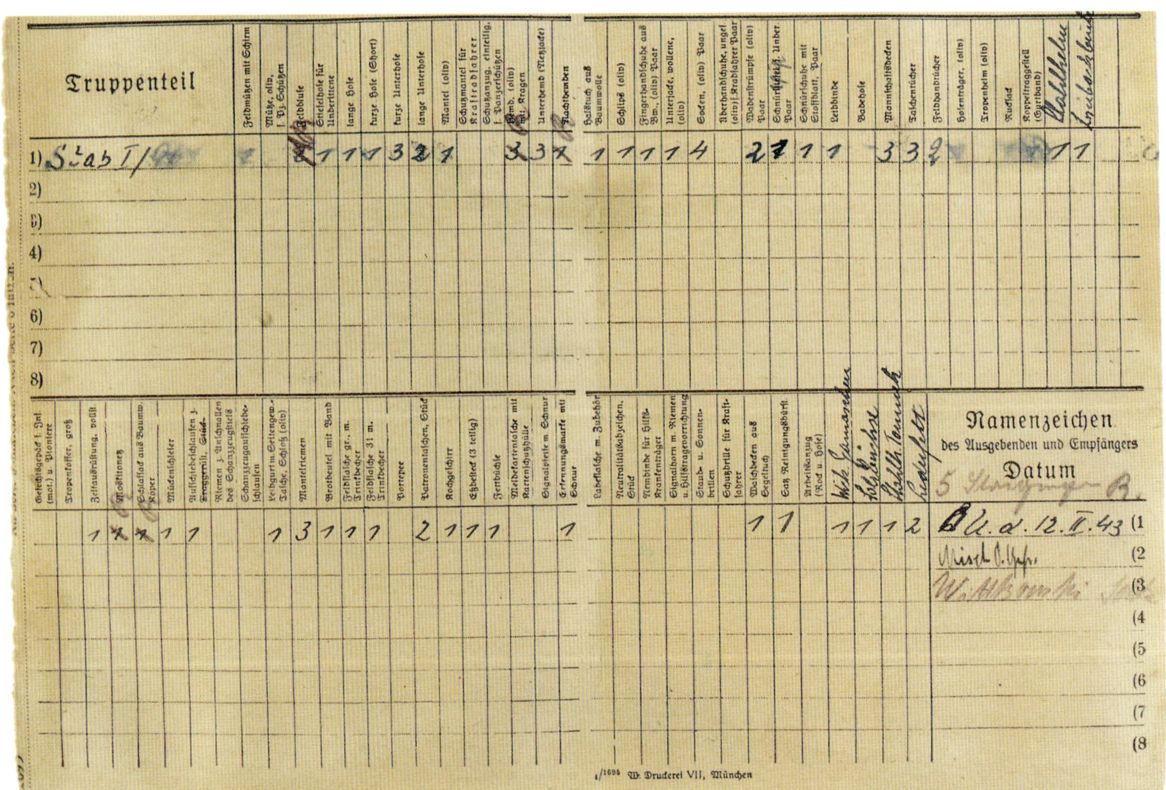

Wegener's *Soldbuch* insert for his tropical clothing and equipment.

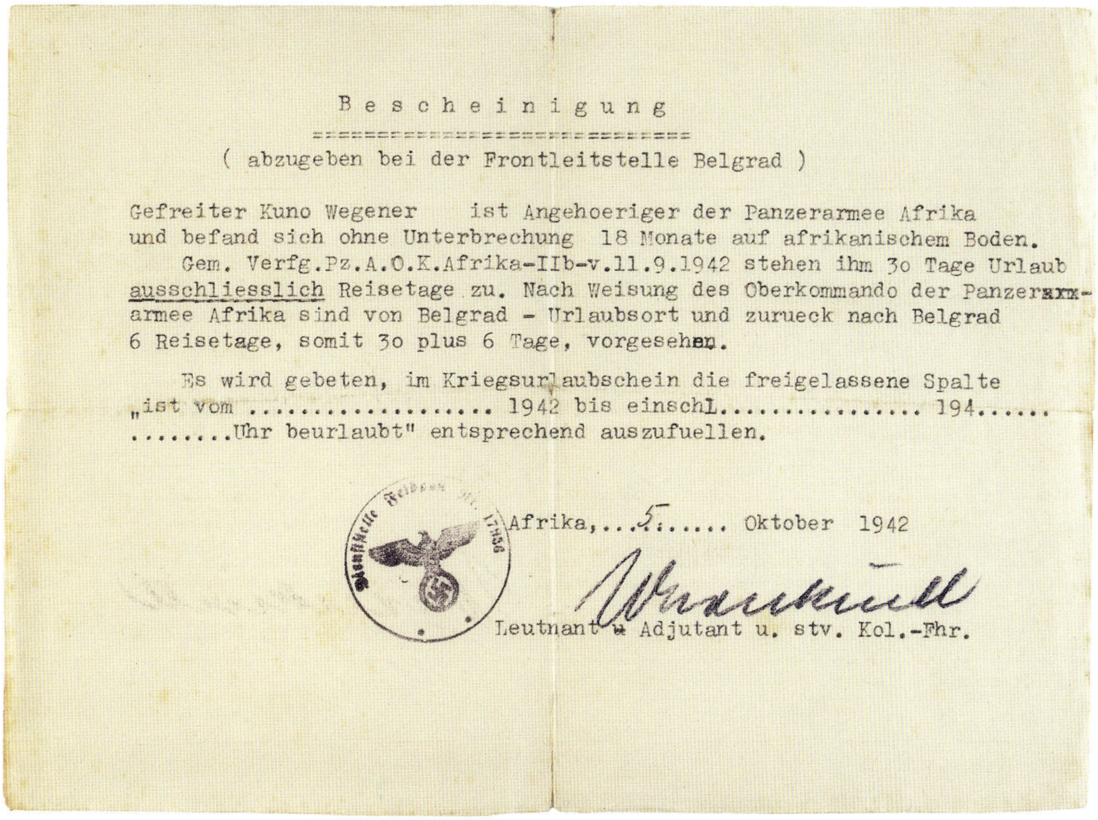

Bescheinigung

(abzugeben bei der Frontleitstelle Belgrad)

Gefreiter Kuno Wegener ist Angehoeriger der Panzerarmee Afrika und befand sich ohne Unterbrechung 18 Monate auf afrikanischem Boden.
Gem. Verfg.Pz.A.O.K.Afrika-IIb-v.11.9.1942 stehen ihm 30 Tage Urlaub ausschliesslich Reisetage zu. Nach Weisung des Oberkommando der Panzerarmee Afrika sind von Belgrad - Urlaubsort und zurueck nach Belgrad 6 Reisetage, somit 30 plus 6 Tage, vorgesehen.

Es wird gebeten, im Kriegsurlaubschein die freigelassene Spalte „ist vom .... 1942 bis einschl................ 194............Uhr beurlaubt" entsprechend auszufuellen.

Afrika,...5...... Oktober 1942

Leutnant u. Adjutant u. stv. Kol.-Fhr.

Leave Authorization issued to *Gefreiter* Kuno Wegener. It states that he is a member of *Panzerarmee Afrika* and has been in Africa for eighteen months without interruption, and is therefore entitled to thirty days leave plus six days travel time. The authorization was to be presented to the transit station in Belgrade, from where he would then travel to his ultimate destination.

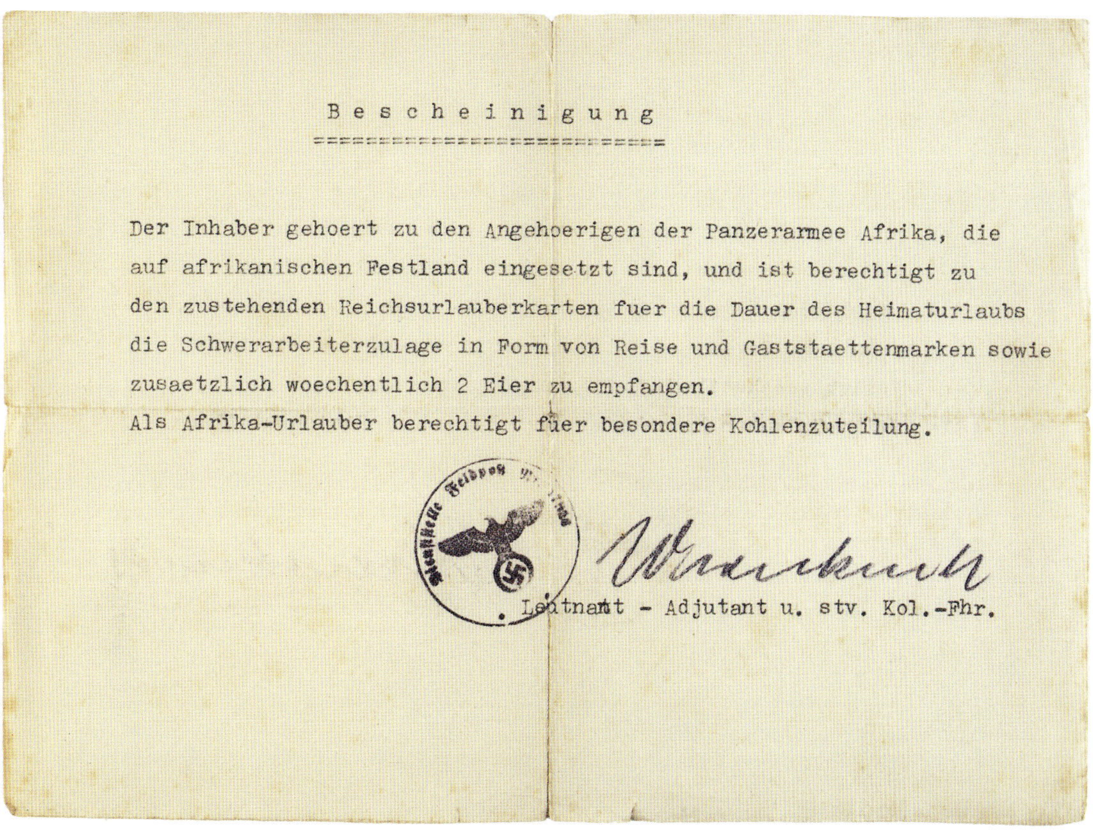

Bescheinigung

Der Inhaber gehoert zu den Angehoerigen der Panzerarmee Afrika, die auf afrikanischen Festland eingesetzt sind, und ist berechtigt zu den zustehenden Reichsurlauberkarten fuer die Dauer des Heimaturlaubs die Schwerarbeiterzulage in Form von Reise und Gaststaettenmarken sowie zusaetzlich woechentlich 2 Eier zu empfangen.
Als Afrika-Urlauber berechtigt fuer besondere Kohlenzuteilung.

Leutnant - Adjutant u. stv. Kol.-Fhr.

Certification issued to *Gefreiter* Wegener. It states that he is a member of *Panzerarmee Afrika* and for the duration of his leave is entitled to travel and restaurant vouchers plus two eggs per week. It also states that while he is on leave from the African theater he is entitled to a supplementary coal allocation.

BESITZZEUGNIS

Der Deutsche General
beim Hauptquartier der italienischen Wehrmacht

verleiht dem

Gefreiten
(Dienstgrad)

Kuno W e g e n e r
(Vor- und Zuname)

Nachschubstab z.b.V.264
(Truppenteil)
(ehem.Kfz.E.Abt.7/686)

das Ärmelband „Afrika"

Rom, den 31. Juli 1943

(Stempel)

General der Infanterie
und
Deutscher General beim Hauptquartier der
italienischen Wehrmacht (Mil. Att. Rom)

Extremely rare AFRIKA cufftitle award document given to Kuno Wegener from the German General of the Headquarters of the Italian Army in Rome. Appropriately signed and stamped, there are only two original examples of this unique variant of the AFRIKA cufftitle award document known to exist today.

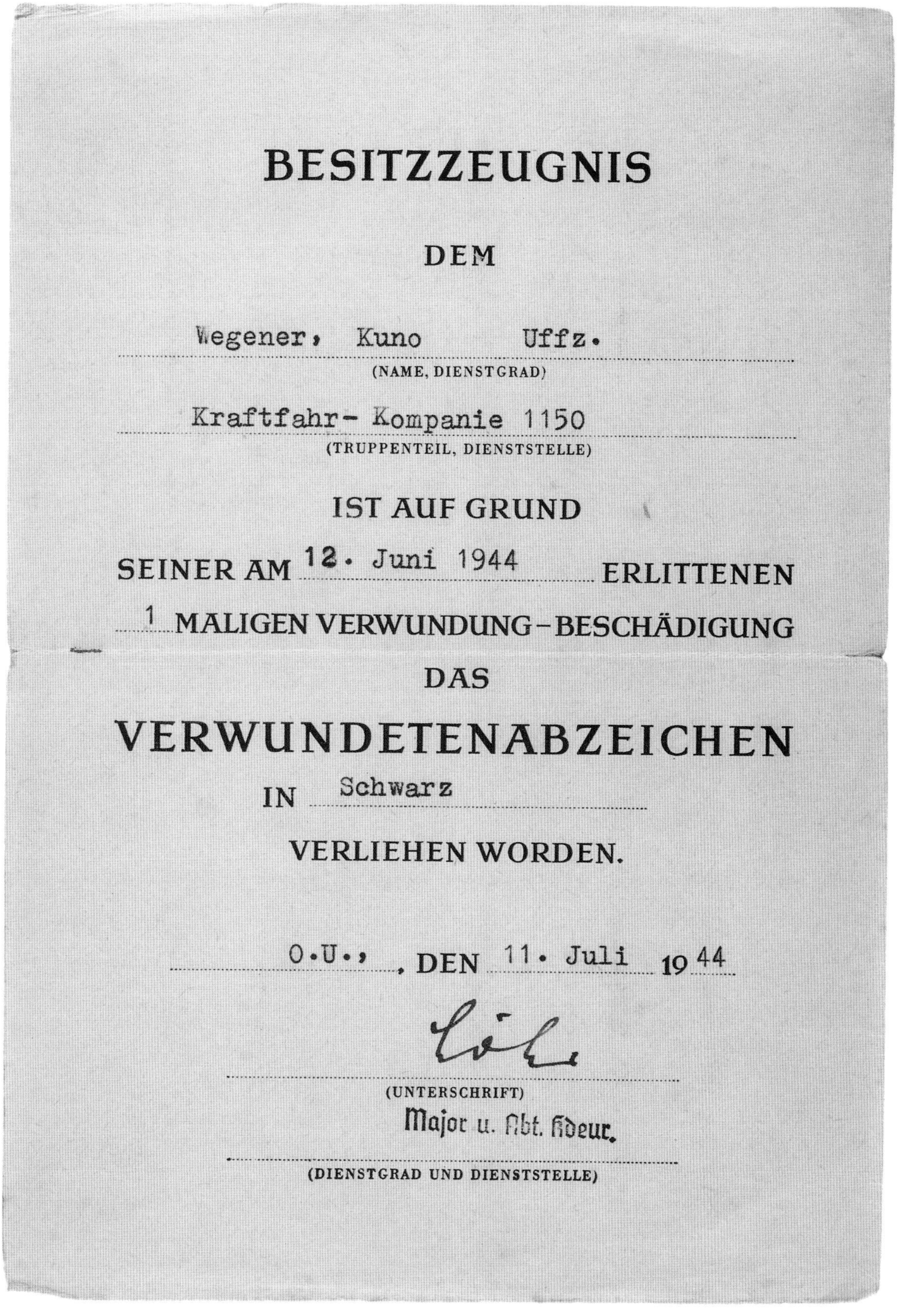

BESITZZEUGNIS

DEM

Wegener, Kuno Uffz.

(NAME, DIENSTGRAD)

Kraftfahr- Kompanie 1150

(TRUPPENTEIL, DIENSTSTELLE)

IST AUF GRUND

SEINER AM 12. Juni 1944 ERLITTENEN

1 MALIGEN VERWUNDUNG-BESCHÄDIGUNG

DAS

VERWUNDETENABZEICHEN

IN Schwarz

VERLIEHEN WORDEN.

O.U., DEN 11. Juli 1944

(UNTERSCHRIFT)

Major u. Abt. Kdeur.

(DIENSTGRAD UND DIENSTSTELLE)

Award document stating that *Unteroffizier (Uffz.)* Kuno Wegener, a member of the 1150th Motor Transport Company, was awarded the Wound Badge in Black after being injured on June 12, 1944.

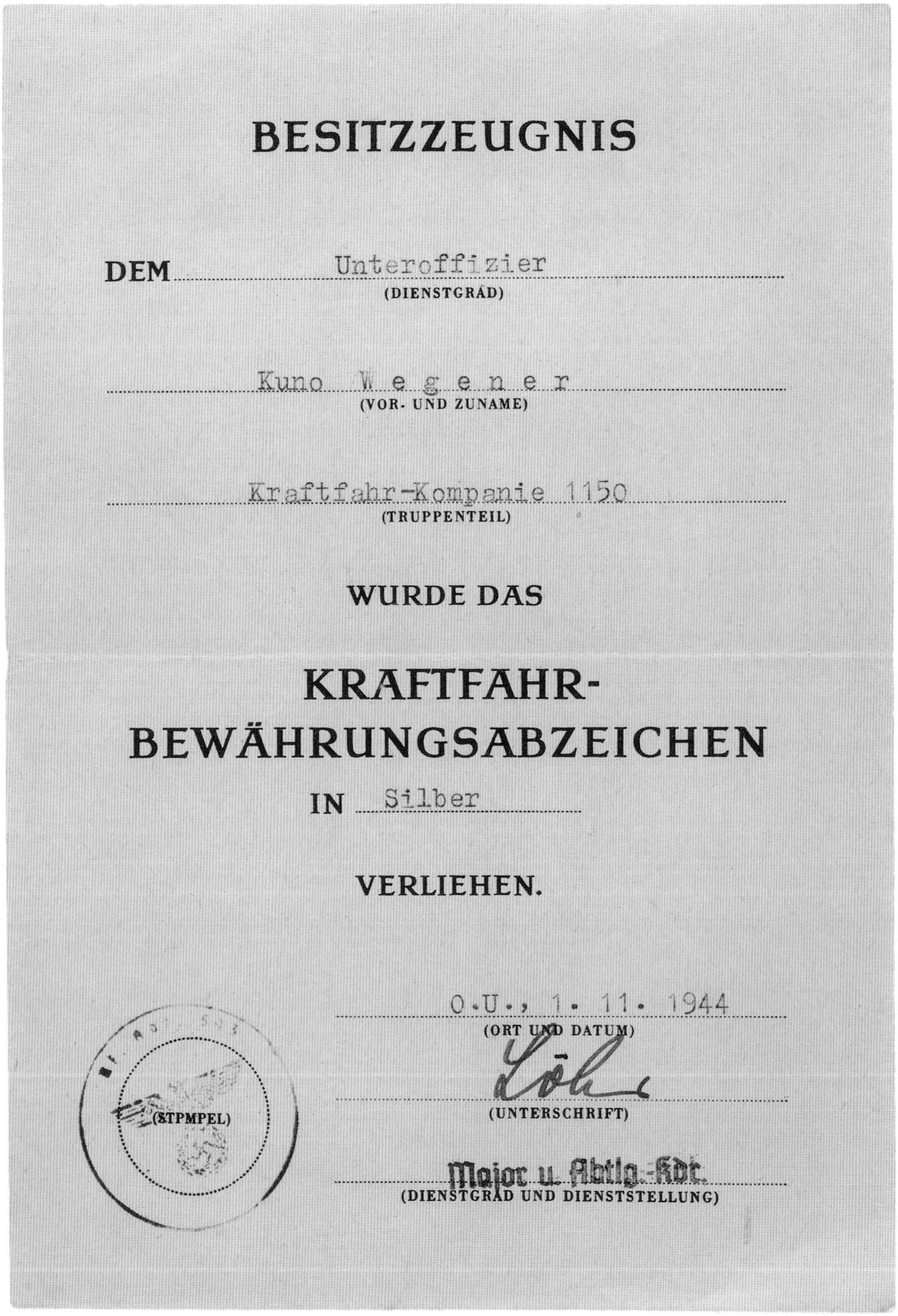

BESITZZEUGNIS

DEM Unteroffizier
(DIENSTGRAD)

Kuno W e g e n e r
(VOR- UND ZUNAME)

Kraftfahr-Kompanie 1150
(TRUPPENTEIL)

WURDE DAS

KRAFTFAHR-
BEWÄHRUNGSABZEICHEN

IN Silber

VERLIEHEN.

O.U., 1. 11. 1944
(ORT UND DATUM)

(STEMPEL)

(UNTERSCHRIFT)

Major u. Abtlg.-Kdr.
(DIENSTGRAD UND DIENSTSTELLUNG)

Award document stating that *Uffz.* Kuno Wegener, a member of the 1150th Motor Transport Company, was awarded the Motor Transport Proficiency Badge in Silver on November 1, 1944.

BESITZZEUGNIS

DEM

Unteroffizier Kuno W e g e n e r
(NAME, DIENSTGRAD)

Kraftfahr-Kompanie 1150
(TRUPPENTEIL, DIENSTSTELLE)

IST AUF GRUND

SEINER AM 17.12.1944 ERLITTENEN

2 MALIGEN VERWUNDUNG - BESCHÄDIGUNG

DAS

VERWUNDETENABZEICHEN

IN S i l b e r

VERLIEHEN WORDEN.

A.H.Qu., DEN 8. 2. 1945

Armeeoberkommando 14

von Heimendahl
(UNTERSCHRIFT)

Oberst und 1.Adjutant
(DIENSTGRAD UND DIENSTSTELLE)

Award document stating that *Uffz.* Kuno Wegener, a member of the 1150 Motor Transport Company, was awarded the Wound Badge in Silver on February 8, 1945.

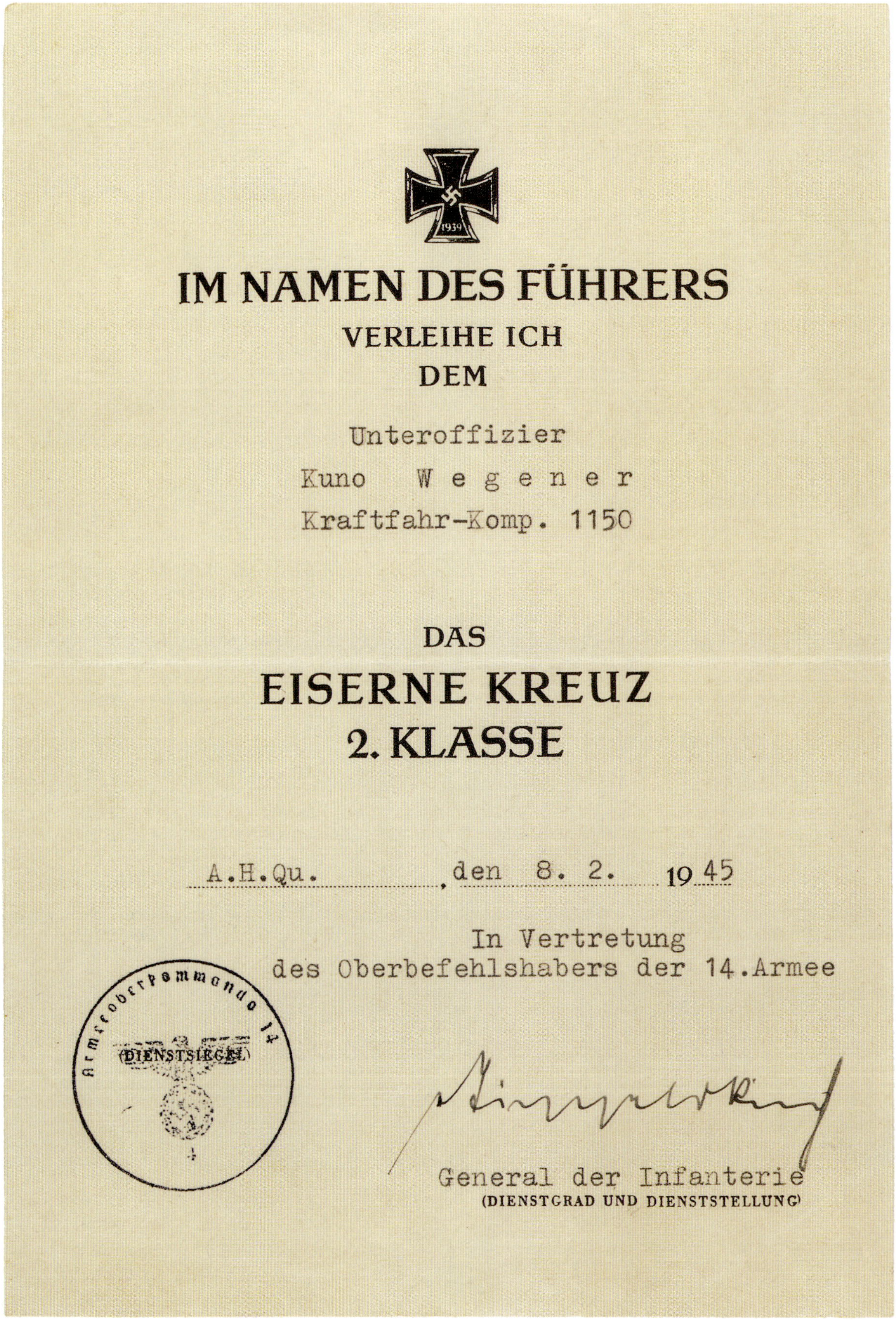

IM NAMEN DES FÜHRERS

VERLEIHE ICH

DEM

Unteroffizier

Kuno W e g e n e r

Kraftfahr-Komp. 1150

DAS

EISERNE KREUZ

2. KLASSE

A.H.Qu. , den 8. 2. 1945

In Vertretung

des Oberbefehlshabers der 14.Armee

Armeeoberkommando 14

DIENSTSIEGEL

General der Infanterie

(DIENSTGRAD UND DIENSTSTELLUNG)

On the same day Kuno Wegener was awarded the Silver Wound Badge, he was also awarded the Iron Cross Second Class. This document is signed and unit stamped by the Commanding General of the Fourteenth Army.

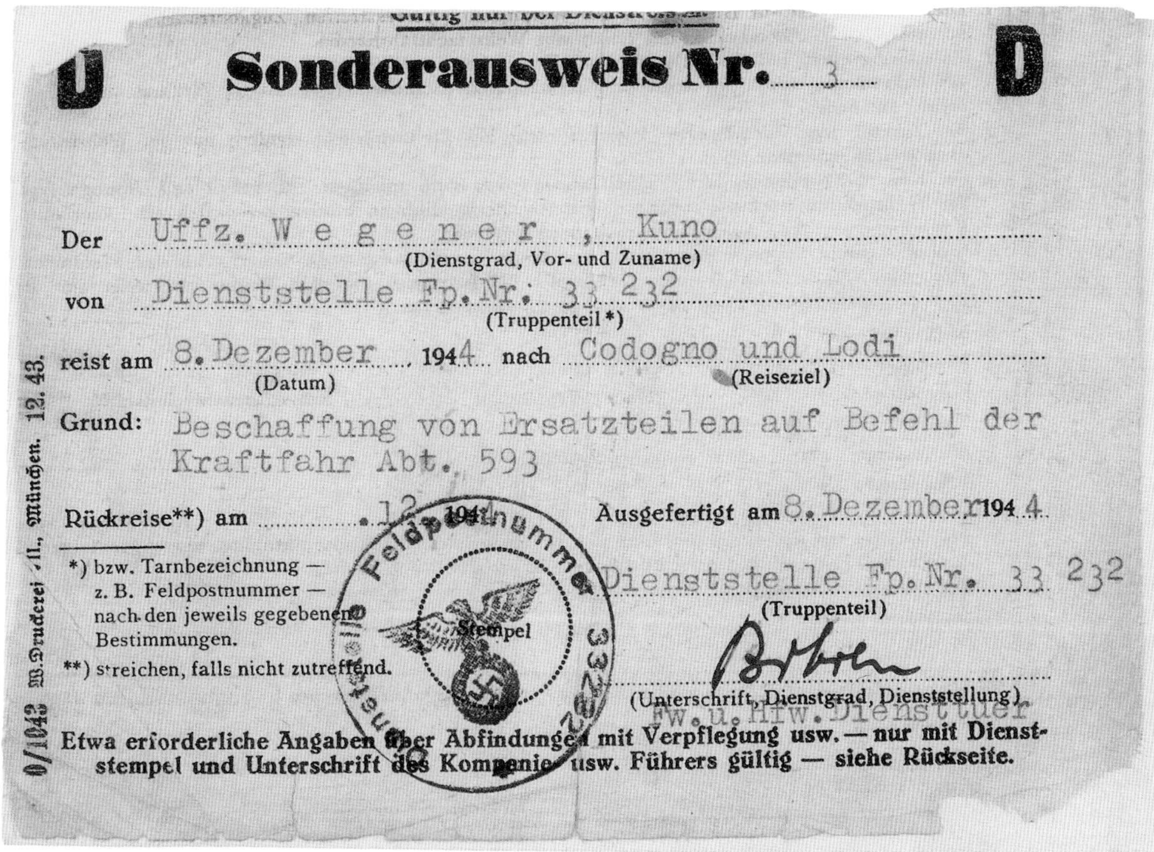

Gültig nur bei Dienstreisen

Sonderausweis Nr. 3 **D**

Der Uffz. W e g e n e r , Kuno
(Dienstgrad, Vor- und Zuname)

von Dienststelle Fp.Nr. 33 232
(Truppenteil*)

reist am 8.Dezember 1944 nach Codogno und Lodi
(Datum) (Reiseziel)

Grund: Beschaffung von Ersatzteilen auf Befehl der Kraftfahr Abt. 593

Rückreise**) am 12. 1944 Ausgefertigt am 8.Dezember 1944

*) bzw. Tarnbezeichnung — z. B. Feldpostnummer — nach den jeweils gegebenen Bestimmungen.

**) streichen, falls nicht zutreffend.

Dienststelle Fp.Nr. 33 232
(Truppenteil)

Fw.u.Hiw.Dienstuer
(Unterschrift, Dienstgrad, Dienststellung)

Stempel: Feldpostnummer 33232 Dienststelle

Etwa erforderliche Angaben über Abfindungen mit Verpflegung usw. — nur mit Dienststempel und Unterschrift des Kompanie- usw. Führers gültig — siehe Rückseite.

0/1043 W. Druckerei ..., München. 12. 43.

Special travel pass issued to *Uffz.* Kuno Wegener, authorizing him to travel to Codogno and Lodi to procure replacement parts for the 593rd Motor Transport Battalion.

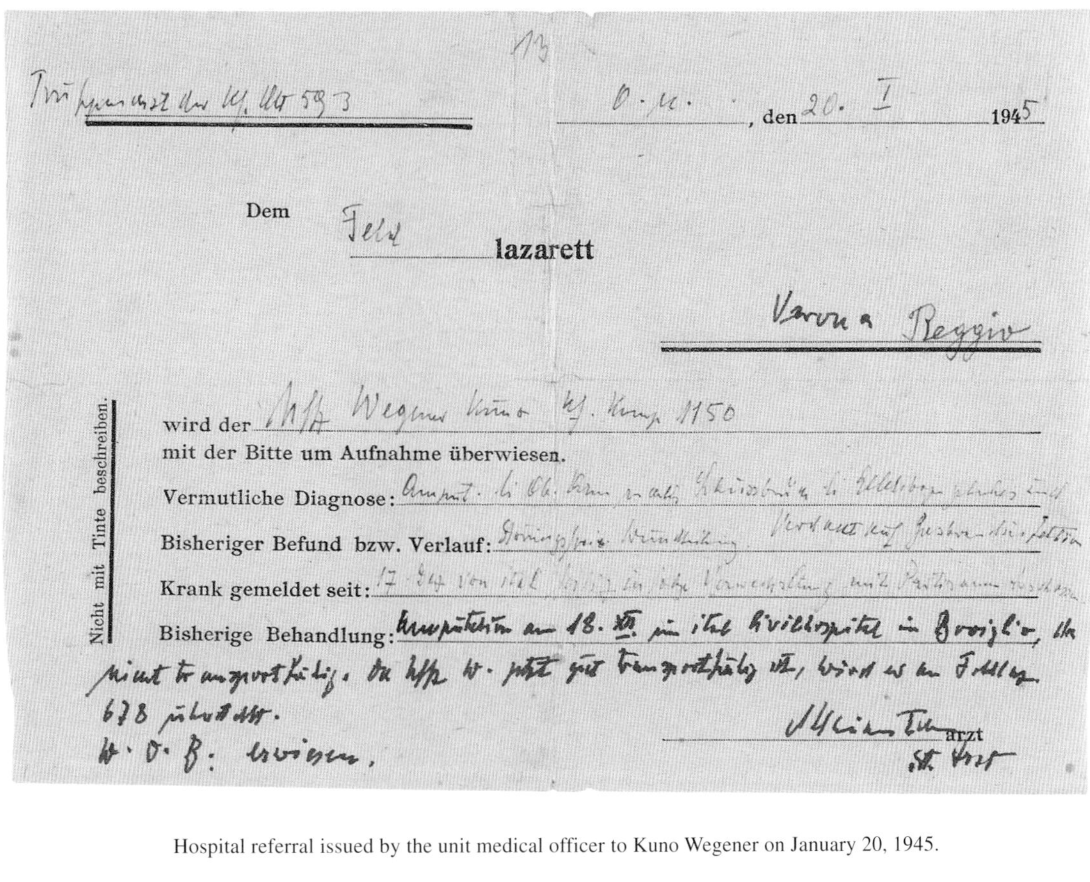

Truppenarzt der Kf. Abt 593 O.U., den 20. I 1945

Dem Feld lazarett

Verona Reggio

wird der Uffz Wegener Kuno Kf. Komp. 1150
mit der Bitte um Aufnahme überwiesen.

Vermutliche Diagnose:

Bisheriger Befund bzw. Verlauf:

Krank gemeldet seit:

Bisherige Behandlung:

arzt

Nicht mit Tinte beschreiben.

Hospital referral issued by the unit medical officer to Kuno Wegener on January 20, 1945.

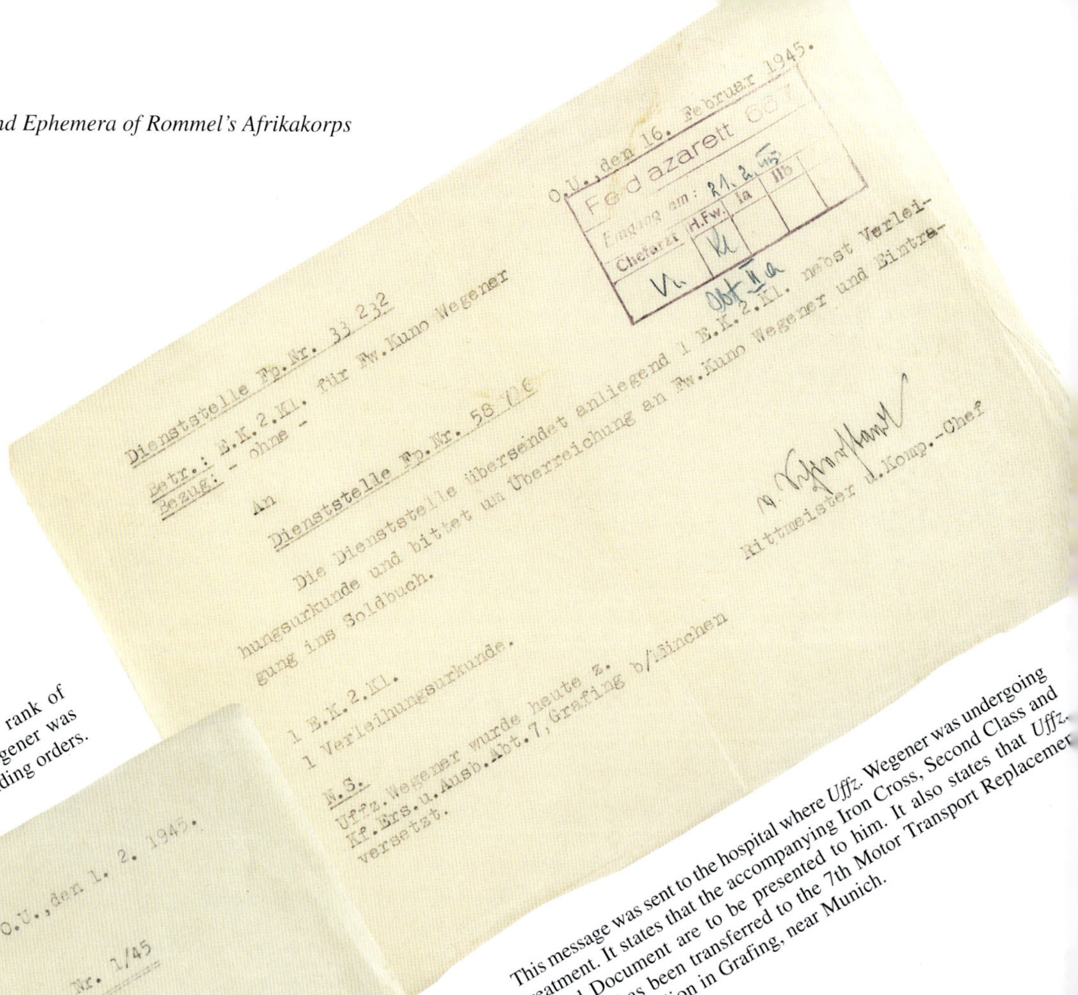

O.U., den 16. Februar 1945.

Feldlazarett 667
Eingang am: 21.2.45
Chefarzt | H.Fw. | Ia | IIb

Dienststelle Fp.Nr. 33 232

Betr.: E.K.2.Kl. für Fw.Kuno Wegener
Bezug: - ohne -

An

Dienststelle Fp.Nr. 58 706

Die Dienststelle übersendet anliegend 1 E.K.2.Kl. nebst Verleihungsurkunde und bittet um Überreichung an Fw.Kuno Wegener und Eintragung ins Soldbuch.

Rittmeister u.Komp.-Chef

1 E.K.2.Kl.
1 Verleihungsurkunde.

N.S.
Uffz.Wegener wurde heute z. Kf.Ers.u.Ausb.Abt.7,Grafing b/München versetzt.

This message was sent to the hospital where *Uffz.* Wegener was undergoing treatment. It states that the accompanying Iron Cross, Second Class and Award Document are to be presented to him. It also states that *Uffz.* Wegener has been transferred to the 7th Motor Transport Replacement Training Battalion in Grafing, near Munich.

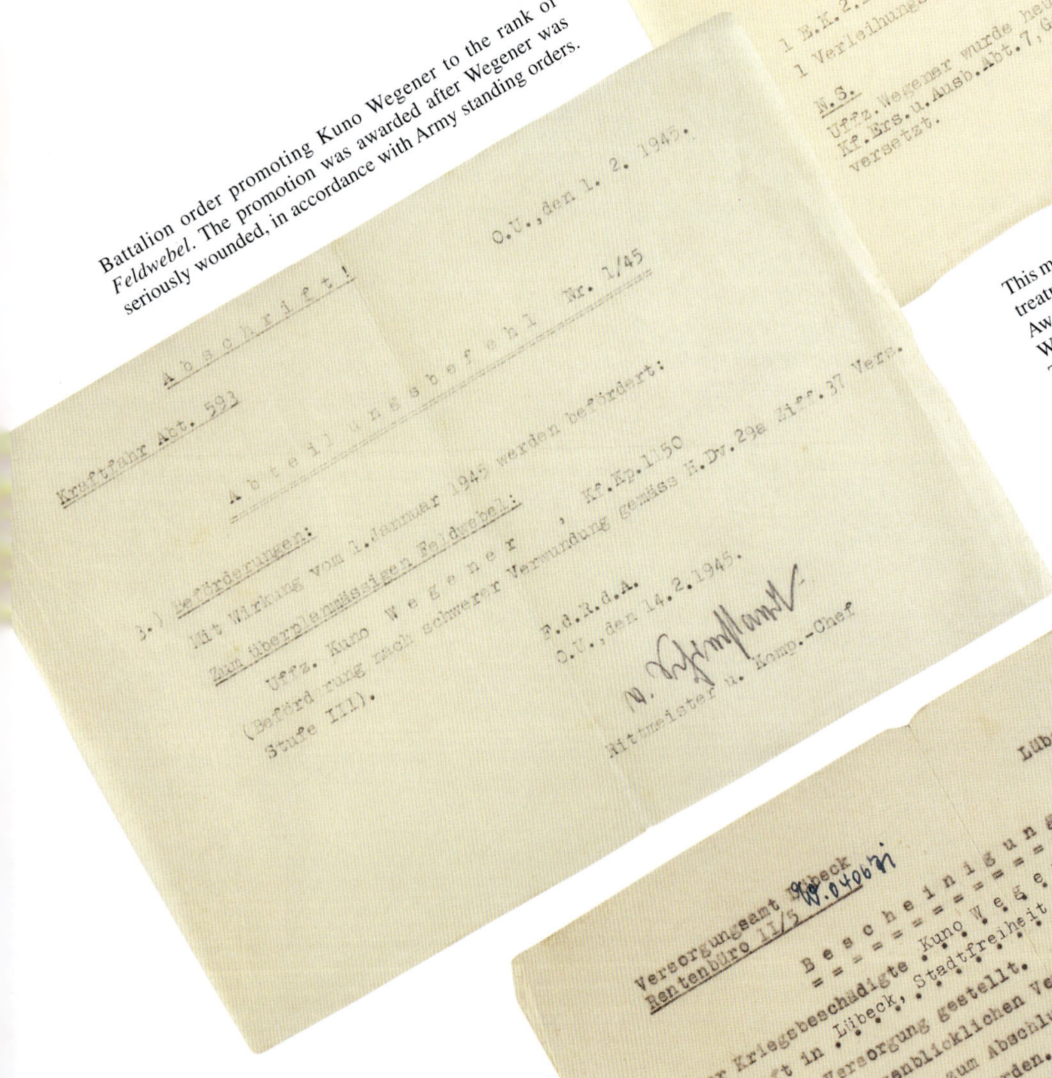

Abschrift!

O.U., den 1. 2. 1945.

Kraftfahr Abt. 593

Abteilungsbefehl Nr. 1/45

3.) Beförderungen:
Mit Wirkung vom 1.Januar 1945 werden befördert:
Zum überplanmässigen Feldwebel:
Uffz. Kuno Wegener , Kf.Kp.1150
(Beförderung nach schwerer Verwundung gemäss H.Dv.29a Ziff.37 Vers.Stufe III).

F.d.R.d.A.
O.U., den 14.2.1945.

Rittmeister u. Komp.-Chef

Battalion order promoting Kuno Wegener to the rank of *Feldwebel*. The promotion was awarded after Wegener was seriously wounded, in accordance with Army standing orders.

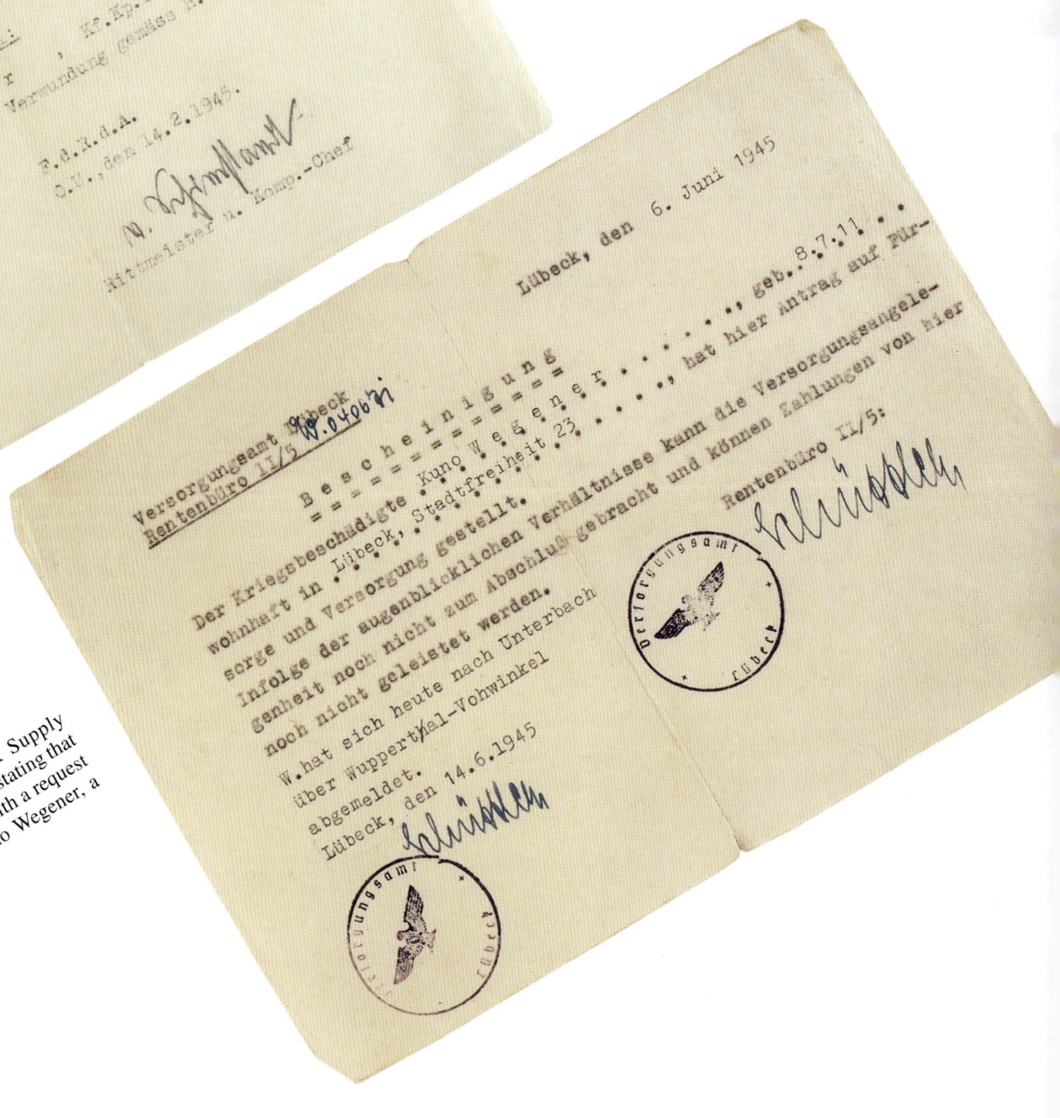

Lübeck, den 6. Juni 1945

Versorgungsamt Lübeck
Rentenbüro II/5 W.040671

Bescheinigung

Der Kriegsbeschädigte Kuno Wegener, geb. 8.7.11 wohnhaft in Lübeck, Stadtfreiheit 23, hat hier Antrag auf Fürsorge und Versorgung gestellt.
Infolge der augenblicklichen Verhältnisse kann die Versorgungsangelegenheit noch nicht zum Abschluß gebracht und können Zahlungen von hier noch nicht geleistet werden.

Rentenbüro II/5:

Versorgungsamt Lübeck

W. hat sich heute nach Unterbach über Wuppertal-Vohwinkel abgemeldet.
Lübeck, den 14.6.1945

Versorgungsamt Lübeck

A letter from the Lübeck Supply Office dated June 6, 1945 stating that it is unable to comply with a request for assistance for Kuno Wegener, a disabled veteran.

Photograph of Kuno Wegener sitting utside his truck getting his tropical boots ned by a young local Arab.

Dem Kraftfahrer Kuno Wegener

wird diese Urkunde für eine Strecke von 70000 km, die er mit demselben Kraftfahrzeug trotz ungünstigen Straßen- und Witterungsverhältnissen in Afrika zurückgelegt hat und für gute Wagenpflege als besondere Anerkennung für diese Leistung verliehen.

Afrika den 1.6.1942

Rommel

Generaloberst und Oberbefehlshaber der Panzerarmee Afrika.

Rare and colorful *Afrikakorps* Drivers Certificate awarded to Kuno Wegener on June 1, 1942 in recognition of having driven 70,000 kilometers in North Africa. Supply was a constant problem in the desert and these documents ere printed to recognize those brave drivers that had driven exceptionally long distances and survived the stant Allied air attacks. The certificate was printed with a facsimile of Rommel's signature.

Colorized studio portrait of Kuno Wegener in his tropical uniform and visored field cap.

Nice *Afrikakorps Soldbuch* to an *Obergefreiter* in *Panzergrenadier Regiment 104*. This *Soldbuch* was picked up by a New Zealand soldier at El Alamein. The holder arrived in Africa on July 31, 1942. His *Soldbuch* also has the rare insert for full issuance of tropical uniform and field gear (issued July 9, 1942). There were also inserts for buying additional *Wehrmacht* clothing, tips for healthy living in extreme climates and how to prevent ill health. (David Bunch)

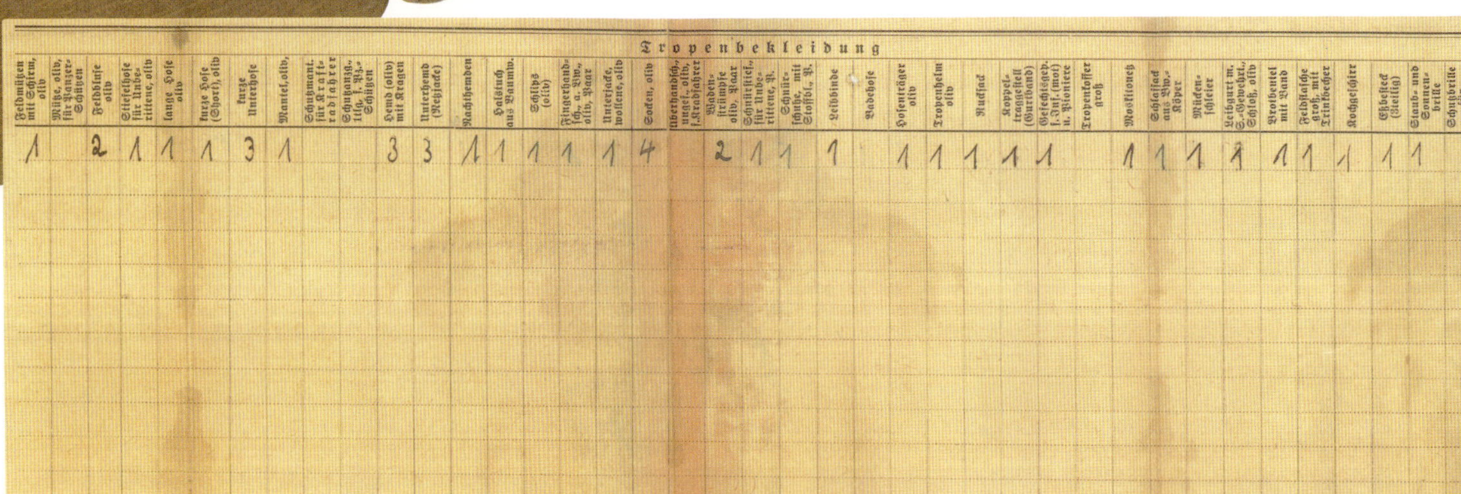
Tropenbekleidung

Anmerkung: Stücke, die nicht vorgedruckt sind, sind in freie Spalten einzutragen. Vorhandene Spalten können auch berichtigt werden. Alle Änderungen sind durch Namenzeichen zu bescheinigen.

***Afrikakorps Wehrpass*. While on active duty, the *Wehrpass* typically followed the holder to his various duty stations, and was retained there by the administrative unit.** (David Bunch)

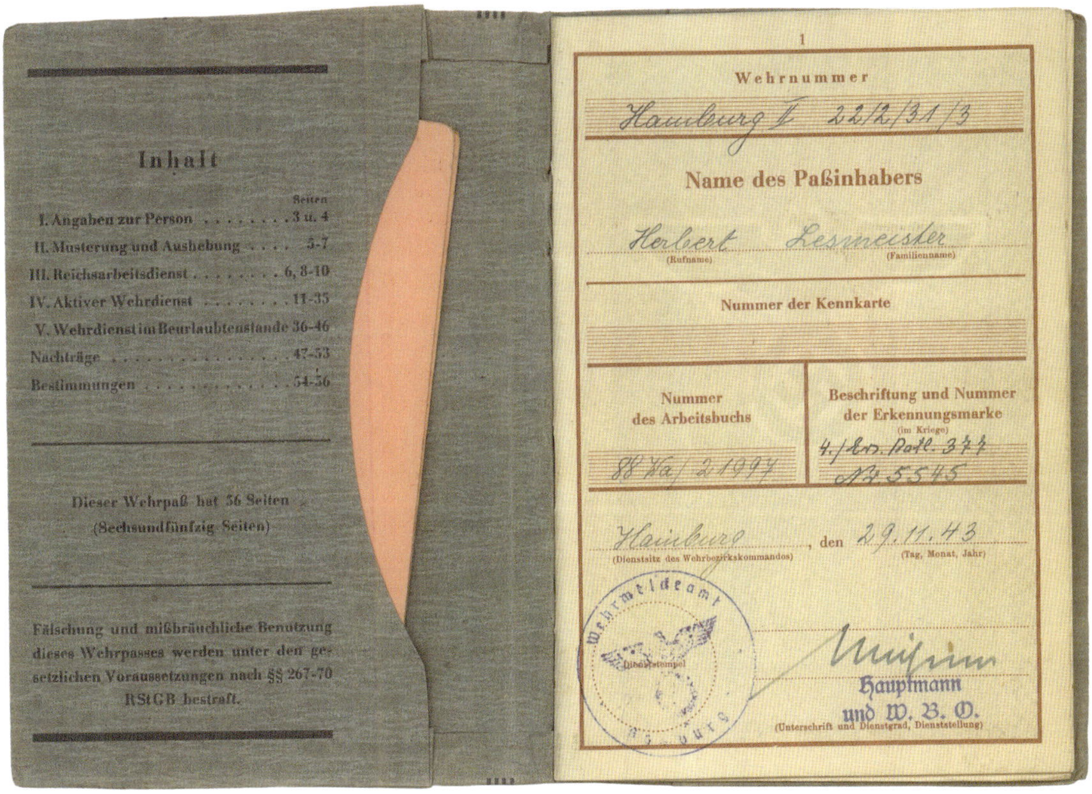

The *Wehrpass* of this holder was re-issued in Hamburg after the fighting had ended in Africa but was still completed to reflect his previous duties in Africa.

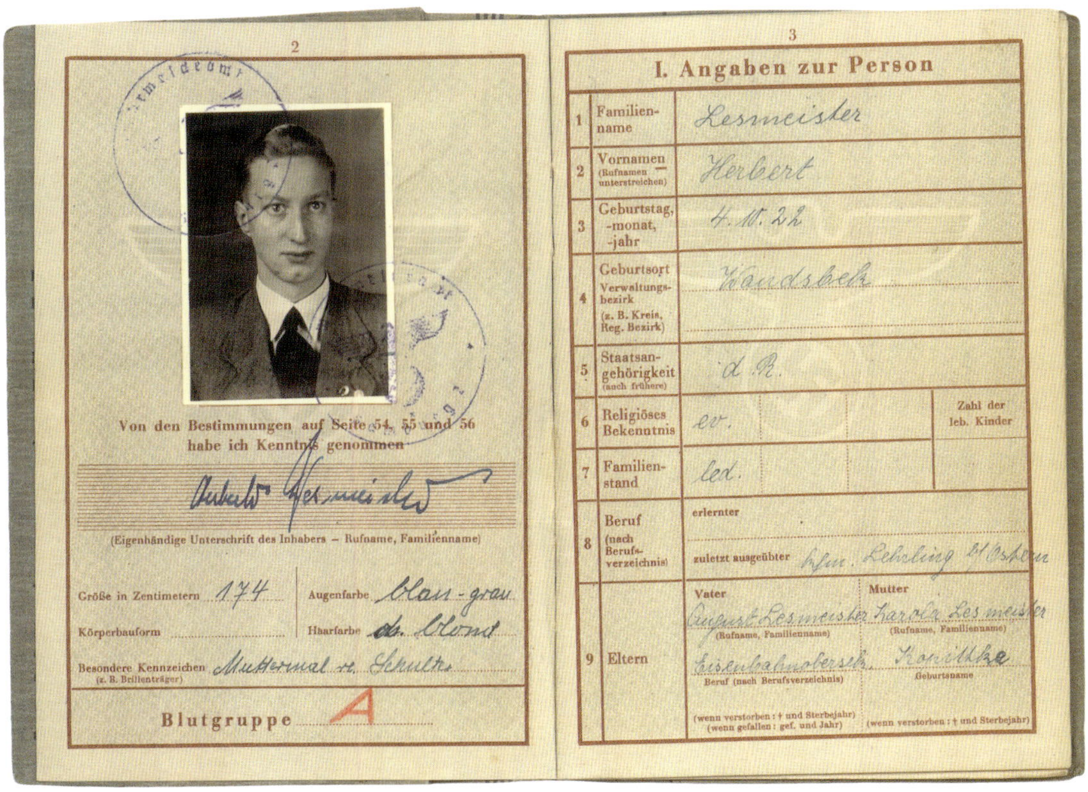

Page 2 contains a photo of the holder and his signature. Page 3 contained personal information.

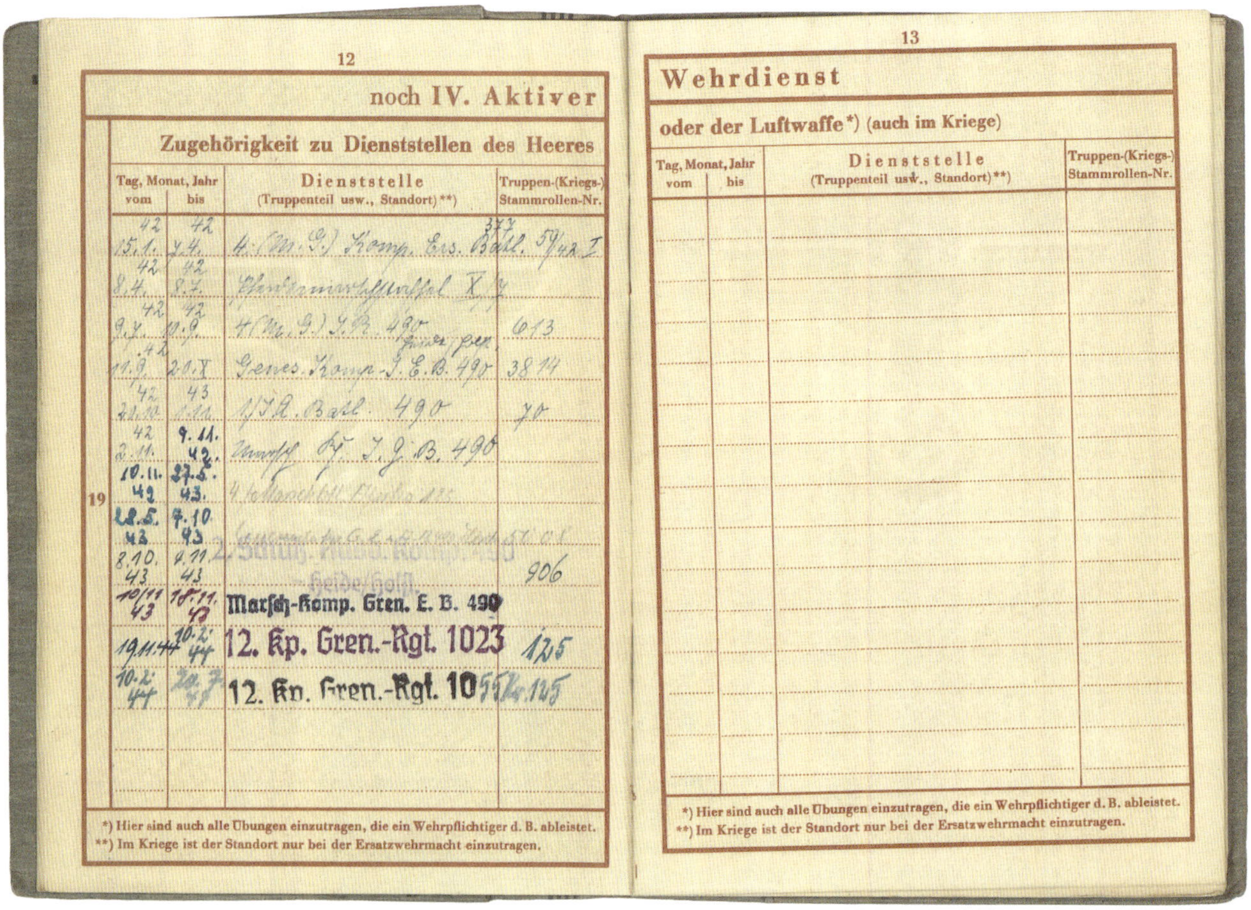

12

noch IV. Aktiver

Zugehörigkeit zu Dienststellen des Heeres

Tag, Monat, Jahr vom	bis	Dienststelle (Truppenteil usw., Standort) **)	Truppen-(Kriegs-) Stammrollen-Nr.
10/11 43	18.11. 43	Marsch-Komp. Gren. E. B. 490	
19.11.43	10.2. 44	12. Kp. Gren.-Rgt. 1023	125
10.2. 44	20.7 44	12. Kp. Gren.-Rgt. 10[illegible]	125

*) Hier sind auch alle Übungen einzutragen, die ein Wehrpflichtiger d. B. ableistet.
**) Im Kriege ist der Standort nur bei der Ersatzwehrmacht einzutragen.

13

Wehrdienst

oder der Luftwaffe *) (auch im Kriege)

Tag, Monat, Jahr vom	bis	Dienststelle (Truppenteil usw., Standort) **)	Truppen-(Kriegs-) Stammrollen-Nr.

*) Hier sind auch alle Übungen einzutragen, die ein Wehrpflichtiger d. B. ableistet.
**) Im Kriege ist der Standort nur bei der Ersatzwehrmacht einzutragen.

Page 12 lists the active duty assignments. This soldier arrived in Africa on November 10, 1942 and was able to depart the day before the *Afrikakorps* surrendered!

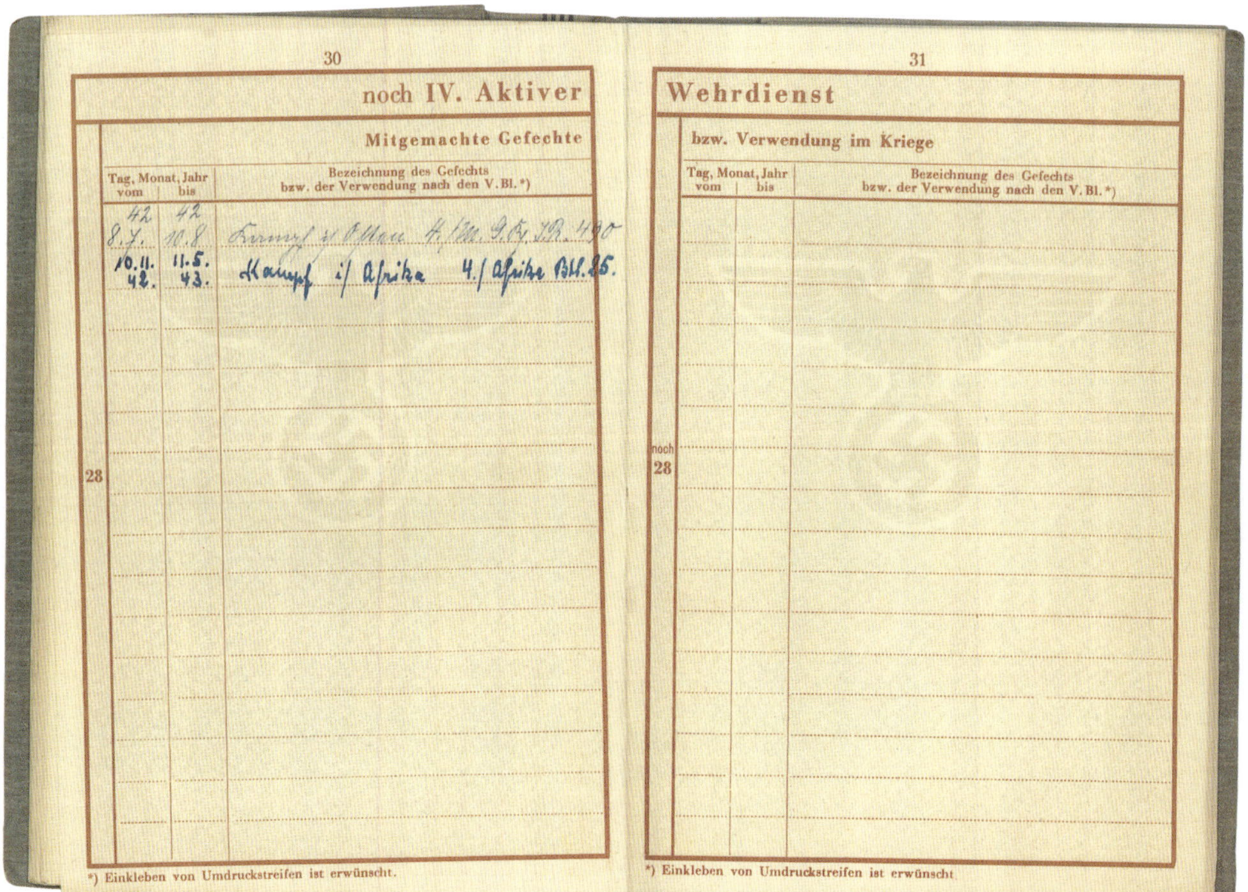

30

noch IV. Aktiver

Mitgemachte Gefechte

Tag, Monat, Jahr vom	bis	Bezeichnung des Gefechts bzw. der Verwendung nach den V. Bl. *)
10.11. 42.	11.5. 43.	Kampf i/ Afrika 4./ Afrika Btl. 25.

*) Einkleben von Umdruckstreifen ist erwünscht.

31

Wehrdienst

bzw. Verwendung im Kriege

Tag, Monat, Jahr vom	bis	Bezeichnung des Gefechts bzw. der Verwendung nach den V. Bl. *)

*) Einkleben von Umdruckstreifen ist erwünscht.

***Afrikakorps Wehrpass* to a *Gefreiter* in *Reconnaissance Abteilung*. Issued June 13, 1939 in Berlin to a soldier promoted to *Gefreiter* in December 1940, this *Wehrpass* has a clear photo of the young man in civilian clothing. This soldier saw service on the Western front and was certified fit for tropical service on May 8, 1941. Holder was wounded in May 1942 and returned to Germany for a month. This *Wehrpass* was found at El Alamein by a New Zealander. His last unit post was on August 1, 1942 to a Reconnaissance unit attached to Army Headquarters. Before this posting, he was attached to an Artillery battalion in the *15th Panzer Division*.** (David Bunch)

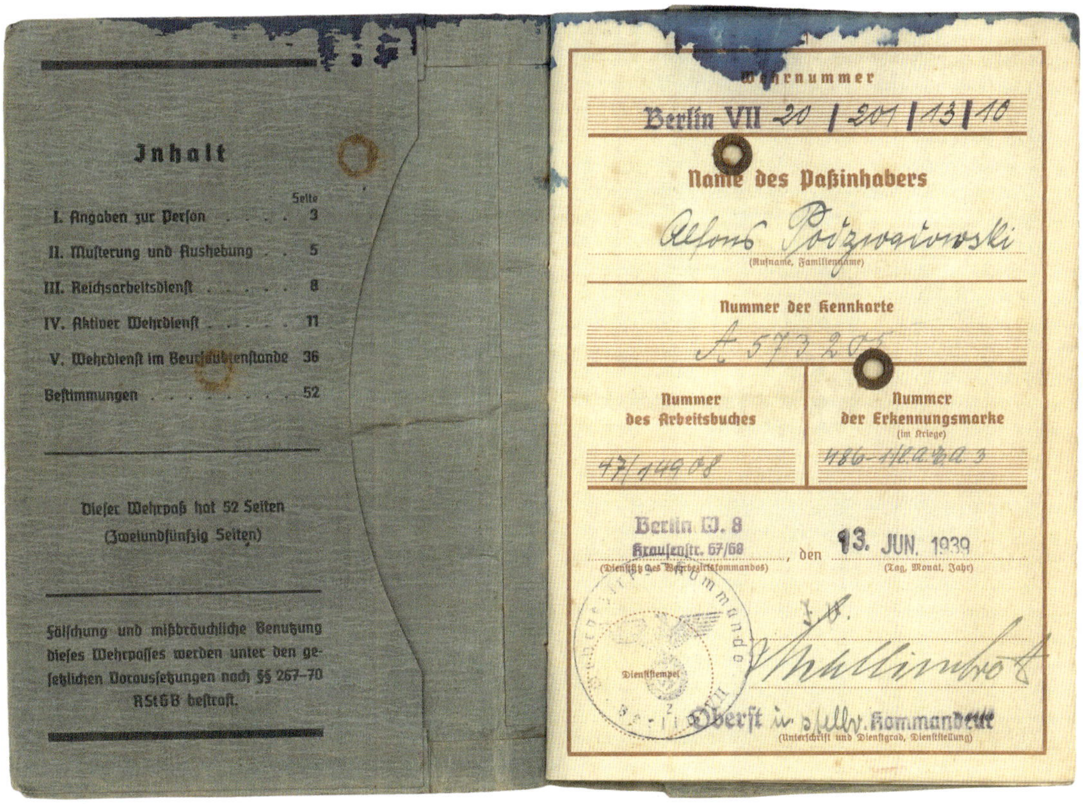

Inhalt

	Seite
I. Angaben zur Person	3
II. Musterung und Aushebung	5
III. Reichsarbeitsdienst	8
IV. Aktiver Wehrdienst	11
V. Wehrdienst im Beurlaubtenstande	36
Bestimmungen	52

Dieser Wehrpaß hat 52 Seiten (Zweiundfünfzig Seiten)

Fälschung und mißbräuchliche Benutzung dieses Wehrpasses werden unter den gesetzlichen Voraussetzungen nach §§ 267–70 RStGB bestraft.

Wehrnummer

Berlin VII 20 / 201 / 13 / 10

Name des Paßinhabers

Alfons Podzwadowski

(Rufname, Familienname)

Nummer der Kennkarte

A 573205

Nummer des Arbeitsbuches	Nummer der Erkennungsmarke (im Kriege)
47/14908	486-1/1.A.A.A.9

Berlin W. 8 Kronenstr. 67/68 (Dienstsitz des Wehrbezirkskommandos), den 13. JUN. 1939 (Tag, Monat, Jahr)

Dienststempel

I.V. Mallinckrodt

Oberst u. stellv. Kommandeur

(Unterschrift und Dienstgrad, Dienststellung)

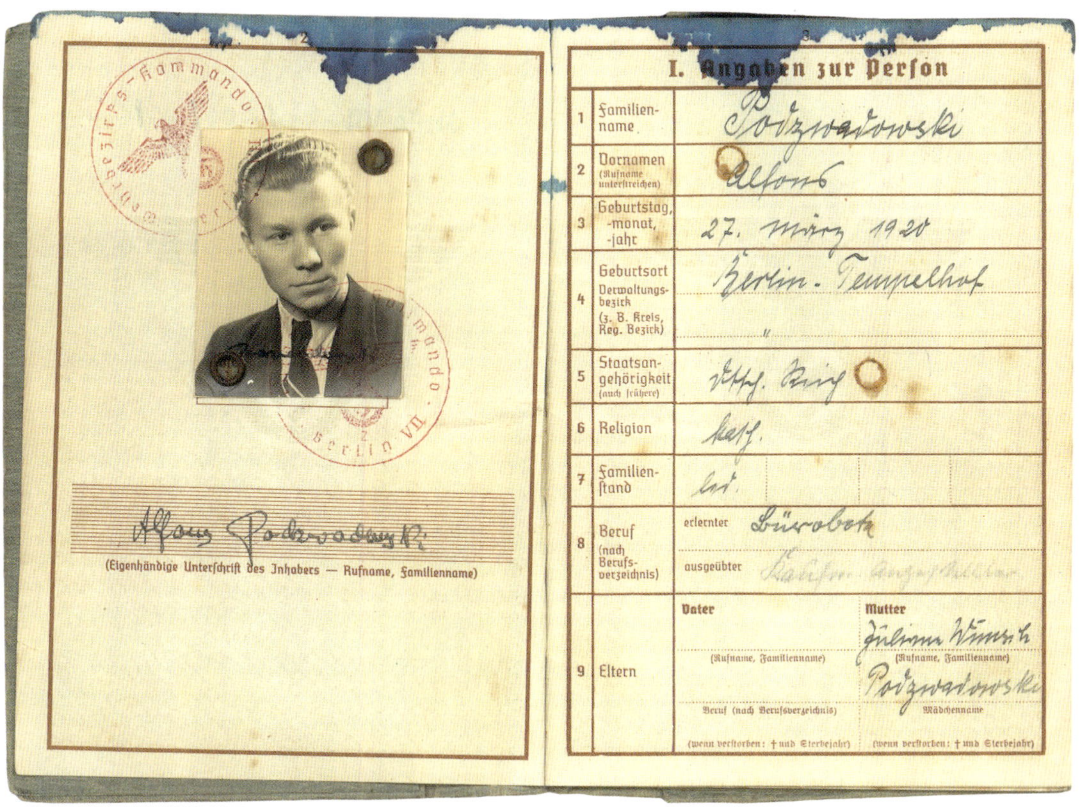

Wehrbezirks-Kommando Berlin VII

Alfons Podzwadowski

(Eigenhändige Unterschrift des Inhabers — Rufname, Familienname)

I. Angaben zur Person

1	Familienname	Podzwadowski
2	Vornamen (Rufname unterstreichen)	Alfons
3	Geburtstag, -monat, -jahr	27. März 1920
4	Geburtsort Verwaltungsbezirk (z. B. Kreis, Reg. Bezirk)	Berlin-Tempelhof
5	Staatsangehörigkeit (auch frühere)	Dtsch. Reich
6	Religion	kath.
7	Familienstand	led.
8	Beruf (nach Berufsverzeichnis)	erlernter: Bürobote; ausgeübter: Kaufm. Angestellter
9	Eltern	Vater: (Rufname, Familienname); Beruf (nach Berufsverzeichnis) — Mutter: Juliane Wunsch (Rufname, Familienname) Podzwadowski Mädchenname

(wenn verstorben: † und Sterbejahr) (wenn verstorben: † und Sterbejahr)

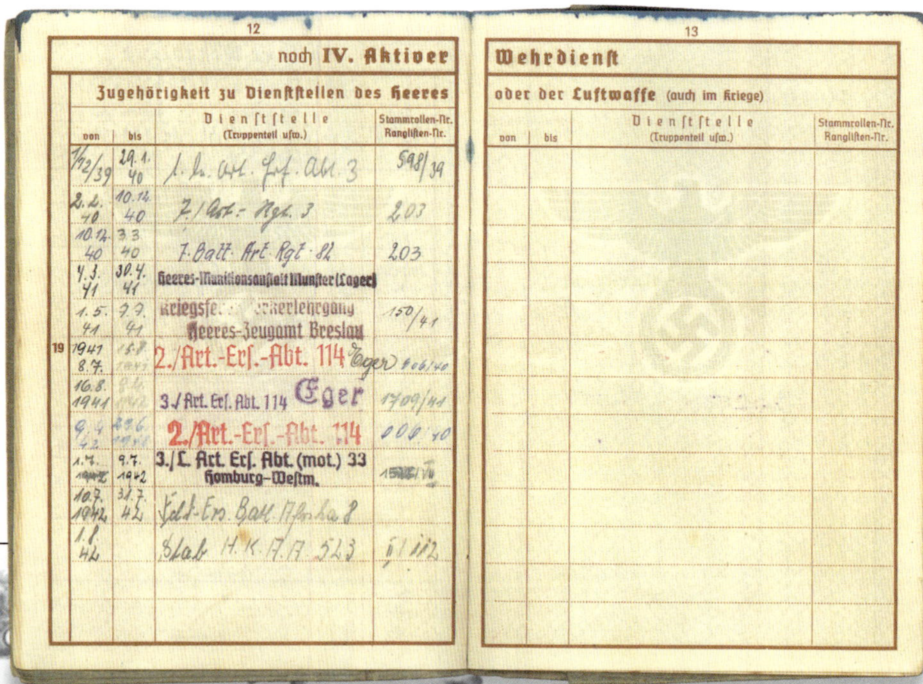

12 — noch IV. Aktiver Wehrdienst — 13

Zugehörigkeit zu Dienststellen des Heeres oder der Luftwaffe (auch im Kriege)

von	bis	Dienststelle (Truppenteil usw.)	Stammrollen-Nr. Ranglisten-Nr.
1/12/39	29.1.40	1. le. Art. Ers. Abt. 3	598/39
2.2.40	10.12.40	7./Art.-Rgt. 3	203
10.12.40	3.3.40	7. Batt. Art. Rgt. 82	203
4.3.41	30.4.41	Heeres-Munitionsanstalt Münster (Lager)	
1.5.41	7.7.41	Kriegsfe[illegible]lehrgang Heeres-Zeugamt Breslau	150/41
1941 8.7.		2./Art.-Ers.-Abt. 114 Eger	
16.8.1941		3./Art. Ers. Abt. 114 Eger	1709/41
		2./Art.-Ers.-Abt. 114	006/40
1.7.1942	9.7.1942	3./L. Art. Ers. Abt. (mot.) 33 Homburg-Westm.	
10.7.1942	31.7.42	Feld-Ers. Batl. Afrika 8	
1.8.42		Stab H.K. A.A. 523	

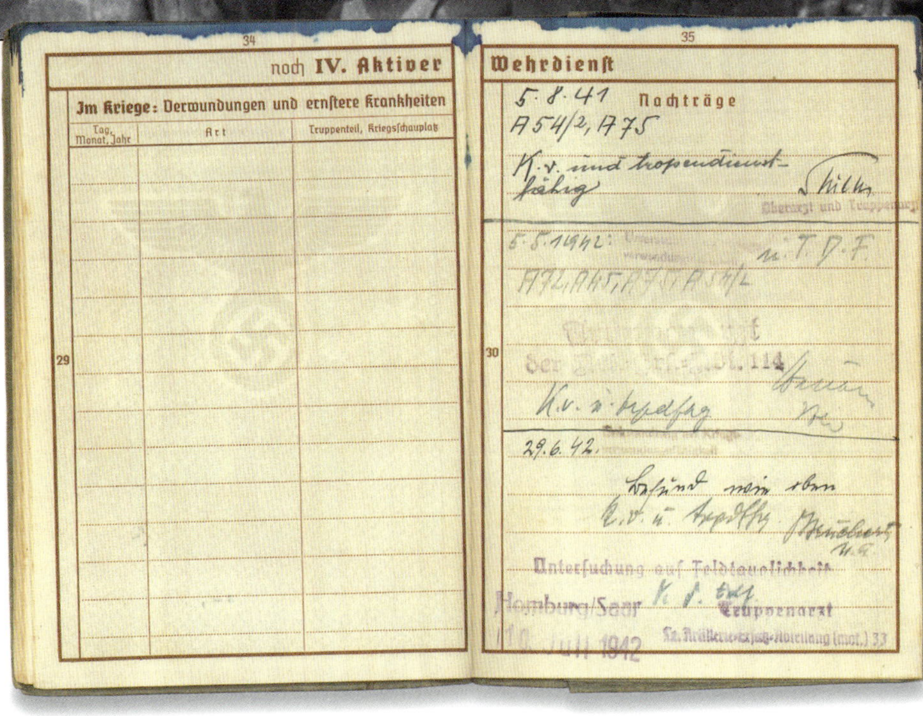

34 — noch IV. Aktiver Wehrdienst — 35

Im Kriege: Verwundungen und ernstere Krankheiten

Tag, Monat, Jahr	Art	Truppenteil, Kriegsschauplatz

Nachträge

5.8.41 A54/2, A75 K.v. und tropendienstfähig — Oberarzt und Truppenarzt

5.8.1942: m. T. D. F.

Der [illegible] 114 K.v. u. tropdfg.

29.6.42. Gesund wie oben K.v. u. tropdfg.

Untersuchung auf Feldtauglichkeit

Homburg/Saar 10. Juli 1942 — Truppenarzt — L. Artillerie-Ersatz-Abteilung (mot.) 33

Above
Before surrendering, the men of the *Afrikakorps* were ordered to destroy certain pages from their *Soldbuchs*.

CHAPTER TWO

Awards and Misc. Documents

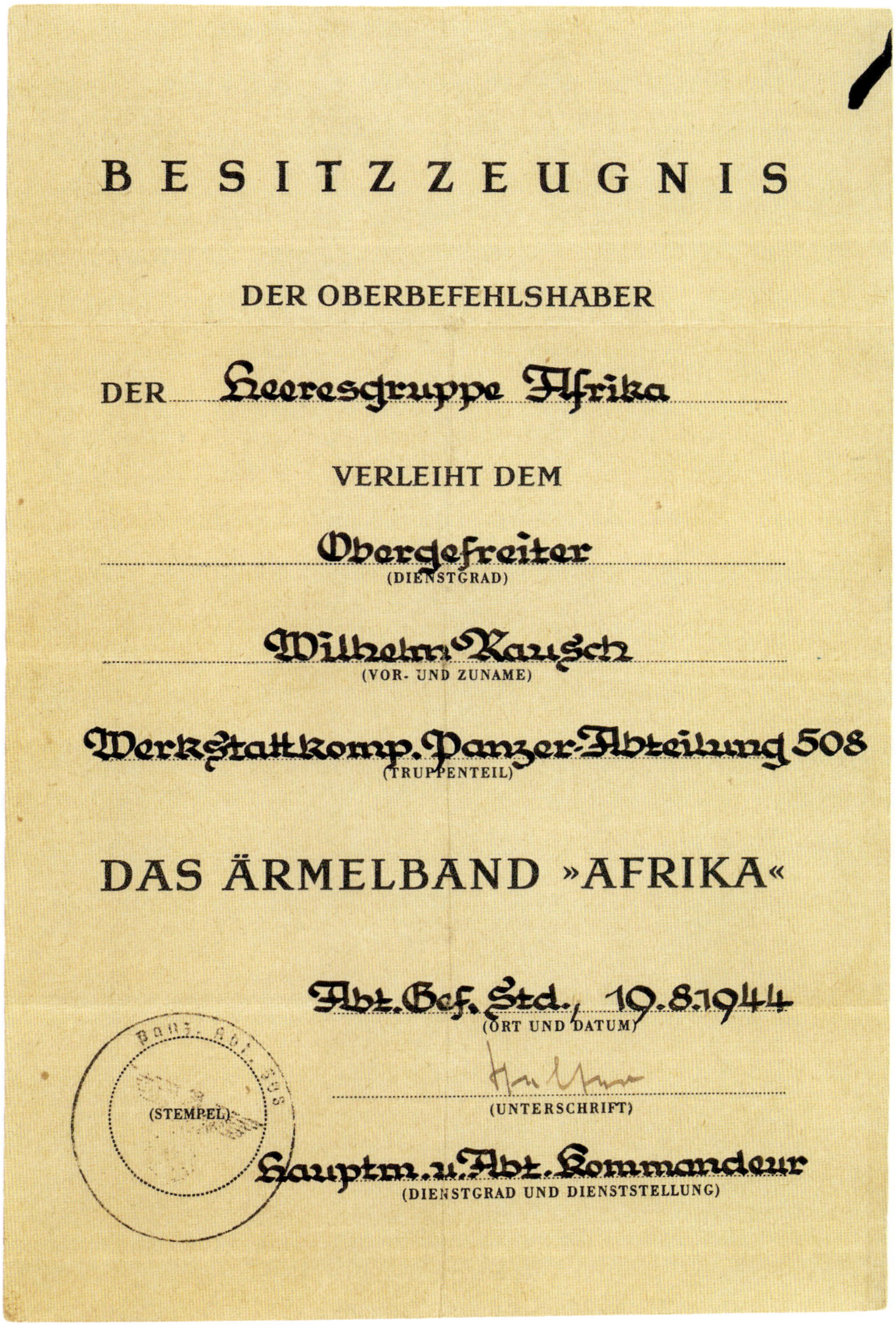

BESITZZEUGNIS

DER OBERBEFEHLSHABER

DER Heeresgruppe Afrika

VERLEIHT DEM

Obergefreiter
(DIENSTGRAD)

Wilhelm Rausch
(VOR- UND ZUNAME)

Werkstattkomp. Panzer-Abteilung 508
(TRUPPENTEIL)

DAS ÄRMELBAND »AFRIKA«

Abt. Gef. Std., 19.8.1944
(ORT UND DATUM)

(STEMPEL)

(UNTERSCHRIFT)

Hauptm. u. Abt. Kommandeur
(DIENSTGRAD UND DIENSTSTELLUNG)

Wehrmacht issued AFRIKA cufftitle award document to an *Obergefreiter* in *Werkstatt-Kompanie* (Maintenance Company) *Panzer-Abteilung 508*. This document has a very nice unit stamp and signature from the company commander dated August 19, 1944. No foreigner was eligible for the AFRIKA cufftitle. (David Bunch)

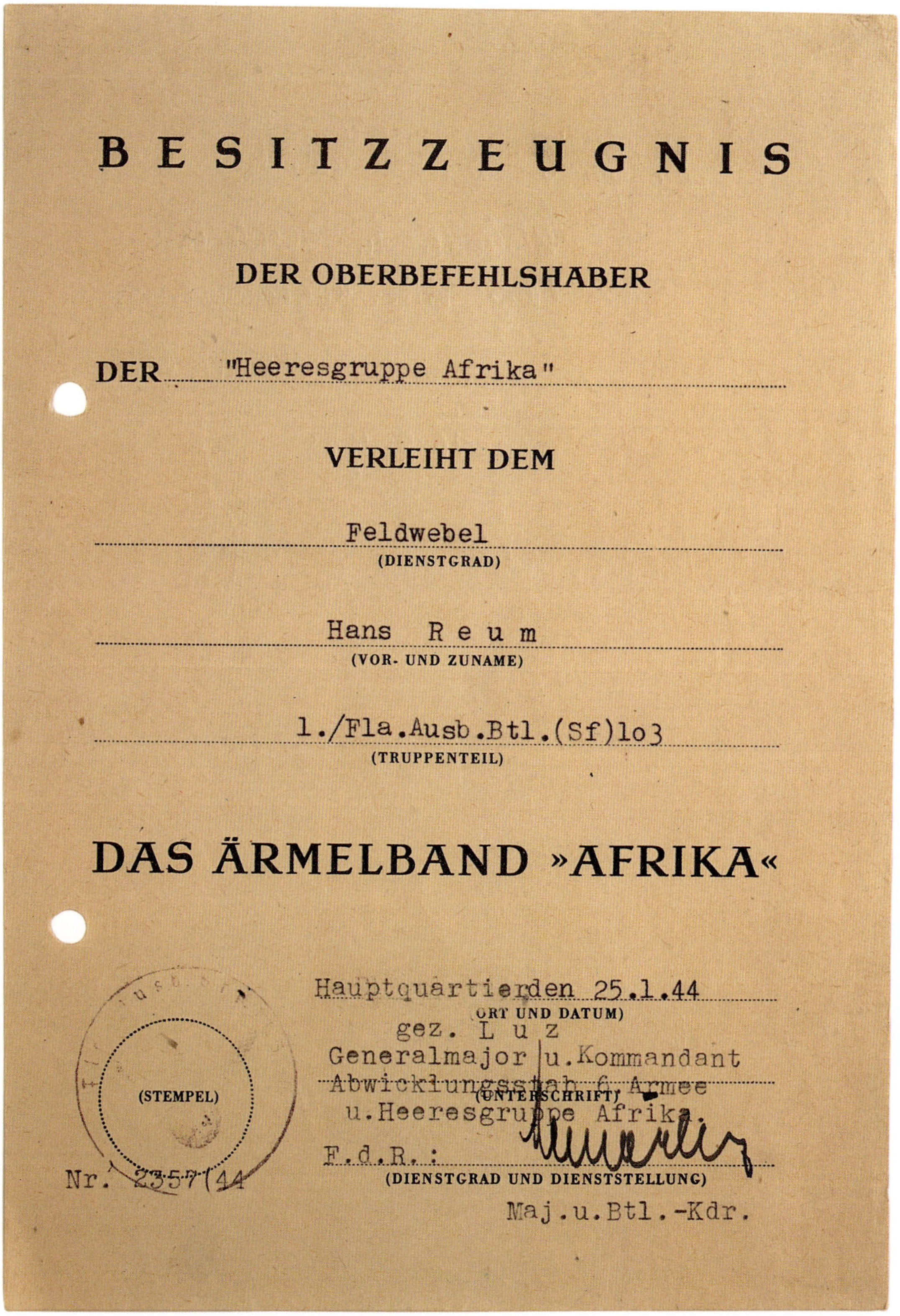

BESITZZEUGNIS

DER OBERBEFEHLSHABER

DER "Heeresgruppe Afrika"

VERLEIHT DEM

Feldwebel
(DIENSTGRAD)

Hans Reum
(VOR- UND ZUNAME)

1./Fla.Ausb.Btl.(Sf)1o3
(TRUPPENTEIL)

DAS ÄRMELBAND »AFRIKA«

Hauptquartier den 25.1.44
(ORT UND DATUM)

(STEMPEL)

gez. L u z
Generalmajor u.Kommandant
Abwicklungsstab 6. Armee
u.Heeresgruppe Afrika.
(UNTERSCHRIFT)

F.d.R.:
(DIENSTGRAD UND DIENSTSTELLUNG)
Maj.u.Btl.-Kdr.

Nr. 2357/44

Rare *Sonderverband* 288 document grouping. Hans Reum served in *Sonderverband* 288's 6th Company and was awarded the War Merit Cross with Swords in February 1942 by *Generalmajor* Richard Veith of the 90th *Leichte* Africa Division. The document incorrectly names the unit as "*Sperrverband* 288" or "Blocking Unit 288" which, given its combat role, is understandable. *Sonderverband* translates as "Special Unit." Reum was awarded his AFRIKAKORPS cufftitle in 1944. (Gary Armitage)

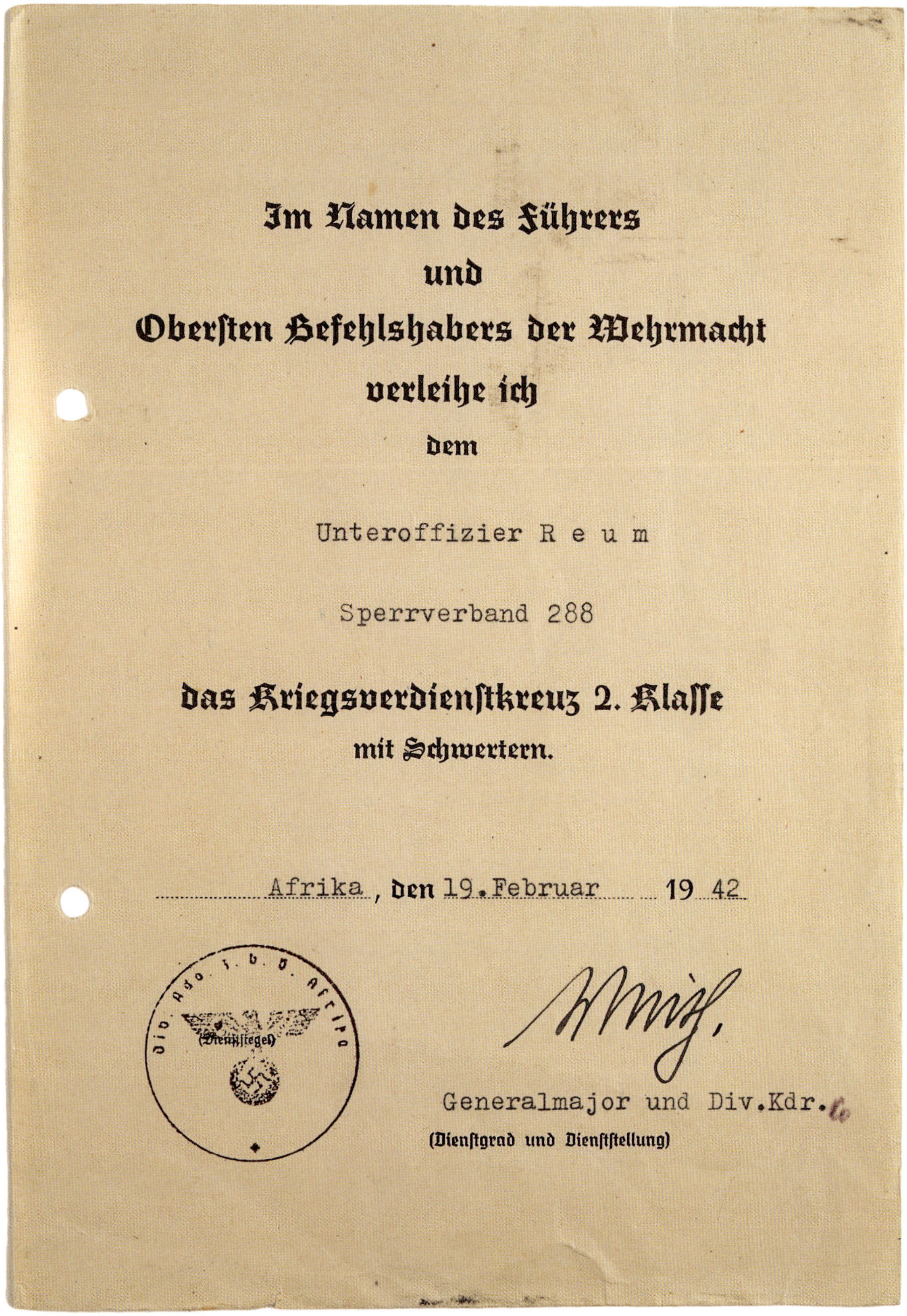
Im Namen des Führers
und
Obersten Befehlshabers der Wehrmacht
verleihe ich
dem

Unteroffizier R e u m

Sperrverband 288

das Kriegsverdienstkreuz 2. Klasse
mit Schwertern.

Afrika, den 19. Februar 1942

(Dienstsiegel)

Generalmajor und Div.Kdr.
(Dienstgrad und Dienststellung)

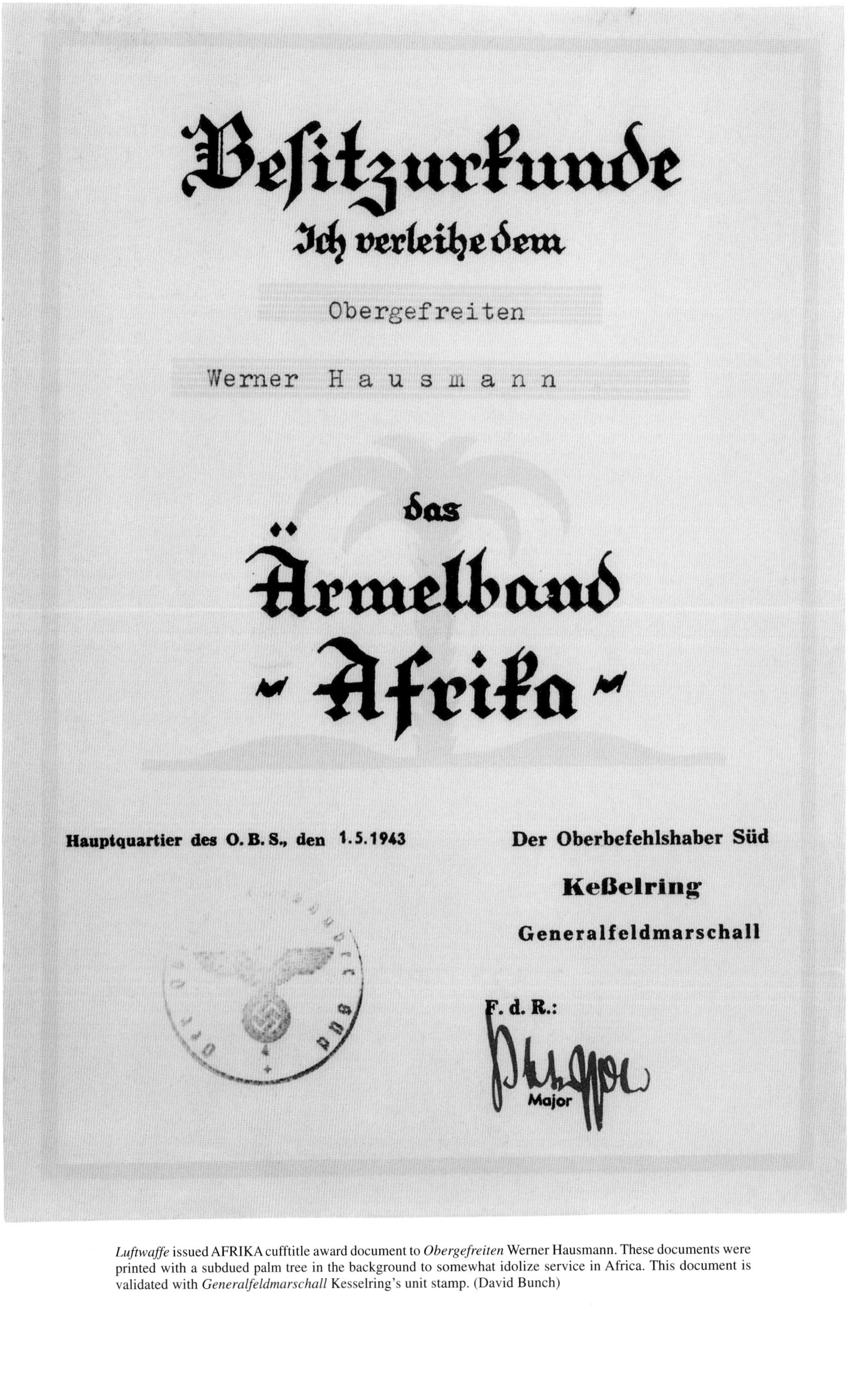
Besitzurkunde

Ich verleihe dem

Obergefreiten

Werner H a u s m a n n

das

Ärmelband

- Afrika -

Hauptquartier des O. B. S., den 1.5.1943

Der Oberbefehlshaber Süd

Keßelring

Generalfeldmarschall

F. d. R.:

Major

Luftwaffe issued AFRIKA cufftitle award document to *Obergefreiten* Werner Hausmann. These documents were printed with a subdued palm tree in the background to somewhat idolize service in Africa. This document is validated with *Generalfeldmarschall* Kesselring's unit stamp. (David Bunch)

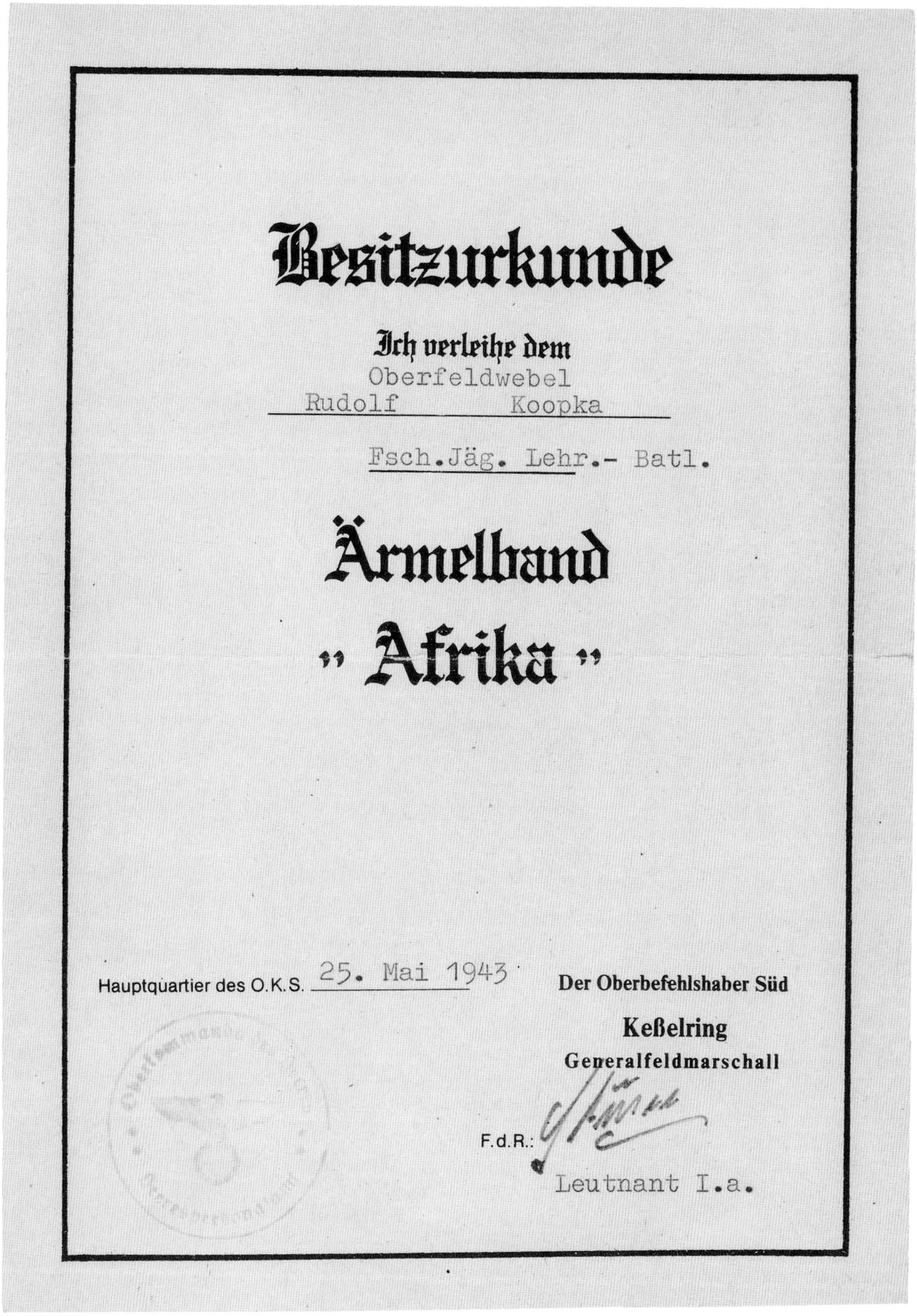

Besitzurkunde

Ich verleihe dem

Oberfeldwebel

Rudolf Koopka

Fsch.Jäg. Lehr.- Batl.

Ärmelband

„Afrika“

Hauptquartier des O.K.S. 25. Mai 1943

Der Oberbefehlshaber Süd

Keßelring

Generalfeldmarschall

F.d.R.:

Leutnant I.a.

An extremely rare *Luftwaffe Fallschirmjäger* variant of the AFRIKA cufftitle award document awarded to an *Oberfeldwebel* of a *Fallschirmjäger Lehr* (Paratrooper Training) *Bataillon*. (David Bunch via George Petersen)

Besitzzeugnis.

Auf Grund der Ermächtigung

des Oberbefehlshabers der Kriegsmarine

verleihe ich dem

Sdf. Oberleutnant M.A.

Walter B a r t e l s

das Ärmelband " Afrika "

R o m, den 15. Juli 1943

Ort und Datum

(Dienstsiegel)

Konteradmiral
~~Vizeadmiral~~
und Befehlshaber des Deutschen
Marinekommandos Italien

Dienstgrad und Dienststellung
des Verleihungsberechtigten

OQu H 4848 PI

Rare *Kriegsmarine* version of the AFRIKA cufftitle award document. Few *Kriegsmarine* personnel were awarded the AFRIKA cufftitle. This award was given to Walter Bartels who came to Africa in 1941 and was promoted to *harbourmaster*, officer and eventually *Sonderführer* while in Africa. The document is dated July 15, 1943 and signed by an Admiral in command of German navy personnel in Italy. Photograph at top left shows *Sonderführer* Walter Bartels wearing his AFRIKA cufftitle while on leave in Germany. (David Bunch)

This is an official Italian-German Africa campaign medal award document issued by the Italian Military Command and only awarded to German personnel in Africa. The first awards were given in early 1942. This award was given to a *Flieger* in the *Luftwaffe* on March 1, 1943. To the right of the award document is an early bronze medal with a very rare Italian maker-titled cellophane packet. At left is an Italian-German Africa campaign medal Stickpin. Produced by the Italians in very limited quantities and offered to recipients of the campaign medal, this small stickpin is a bronze metal replica of the campaign medal with an armored German and Italian soldier holding a crocodile's jaws closed. The crocodile is representative of the British Empire. (David Bunch)

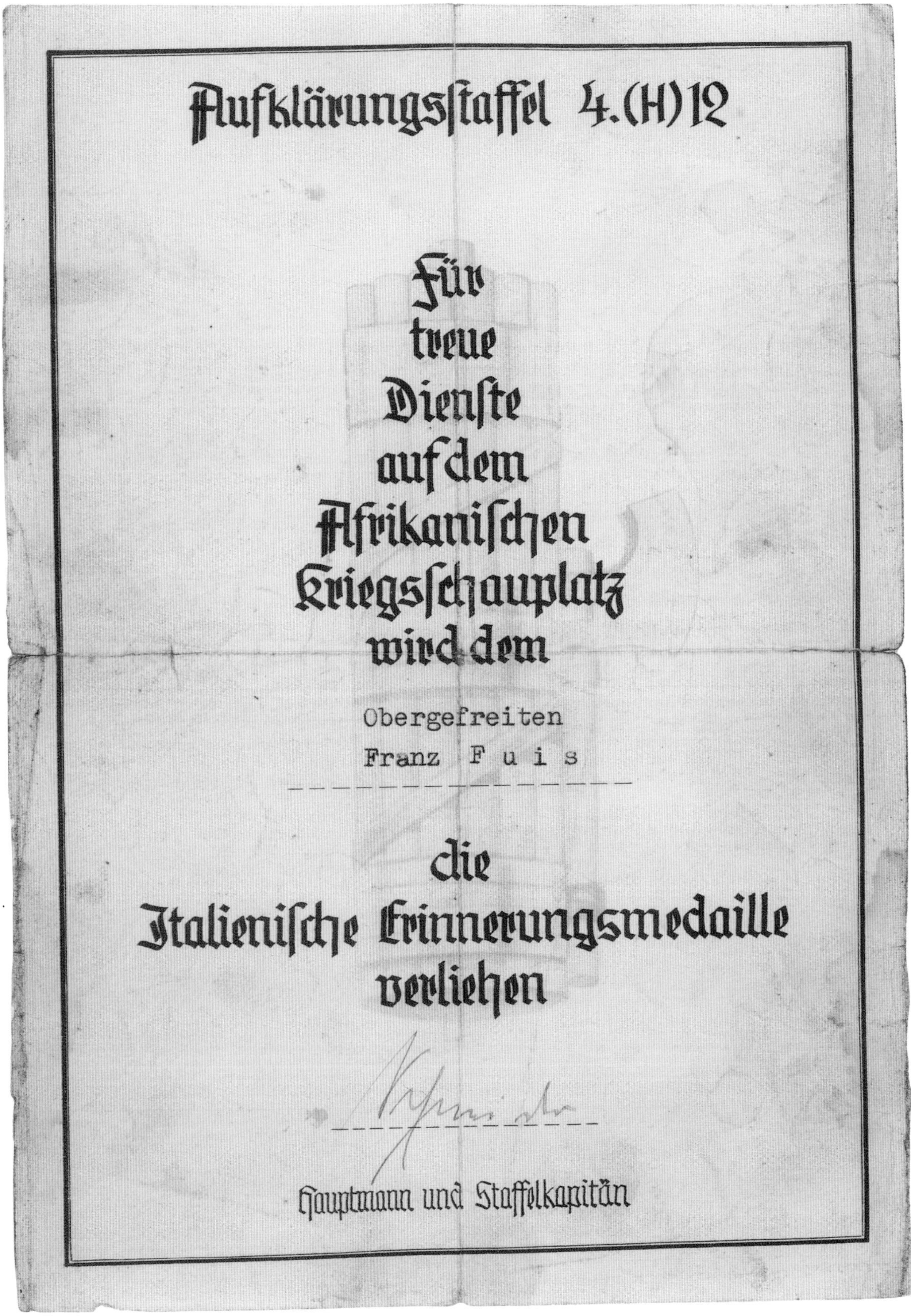

Aufklärungsstaffel 4.(H)12

Für
treue
Dienste
auf dem
Afrikanischen
Kriegsschauplatz
wird dem

Obergefreiten
Franz F u i s

die
Italienische Erinnerungsmedaille
verliehen

Hauptmann und Staffelkapitän

Very interesting and rare version of the Italian-German Africa campaign medal award document issued to Franz Fuis of *Reconnaissance Staffel 4.(H)12*. The document has a subdued Italian Fascist party symbol and was awarded, "for faithful service in the African theater of war." This is the same unit associated with the Me 109 "war trophy" shown on pages 300-303 of volume one. (David Bunch)

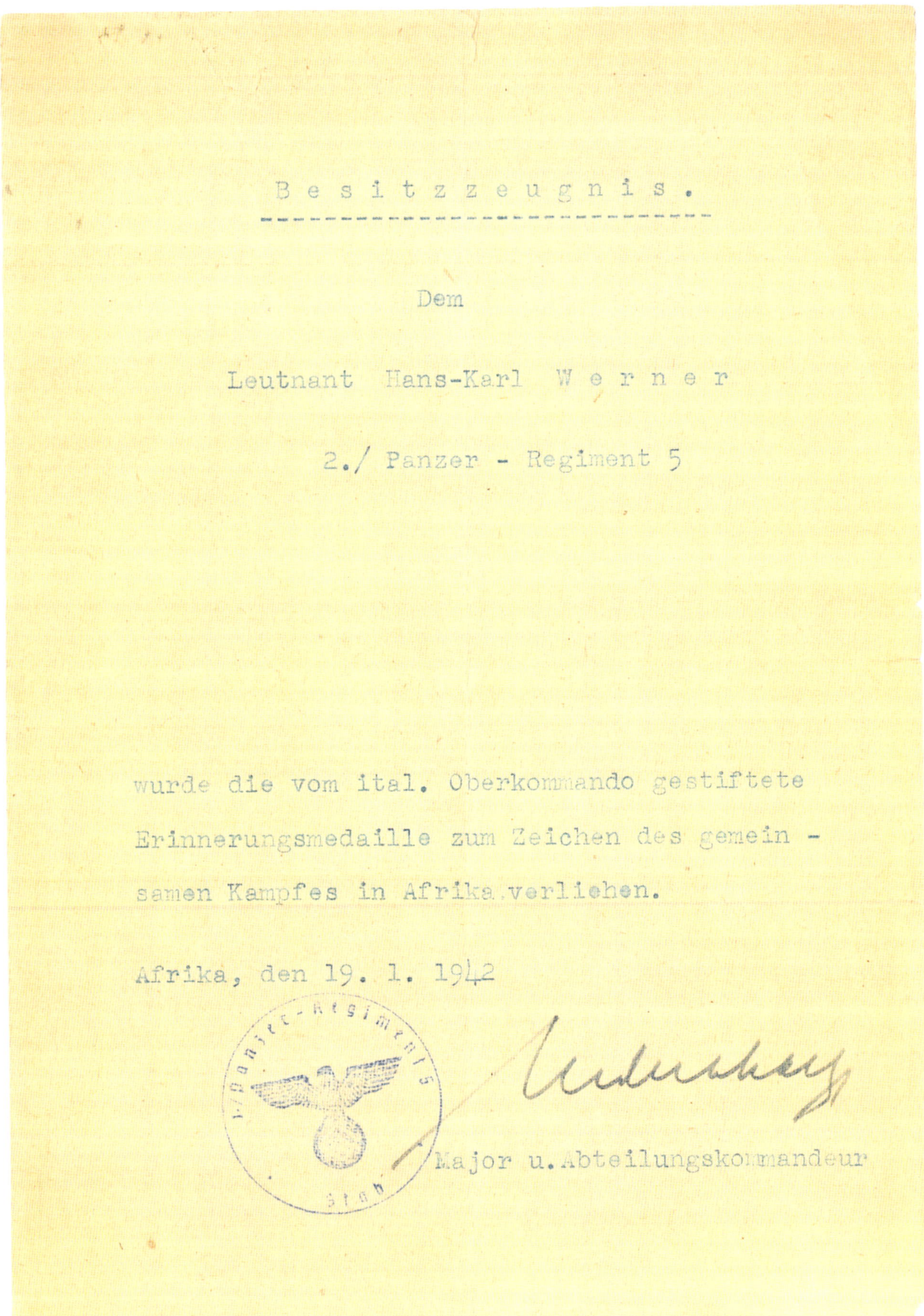

Besitzzeugnis.

Dem

Leutnant Hans-Karl Werner

2./ Panzer - Regiment 5

wurde die vom ital. Oberkommando gestiftete Erinnerungsmedaille zum Zeichen des gemein - samen Kampfes in Afrika verliehen.

Afrika, den 19. 1. 1942

Major u. Abteilungskommandeur

Leutnant Hans-Karl Werner of *2nd Kompanie, 5th Panzer Regiment (5th leichte Division)* is awarded the Italian Commemorative Medal created by the Italian High Command as a symbol of "our common struggle" in Africa. Based on the date, this is a very early field-made version of the award document. (David Bunch)

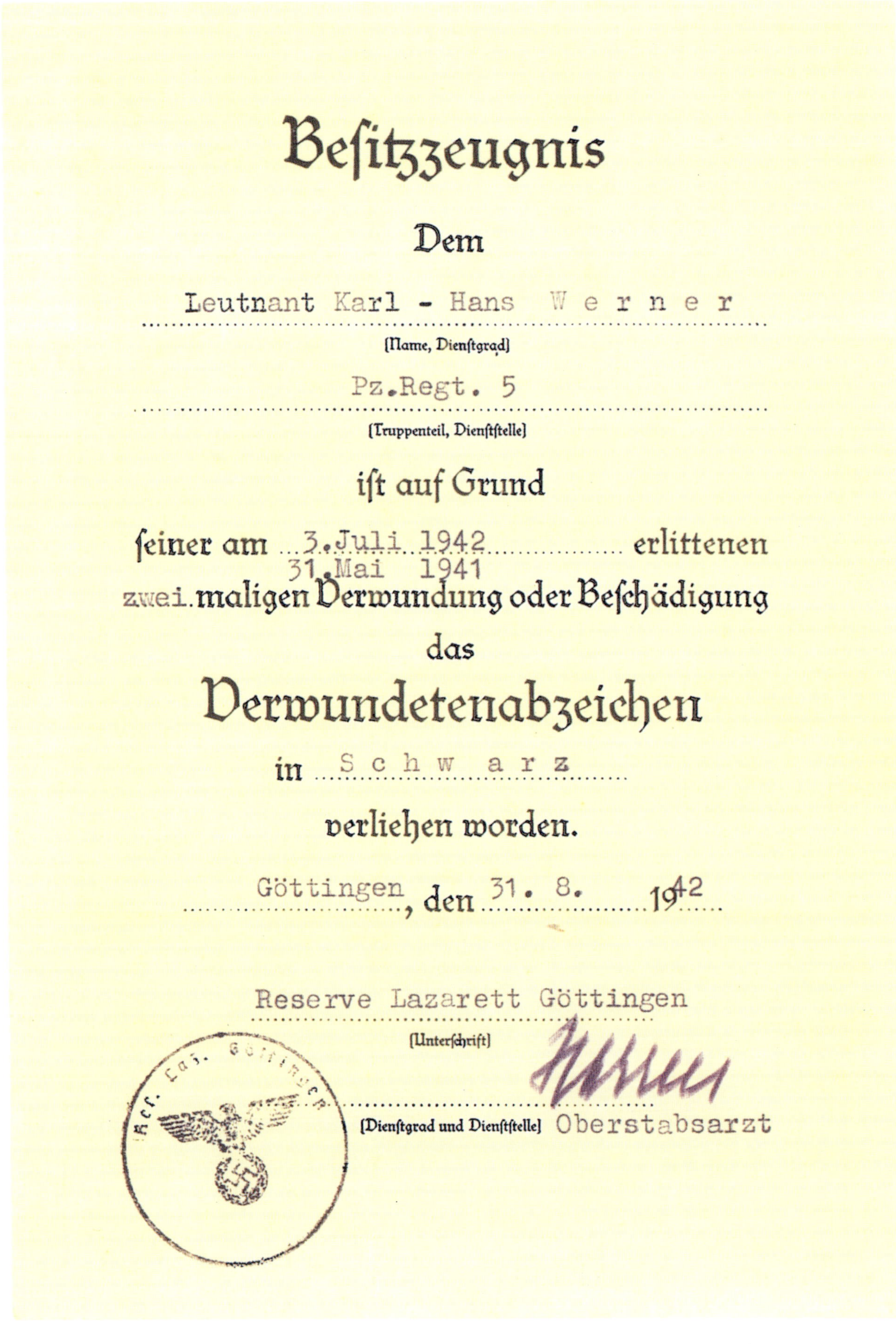

Besitzzeugnis

Dem

Leutnant Karl - Hans Werner

(Name, Dienstgrad)

Pz.Regt. 5

(Truppenteil, Dienststelle)

ist auf Grund

seiner am 3.Juli 1942 / 31.Mai 1941 erlittenen

zwei.maligen Verwundung oder Beschädigung

das

Verwundetenabzeichen

in Schwarz

verliehen worden.

Göttingen, den 31. 8. 1942

Reserve Lazarett Göttingen

(Unterschrift)

(Dienstgrad und Dienststelle) Oberstabsarzt

Leutnant Werner was wounded in Africa on May 31, 1941 and July 3, 1942 earning him the Black Wound Badge on August 31, 1942 while recuperating in Göttingen, Germany. (David Bunch)

Dem Obergefreiten Frido Meyer

wird diese Urkunde für eine Strecke von 68 000 km, die er mit demselben Kraftfahrzeug trotz ungünstigen Straßen- und Witterungsverhältnissen in Afrika zurückgelegt hat und für gute Wagenpflege als besondere Anerkennung für diese Leistung verliehen.

Afrika, den 10. Juni 1942

Rommel

Generaloberst
und Oberbefehlshaber der Panzerarmee Afrika.

A rare and artistic *Afrikakorps* driver's award document designed to herald the success of those transport units critical to supplying Rommel's army in North Africa. These documents were printed by the same propaganda unit responsible for printing *Die Oase*. This award was given to *Obergefreiten* Frido Meyer on June 10, 1942 in recognition of driving 68,000 kilometers in Africa. (David Bunch)

GETREU SEINEM FAHNENEID
STARB IM KAMPF UM DIE
FREIHEIT GROSSDEUTSCHLANDS

Josef Schmidt

Panzerschütze in der 7.Kompanie
Panzer-Regiment 7

DEN HELDENTOD FÜR
FÜHRER, VOLK UND VATERLAND

O.U.,den 10.März 1943.

Panzer-Regiment 7 · 7. Kompanie

Hauptmann und Kp.-Chef

O 1350

Afrikakorps Heldentod or "Hero's Death Certificate" in recognition of one's sacrifice in fighting for the "*Führer*, People and Fatherland." This unique document is dated March 10, 1943 in honor of *Panzerschütze* Josef Schmidt of the *7th Kompanie, Panzer-Regiment 7 (10th Panzer Division)*. The certificate also has the 7th Company unit stamp and was signed by its commander. (David Bunch)

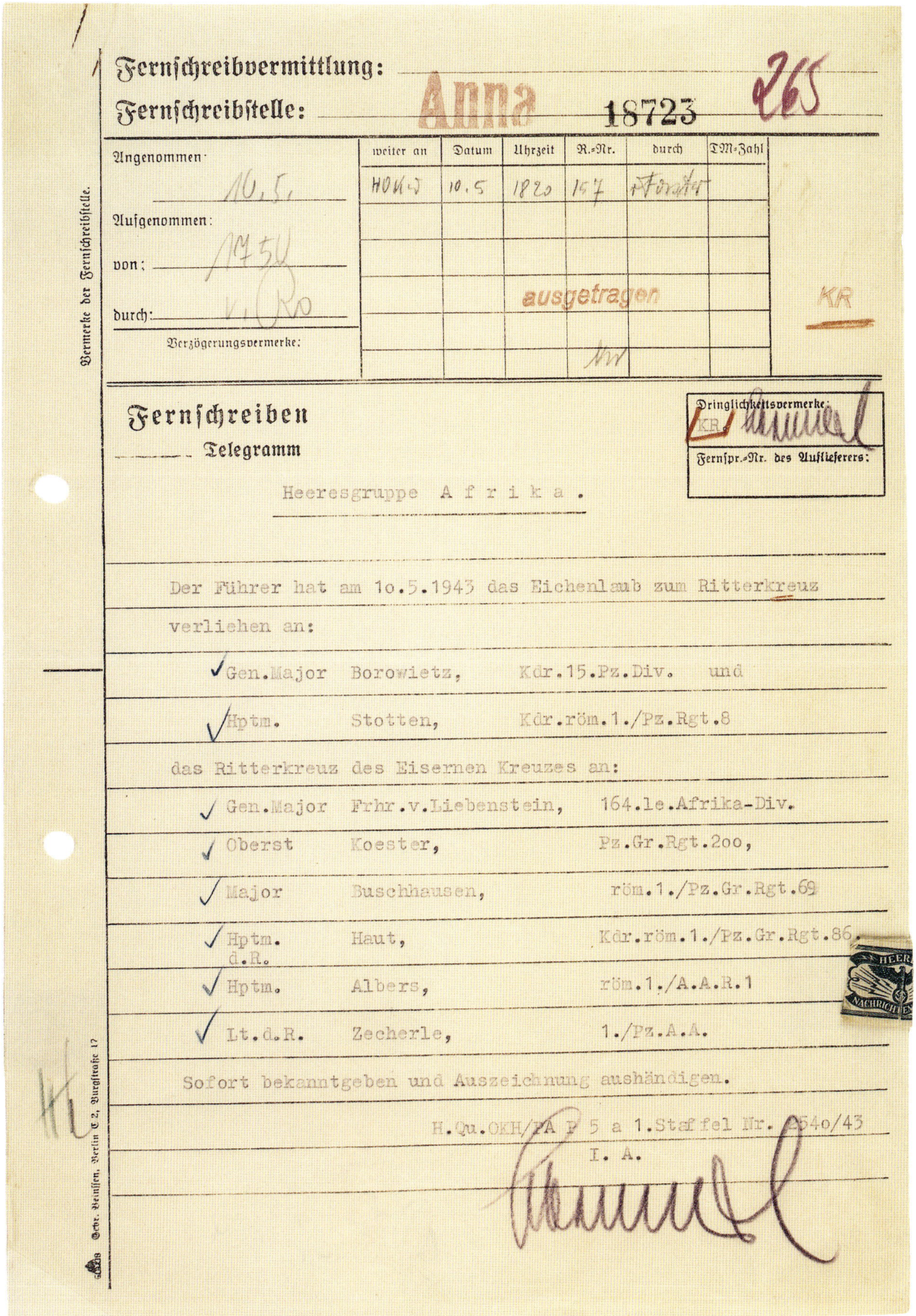

Fernschreibvermittlung:
Fernschreibstelle: Anna 18723 265

Angenommen: 10.5.	weiter an	Datum	Uhrzeit	R.-Nr.	durch	TM-Zahl
Aufgenommen:	HOK-J	10.5	1820	157		
von: 1754						
durch: v. Ro						

ausgetragen KR

Verzögerungsvermerke:

Vermerke der Fernschreibstelle.

Fernschreiben
Telegramm

Dringlichkeitsvermerke:
Fernspr.-Nr. des Auflieferers:

Heeresgruppe A f r i k a .

Der Führer hat am 10.5.1943 das Eichenlaub zum Ritterkreuz verliehen an:

✓Gen.Major	Borowietz,	Kdr.15.Pz.Div. und
✓Hptm.	Stotten,	Kdr.röm.1./Pz.Rgt.8

das Ritterkreuz des Eisernen Kreuzes an:

✓Gen.Major	Frhr.v.Liebenstein,	164.le.Afrika-Div.
✓Oberst	Koester,	Pz.Gr.Rgt.200,
✓Major	Buschhausen,	röm.1./Pz.Gr.Rgt.69
✓Hptm. d.R.	Haut,	Kdr.röm.1./Pz.Gr.Rgt.86
✓Hptm.	Albers,	röm.1./A.A.R.1
✓Lt.d.R.	Zecherle,	1./Pz.A.A.

Sofort bekanntgeben und Auszeichnung aushändigen.

H.Qu.OKH/PA P 5 a 1.Staffel Nr. 2540/43
I. A.

A historically significant telegram transmission from OKH (*Oberkommando des Heeres* or Army High Command) to Army Group *Afrika* formally announcing the awards of two Oak Leaf (*Eichenlaub zum Ritterkreuz*) recipients and six Knight's Cross (*Ritterkreuz des Eiserner Kreuzes*) recipients. Among the distinguished names on this list are the commanders of the *15th Panzer Division* and *164th leichte Afrika Division*. The most amazing fact is that this telegram was received on one of the last day of fighting in Africa, May 10, 1943. (David Bunch)

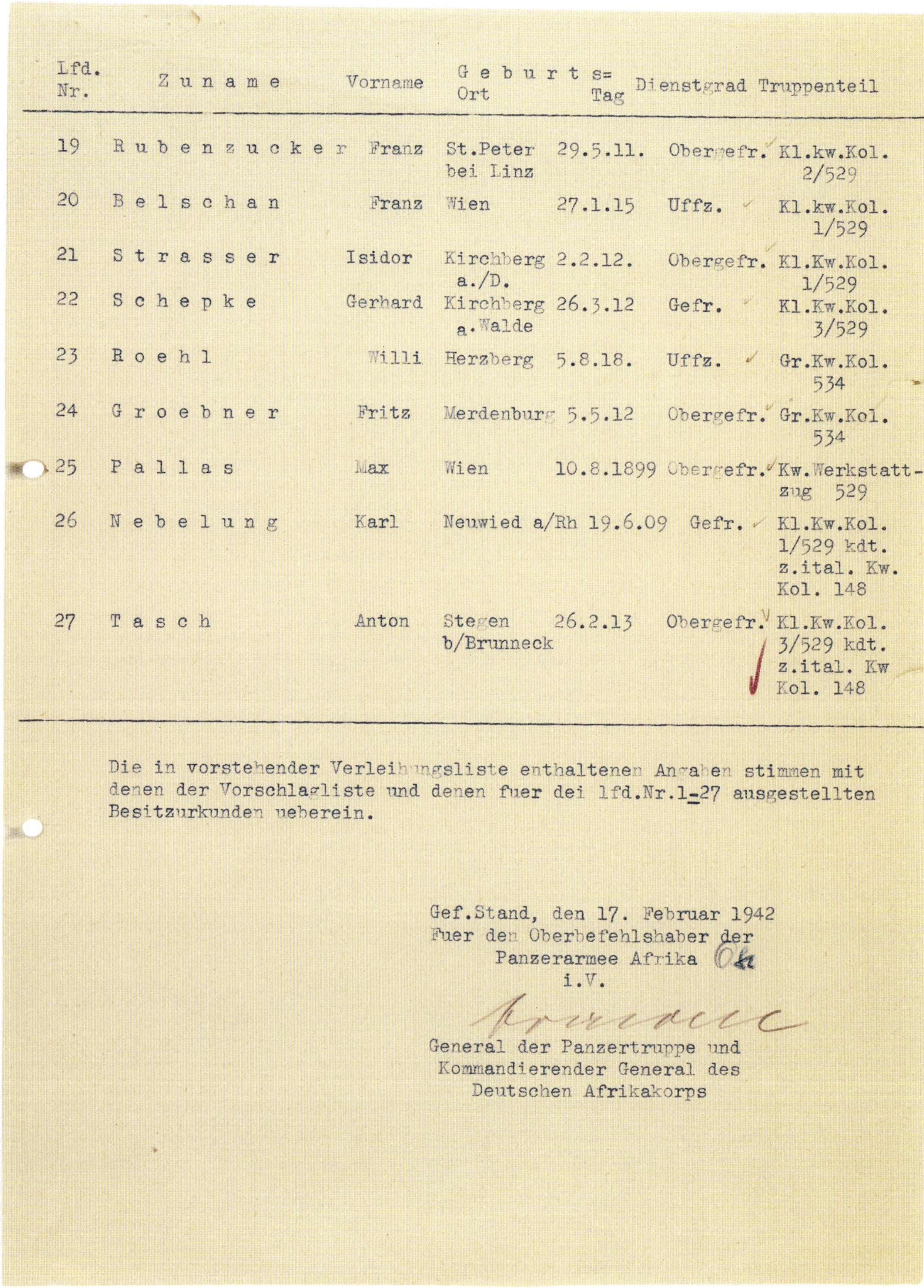

Lfd. Nr.	Zuname	Vorname	Geburts= Ort	Tag	Dienstgrad	Truppenteil
19	Rubenzucker	Franz	St.Peter bei Linz	29.5.11.	Obergefr.	Kl.kw.Kol. 2/529
20	Belschan	Franz	Wien	27.1.15	Uffz.	Kl.kw.Kol. 1/529
21	Strasser	Isidor	Kirchberg a./D.	2.2.12.	Obergefr.	Kl.Kw.Kol. 1/529
22	Schepke	Gerhard	Kirchberg a.Walde	26.3.12	Gefr.	Kl.Kw.Kol. 3/529
23	Roehl	Willi	Herzberg	5.8.18.	Uffz.	Gr.Kw.Kol. 534
24	Groebner	Fritz	Merdenburg	5.5.12	Obergefr.	Gr.Kw.Kol. 534
25	Pallas	Max	Wien	10.8.1899	Obergefr.	Kw.Werkstatt-zug 529
26	Nebelung	Karl	Neuwied a/Rh	19.6.09	Gefr.	Kl.Kw.Kol. 1/529 kdt. z.ital. Kw. Kol. 148
27	Tasch	Anton	Stegen b/Brunneck	26.2.13	Obergefr.	Kl.Kw.Kol. 3/529 kdt. z.ital. Kw Kol. 148

Die in vorstehender Verleihungsliste enthaltenen Angaben stimmen mit denen der Vorschlagliste und denen fuer dei lfd.Nr.1-27 ausgestellten Besitzurkunden ueberein.

Gef.Stand, den 17. Februar 1942
Fuer den Oberbefehlshaber der
Panzerarmee Afrika
i.V.

General der Panzertruppe und
Kommandierender General des
Deutschen Afrikakorps

This document is a *verleihungsliste* of personnel recommended for decorations. The document is quite rare given the signature of *General* Crüwell as Commander of the *Deutschen Afrikakorps*. In actuality, the *Afrikakorps* only consisted of the *15th* and *21st Panzer Divisions*. Rommel's command was raised to the status of a *Panzergruppe* in August 1941 and included the *Afrikakorps* as well as other German units and six Italian divisions. On May 24, 1942 *Generalleutnant* Crüwell was shot down in his Fieseler Fi 156 *Storch* aircraft while leading an attack on the Gazala line. (David Bunch)

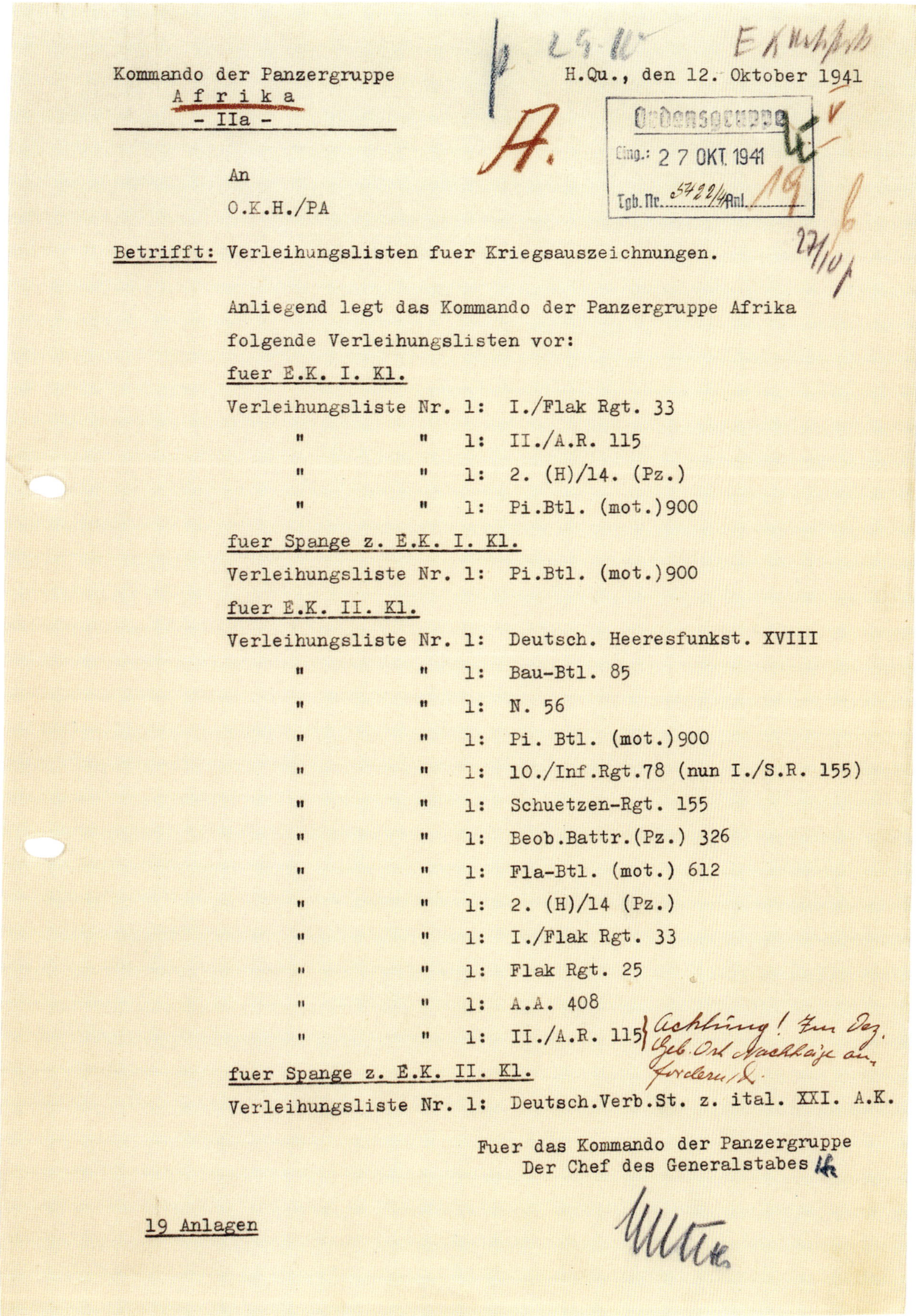

Kommando der Panzergruppe
A f r i k a
- IIa -

H.Qu., den 12. Oktober 1941

Eing.: 27 OKT. 1941

An

O.K.H./PA

Betrifft: Verleihungslisten fuer Kriegsauszeichnungen.

Anliegend legt das Kommando der Panzergruppe Afrika folgende Verleihungslisten vor:

fuer E.K. I. Kl.

Verleihungsliste Nr. 1: I./Flak Rgt. 33
" " 1: II./A.R. 115
" " 1: 2. (H)/14. (Pz.)
" " 1: Pi.Btl. (mot.)900

fuer Spange z. E.K. I. Kl.

Verleihungsliste Nr. 1: Pi.Btl. (mot.)900

fuer E.K. II. Kl.

Verleihungsliste Nr. 1: Deutsch. Heeresfunkst. XVIII
" " 1: Bau-Btl. 85
" " 1: N. 56
" " 1: Pi. Btl. (mot.)900
" " 1: 10./Inf.Rgt.78 (nun I./S.R. 155)
" " 1: Schuetzen-Rgt. 155
" " 1: Beob.Battr.(Pz.) 326
" " 1: Fla-Btl. (mot.) 612
" " 1: 2. (H)/14 (Pz.)
" " 1: I./Flak Rgt. 33
" " 1: Flak Rgt. 25
" " 1: A.A. 408
" " 1: II./A.R. 115

fuer Spange z. E.K. II. Kl.

Verleihungsliste Nr. 1: Deutsch.Verb.St. z. ital. XXI. A.K.

Fuer das Kommando der Panzergruppe
Der Chef des Generalstabes

19 Anlagen

Cover letter from the command of *Panzergruppe Afrika* to the OKH's personnel office listing recommendations for various decorations of the Iron Cross. (David Bunch)

Panzerarmee Afrika

Der Oberbefehlshaber

Gefechtsstand,

Datum des Poststempels.

Aus allen Teilen Deutschlands erhalte ich täglich ausserordentlich viel Post. Ueber diese Grüsse aus der Heimat freue ich mich sehr. Mit dem besten Willen ist es mir jedoch nicht möglich, bei der Grösse der mir gestellten Aufgabe persönlich auf die einzelnen Schreiben einzugehen. Ich bitte deshalb, Verständnis dafür zu haben, dass die Grüsse nur in dieser Form erwidert werden können.

Die den deutschen Truppen hier zugeteilten Kriegsberichter haben so viele Erlebnisse in Wort und Bild wiedergegeben, dass ich hierauf verweisen kann. Desgleichen geben die Wochenschauen ein treffendes Bild von den aussergewöhnlichen Leistungen der Truppen in Nordafrika.

Ich bin stolz darauf, sagen zu können, dass auch unter den ausserordentlich schwierigen Verhältnissen der Wüste der deutsche Soldat vorbildlich tapfer und pflichttreu an der Seite der italienischen Kameraden für den gemeinsamen Sieg kämpft. Auch in Zukunft werden die deutschen Truppen in Nordafrika auf ihrem schweren Posten durchhalten und ihren Beitrag zum Endsieg der Achse leisten.

Heil dem Führer!

Für Jhre Glückwünsche zu meiner
Beförderung danke ich Jhnen sehr.

Rommel

Generaloberst.

Opposite

A very rare *Panzerarmee Afrika* correspondence letter personally signed by *Generaloberst* Rommel. With his growing popularity in Germany, Rommel often found himself receiving adoration from his admirers and letters of encouragement from the families of soldiers fighting in Africa. Due to his time demands on the desert front, Rommel's propaganda staff prepared this form letter for his signature in response to these many letters from home. This particular letter from Rommel also expresses his appreciation for the congratulations received on his promotion to Generaloberst. Note the use of a captured French typewriter in using umlauts! It reads:

> Panzer Army Africa
> The commanding officer
>
> Daily I receive an extraordinary amount of mail from all over Germany. I enjoy these greetings from home very much. As much as I might like to, however, my many responsibilities prevent me from responding personally to every letter. I therefore beg that you understand that I can only reply to the majority of letters in this manner.
>
> The war correspondents assigned to the troops here have described so many events in words and pictures that I can refer you to them. The newsreels also provide an accurate picture of the extraordinary efforts made by the troops in North Africa.
>
> I am proud to be able to say that, even under the extremely difficult conditions of the desert, the German soldier has fought with exemplary bravery and devotion to duty at the side of his Italian comrades in the struggle for the common victory. The German troops in North Africa will continue to hold their isolated posts and contribute to the final victory of the Axis powers.
>
> Hail to the *Führer*!
>
> I am extremely grateful for your congratulations on my promotion.
>
> Rommel,
> *Generaloberst*

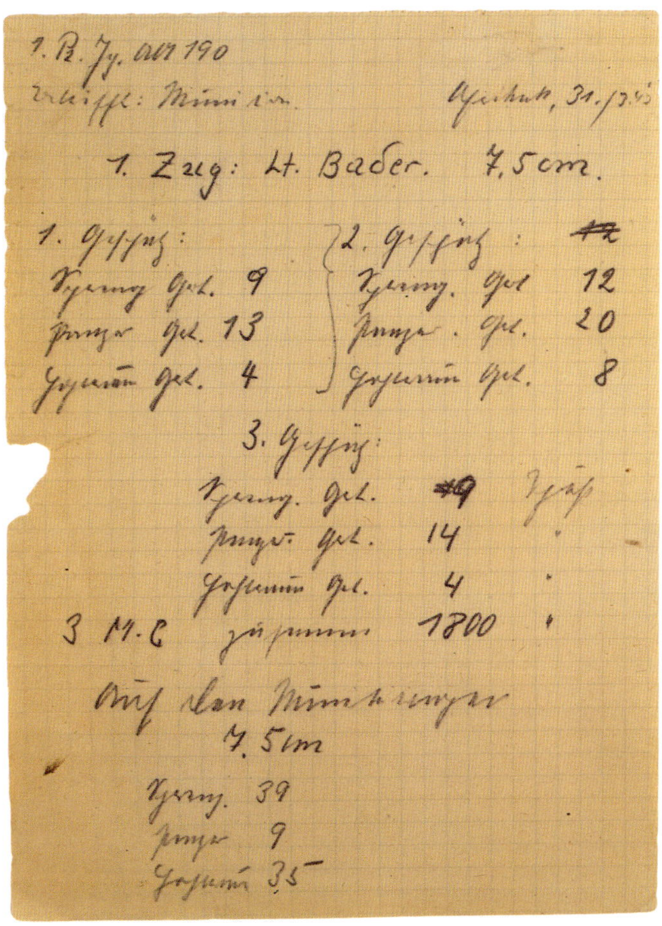

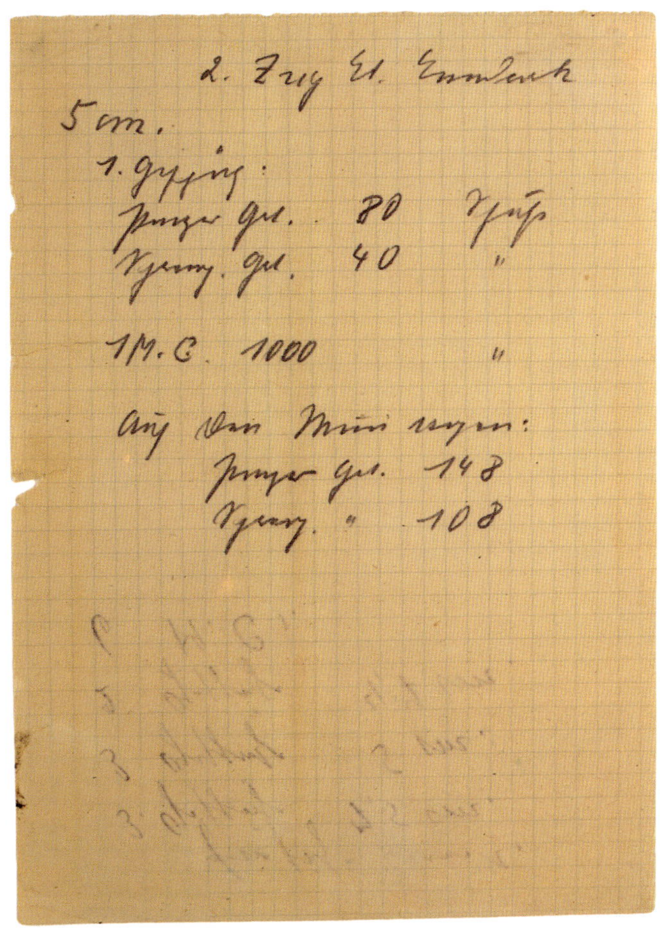

Field dispatches from the 90th *Leichte* Africa Division. This rare document grouping consists of section dispatches from the 1st Company of the 190th *Panzerjäger* Battalion and is dated March 31, 1943 during the battles near El Guettar, Tunisia. The report indicates the ammunition levels for the company's 75mm, 50mm, and heavy machineguns. (Gary Armitage)

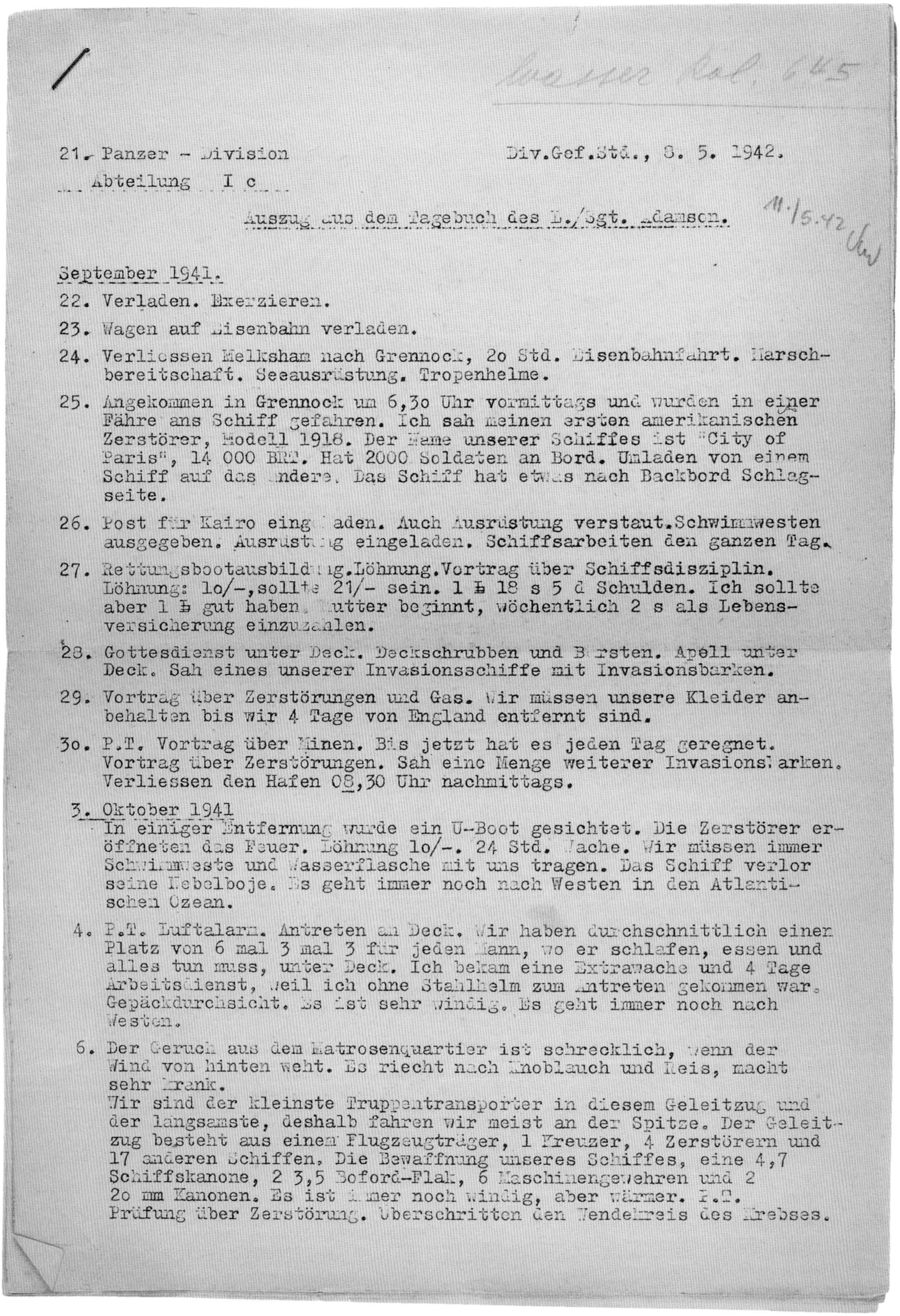

21. Panzer - Division Div.Gef.Std., 8. 5. 1942.
Abteilung I c

Auszug aus dem Tagebuch des L./Sgt. Adamson.

September 1941.

22. Verladen. Exerzieren.

23. Wagen auf Eisenbahn verladen.

24. Verliessen Melksham nach Grennock, 2o Std. Eisenbahnfahrt. Marschbereitschaft. Seeausrüstung. Tropenhelme.

25. Angekommen in Grennock um 6,3o Uhr vormittags und wurden in einer Fähre ans Schiff gefahren. Ich sah meinen ersten amerikanischen Zerstörer, Modell 1918. Der Name unserer Schiffes ist "City of Paris", 14 000 BRT. Hat 2000 Soldaten an Bord. Umladen von einem Schiff auf das andere. Das Schiff hat etwas nach Backbord Schlagseite.

26. Post für Kairo eingeladen. Auch Ausrüstung verstaut. Schwimmwesten ausgegeben. Ausrüstung eingeladen. Schiffsarbeiten den ganzen Tag.

27. Rettungsbootausbildung. Löhnung. Vortrag über Schiffsdisziplin. Löhnung: 1o/-, sollte 21/- sein. 1 ₤ 18 s 5 d Schulden. Ich sollte aber 1 ₤ gut haben. Mutter beginnt, wöchentlich 2 s als Lebensversicherung einzuzahlen.

28. Gottesdienst unter Deck. Deckschrubben und Bürsten. Apell unter Deck. Sah eines unserer Invasionsschiffe mit Invasionsbarken.

29. Vortrag über Zerstörungen und Gas. Wir müssen unsere Kleider anbehalten bis wir 4 Tage von England entfernt sind.

3o. P.T. Vortrag über Minen. Bis jetzt hat es jeden Tag geregnet. Vortrag über Zerstörungen. Sah eine Menge weiterer Invasionsbarken. Verliessen den Hafen 08,30 Uhr nachmittags.

3. Oktober 1941
In einiger Entfernung wurde ein U-Boot gesichtet. Die Zerstörer eröffneten das Feuer. Löhnung 1o/-. 24 Std. Wache. Wir müssen immer Schwimmweste und Wasserflasche mit uns tragen. Das Schiff verlor seine Nebelboje. Es geht immer noch nach Westen in den Atlantischen Ozean.

4. P.T. Luftalarm. Antreten an Deck. Wir haben durchschnittlich einen Platz von 6 mal 3 mal 3 für jeden Mann, wo er schlafen, essen und alles tun muss, unter Deck. Ich bekam eine Extrawache und 4 Tage Arbeitsdienst, weil ich ohne Stahlhelm zum Antreten gekommen war. Gepäckdurchsicht. Es ist sehr windig. Es geht immer noch nach Westen.

6. Der Geruch aus dem Matrosenquartier ist schrecklich, wenn der Wind von hinten weht. Es riecht nach Knoblauch und Reis, macht sehr krank.
Wir sind der kleinste Truppentransporter in diesem Geleitzug und der langsamste, deshalb fahren wir meist an der Spitze. Der Geleitzug besteht aus einem Flugzeugträger, 1 Kreuzer, 4 Zerstörern und 17 anderen Schiffen. Die Bewaffnung unseres Schiffes, eine 4,7 Schiffskanone, 2 3,5 Boford-Flak, 6 Maschinengewehren und 2 2o mm Kanonen. Es ist immer noch windig, aber wärmer. P.T. Prüfung über Zerstörung. Überschritten den Wendekreis des Krebses.

This is a rare mimeographed chronology from the captured diary of a British soldier, describing his embarkation and transport to North Africa between September 1941 and March 1942. This report was prepared by the Intelligence Company attached to the *21st Panzer Division.* (David Bunch)

CHAPTER THREE

Field Newspapers/Newsletters

A fantastic collection of *Afrikakorps* newspapers printed in Africa to promote Germany's perspective of the war and provide news coverage from other fronts as well as the home front. The *Die Oase* ("The Oasis") newspaper (right) is dated March 19, 1941 and was only the second issue of the new publication. The center issue of *Die Oase* is dated May 2, 1943 and the very last edition of the infamous *Afrikakorps* weekly newspaper before German forces collapsed in Africa. *Die Karawane* ("The Caravan"), at left, was a daily field newspaper for German troops in Tunisia and was only in print between December 1942 and April 1943. (David Bunch/John Keener)

An officer reading the *Afrikakorps* field newspaper *Die Oase*.

Opposite

An incredible color photograph of a member o *Afrikakorps* reading the latest issue of *Die Oase* Dohm, P.K. [Propaganda-Kompanie], courtes Peitz Collection)

A *Hauptmann* enjoying a few quite moments as he reads through a magazine while under a tent in the North African desert. Note how he carefully rested his tropical officer visored field cap on the table.

rieg als schöpferische Macht

While waiting for orders, this soldier takes the opportunity to catch up on news from Germany and other war fronts by reading his *Die Oase*. (E. Dohm, P.K. [Propaganda-Kompanie], courtesy B. Peitz Collection)

Die Karawane

Nummer 1. Herausgeber : P. K. Samstag 12. Dezember 1942

ZUM GELEIT UNSERER ZEITUNG

Ich begrüsse die erste Nummer unserer Frontzeitung « Die Karawane ». Sie soll der kæmpfenden Truppe in Tunesien eine Brücke sein zum Weltgeschehen, in dessen Mittelpunkt unsere Heimat und das verbündete Italien stehen.

Meine besten Wünsche begleiten dieses soldatisch kurzgefasste Nachrichtenblatt. Ich weiss, dass es in Zukunft noch manche Siegesmeldung über die angelsæchsischen Mæchte bringen wird.

Der deutsche Soldat aber vergesse nie, dass er dort, wo er auftritt, der Træger der deutschen Kultur und Sitte ist.

Besonders in Tunesien muss jeder von uns sich dessen bewusst sein, dass gerade er als einzelner dem deutschen Namen überall Ehre machen muss.

Der OBERBEFEHLSHABER
der Achsenstreitkæfte in Tunesien

FORTSCHREITEN DES GEGENANGRIFFES

Angriffe und Abwehr im Osten -- In Tunesien oertliche Kaempfe

FUEHRERHAUPTQUARTIER, 10. Dez.

Der Bericht des Oberkommandos der Wehrmacht vom Donnerstag, 10. Dezember hat folgenden Wortlaut :

Im Terek-Gebiet zerschlugen deutsche Truppen in konzrentrischen Angriffen feindliche Kraeftegruppen. Oertliche Unternehmungen des Feindes scheiterten. Zwischen Wolga und Don wurden feindliche Kraefte, denen ein Einbruch geglueckt war eingeschlossen und vernichtet. Im Uebrigen hatten die Sowjets bei der Fortsetzung ihrer vergeblichen Angriffe erneut hohe Verluste. Sie verloren am 8. und 9. Dezember allein in diesem Abschnitt 104 Panzerkampfwagen. Trotz heftiger Gegenwehr warfen Infanterie- und Panzertruppen, den Gegner im grossen Donbogen weiter zurueck, wiesen Gegenangriffe ab und vernichten 16 Sowjetpanzer. Im mittleren Abschnitt der Ostfront wird der eigene Angriff erfolgreich fortzesetzt. Hunderte von Gefangenen wurden eingebracht und zahlreiche Waffen erbeutet. Gegenangriffe des Feindes wurden zurueckgeslagen. Kampf-und Sturzkampfflugzeuze bekaempften feindliche Truppen und Eisenbahnzuege. Stosstrupps einer Luftwaffendivision vernichteten 59 Bunker und Kampfstaende. Bei diesen Kaempfen und suedlich des Ilmensees verloren die Sowjets insgesamt 72 Panzerkampfwagen.

In der Cyrenaika griffen deutsche Kampfflieger den Flugplatz Derna an und zerstoerten sieben Flugzeuge am Boden.

In Tunesien wegen schlechter Wetterlage nur oertliche Kampfhandlungen. Ein feindlicher Panzervorstoss wurde suedwestlich von Tebourba abgewiesen. Panzerkampfwagen zum Teil durch Eingriff der Schlachtflieger in Brand geschossen. Kampfflieger trafen ein Handelsschliff mittlerer Tonnage im Hafen von Bougie mit schweren Bomben und bekaempften feindliche Flugstuetzpunkte mit wichtigen Erfolgen.

Nachtjaeger und Flakartillerie schossen in der vergangenen Nacht bei Durchfluegen britischer Bomber durch die besetzten Westgebiete nach Italien drei Flugzeuge ab.

Am 8. Dezember wurde ein kleiner britischer Sabotagetrupp gestellt und im Kampf niedergemacht.

26.000 BRT. vor Algier

ROM, 10 Dezember.

Artilleriefeuer an der Cyrenaikafront. Waehrend des Angriffes auf einen Flugplatz durch deustche Flugzeuge wurden sieben abgestellte britische Flugzeuge in Brand geworfen.

In Tunesien haben unsere Spaehtrupps Erkundungen durchgefuehrt. Westlich von Tebourba wurde ein Vorstoss feindlicher Panzer, von denen einige vernichtet wurden, zurueckgeworfen.

Turin ist in der vergangenen Nacht von Neuem von feindlichen Flugzeugen bombardiert worden. Zahlreich die getroffenen Gebaeude, die Einstuerze, die Braende, sehr gross die Schaeden. Die Zahl der Opfer des vorhergehenden Luftangriffes ist bisher mit 75 Toten und 112 Verwundeten festgestellt worden. Die Menschenopfer der vergangenen Nacht stehen noch nicht fest.

Ein Verband von Flugzeugen der 150. Staffel der Torpedoflugzeuge unter dem Kommando des Fliegerhauptmanns Urbano Machini fuehrten gestern unter ueberwiegend schlechten Wetterverhaeltnissen einen kuehnen Angriff gegen feindliche Schiffe auf der Reede von Algier aus. Zwei Dampfer von 10.000 BRT und 16.000 BRT erhielten Volltreffer und flogen in die Luft. im nachfolgenden Kampf mit feindlichen Jaegern wurden mehere britische Flugzeuge abgeschossen. Alle Flugzeuge kehrten zu ihren Stuetzpunkten zurueck.

Neuer Generalstabschef General Zeitzler berufen

BERLIN, 11. Dezember.

Wie am Donnerstag bekannt wurde ist als Nachfolger des Generals Halder General der Infanterie Kurt Zeitzler zum Chef des Generalsstabes des Heeres ernannt worden.

Der neue Generalstabschef des Heeres ist 47 Jahre alt und stammt aus Cosmar (Kreis Luckau). Er wurde im Maerz 1914 Soldat und beendete den Weltkrieg als Oberleutnant. seit 31. Mai 1939 ist Zeitzler Oberst 1. G. und seit Beginn des zweiten Weltkrieges Chef des Generalstabes einer Panzergruppe. Mit unverminderter Kraft und Vertrauen auf das Gelingen, traf er die ersten Vorbereitungen einer Panzerbewegung in einer nie dagewesenen Masse, die zum vollen Erfolg fuehrte. General Zeitzler gilt als ein Mann von staendiger Energie. Vor seiner Berufung zum Generalstabschef des Heeres war er Chef des Stabes des O.B.-West, des Generalfeld marschalls v. Rundstaedt. Er organisierte die Verteidigung Frankreichs gegen die englische Invasion, sodass man ihn als den Sieger von Dieppe bezeichnen kann.

Entfesselung der Gefangenen

BERLIN, 10. Dezember.

Amtlich wird bekanntgegeben, dass die Kriegsgefangenen, die in Grossbritannien und Kanada gefesselt wurden, ab 12. Dezember ihrer Fesseln entledigt werden.

Unsere Erfolge in Tunesien

Das Eichenlaub fuer Generalleutnant Fischer

Der Führer hat dem Generalleutnant Fischer, Kommandeur einer Panzerdivision, in Anerkennung des Sieges von Tebourba, das Eichenlaub zum Ritterkreuz des Eisernen Kreuzes verliehen.

Der General macht Gefangene

Auf einer der zahlreichen Frontfahrten des Generals einer bei den Kaempfen in Tunis eingesetzten deutschen Panzerdivision konnte der General selbst einen durchgebrochenen schwerbewaffneten feindlichen LKW jagen und die Besatzung gefangennehmen. Bei dieser Gelegenheit wurden auch drei deutsche Gefangene, die in der Nacht in amerikanische Gefangenschaft geraten waren, durch den General befreit.

Die Beute von Tebourba

In den Kaempfen bei Tebourba vom 1. bis zum 4. dezember wurden 1100 Gefangene gemacht, 76 Panzer, 41 Geschütze, 40 Moerser und 264 Lastwagen erbeutet. Ausserdem sind die feindlichen Nachschublinien insbesondere die Haefen von Bone und Philippeville sowie Eisenbahnknotenpunkte wiederholt bombardiert worden, wodurch erheblicher Schaden an Anlagen, Depots und Rollmaterial angerichtet wurde.

Hafen Tabarca besetzt

Der tunesische Hafen Tabarca wurde in Ausnuetzung des Erfolges bei Tebourba von Truppen der Achse besetzt. Tabarca liegt an der Bahnlinie Bone-Bizerta, etwa 140 Kilometer westlich Bizerta, dem grossen Kriegshafen entfernt. Beim Ausbau von Bizerta wurde es wegen der nahen Erzvorkommen an die von Bone ueber Mateur nach Bizerta fuehrende Eisenbahnstrecke angeschlossen.

SPANIENS HALTUNG

Der spanische Staatschef Generalissimos Franco hiet vor dem Rat der Phalange eine grundsäretzliche Rede, in der er die Stellung Spaniens zur Lage umriss. Spanien, so betonte er, gehoere zu Europa und lehne daher die demokratischen und plutokratischen Ideen ab. In diesem Zusammenhang wies der Caudillo auf die Revolutionen Deutschlands und Italiens hin, wobei er die Notwendigkeit unterstrich die nationale und soziale Erneuerung Spaniens auf dem begonnlnen Wege zu vollenden.

KAMERADEN !

Ein Tisch — ein Stuhl — eine Schreibmaschine und ein guter Wille : damit wurde in den vergangenen Kriegsjahren schon manche Frontzeitung aus dem Boden gestampft.

Wir stellen uns heute vor als eine neue Frontzeitung. Aus einem Nichts haben wir damit begonnen, « die Karawane » aus der Taufe zu heben.

Vielleicht wisst Ihr, wie schwer es ist, in einen fremden Land mit primitiven Mitteln eine Tageszeitung herauszubringen. Wir arbeiten unter anderen technischen Voraussetzungen als unsere Tageszeitungen in der Heimat franzoesiche Setzer reihen Buchstabe an Buchstabe, um muehevoll aus Saetzen, Artikeln und Spalten schliesslich das ganze Nachrichtenblatt zu formen. Es kommt uns nicht darauf an, Euch eine einwandfreie, hieb - und stichfeste Tageszeitung vorzulegen, es geht vielmehr darum, Euch in kurzer Form ueber die wesentlichsten Geschehnisse aus aller Welt zu unterrichten.

Wir arbeiten mit einfachsten Mitteln. Meckert daher, wenn vielleicht von Zeit zu Zeit die eine oder andere Nummer Eurer « Karawane » verspaetet erscheint, sucht keine Druckfehler, sondern arbeitet mit !

Aus der Front fuer die Front soll diese juengste deussche Soldatenzeitung sein; soll vom Geschehen an allen Fronten, wo unsere Kameraden gegen den Feind stehen, berichten und die Verbindung zu ihnen und vor allem auch zur fernen, schoenen deutschen Heimat schaffen.

In diesem Sinne ergeht an Euch die Bitte : Arbeitet mit !

DIE SCHRIFTLEITUNG

Extremely rare first issue of *Die Karawane* dated December 12, 1942! This inaugural issue ("Nummer 1") brings greetings from the new publishers and the German High Command. There is also general war news and an announcement of *General* Fischer receiving the Oak Leaves to his Knight's Cross. (David Bunch)

Die Karawane

Nummer 36 NACHRICHTENBLATT FUER DEUTSCHE SOLDATEN IN TUNESIEN Freitag 29. Januar 1943

Wenn goldne Reden...

Der Casa-blanco-Scheck für STALIN

Stalingrad - Opfermal des deutschen Soldaten des Winterfeldzugs 1942-43

Casablanca, 27. Januar. Der amerikanische Praesident Roosevelt und der englische Ministerpraesident Churchill haben in der Zeit vom 14. bis 24. Januar in der Naehe der Marokkanischen Hafenstadt Casablanca Besprechungen abgehalten, und zwar in Begleitung der Stabschefs der verschiedenen Wehrmachtsteile der beiden Laender. Stalin war, wie es in dem am Mittwochmorgen veroeffentlichten Schlusscommunique heisst, herzlich eingeladen worden, mit dem Praesidenten und dem Premierminister zusammenzutreffen, in welchem Falle das Treffen an einem bedeutend weiter oestlich gelegenen Platze stattgefunden haette.

Aber er war nicht erschienen, was das Communique damit begruendet, das er angesichts der von ihm selbst als Oberkommandierenden geleiteten grossen Offensive Russland zur Zeit nicht verlassen koenne. Das Communique besteht zum groessten Teil aus Personalangaben ueber die Besprechungsteilnehmer und die von Roosevelt und Churchill empfangenen Besuche, unter denen auch Murphy und General Eisenhower von amerikanischer, Mac Millan, General Alexander und Admiral Cunningham von englischer Seite aufgefuehrt werden. Die konkreten Angaben sind sehr mager. Es wird lediglich erklaert das die Operationen auf allen Kriegsschauplaetzen besprochen und alle Hilfskraefte in Erwaegung gezogen worden seien fuer eine intensivere Fortfuehrung des Krieges zur See zu Lande und in der Luft, wobei versichert wird, dass eine vollstaendige Uebereinstimmung zwischen den leitenden Maennern der beiden Laender und ihren Generalstaeben in Bezug auf die Feldzugsplaene fuer 1943 erzielt worden sei. Besondere Anerkennung wird in dem Communique dem sowjetrussischen Kriegspartner gezollt, dem in ziemlich vager Form Entlastung versprochen wird. Ferner wird der unermuedliche Kampf Chiangkaischeks fuer die gemeinsame Sache geruehmt. Zum Schluss wird erklaert, das Treffen habe die geeignete Gelegenheit geboten, General Giraud zu einer Besprechung mit den vereinigten Generalstaeben einzuladen und auch ein Zusammenkommen zwischen ihm und General de Gaulle herbeizufuehren. Beide Generale haben in staendiger Beratung gestanden.

Das Oberkommando der Wehrmacht gibt bekannt

Fuehrerhauptquartier, 27. Januar. Die grosse Winterschlacht an der Ostfront dauert mit unverminderter Staerke an und weitet sich auf neue Raeume aus. Die noch kampffaehigen Teile der 6. Armee verkrallten sich in die Truemmer der Stadt Stalingrad. Unter Aufbietung aller Verteidigungsmoeglichkeiten Sowjets auf der Erde und aus der Luft binden sie die Kraefte mehrere Sowjetarmeen. Eine in die Stadt vorgedrungene feindliche Kraeftegruppe wurde in erbitterten Kaempfen zerschlagen.

Im Kubangebiet verlaufen die eigenen Bewegungen voellig planmaessig. Dem Angriff der deutschen Divisionen zwischen Donez und Don setzte der Feind verstaerkt erbitterten Widerstand entgegen. Weiterer Gelaendegewinn wurde erzielt. Der Versuch des Gegners, den Aufbau der neuen Abwehrfront westlich von Woronesch zu verhindern und in die Stellung mit starken Infanterie- und Panzerkraeften einzubrechen wurde blutig abgewiesen. In der Schlacht am Ladogasee wurden starke Infanterie- und Panzerangriffe die sich an einer Stelle 10, an einer anderen 8 mal wiederholten, von unseren Truppen unter schwersten feindlichen Verlusten abgewiesen. Einzelne kleinere Einbrueche wurden im sofortigen Gegenstoss bereinigt. Die Luftwaffe entlastete die Verbaende des Heeres durch zahlreiche Angriffe auf Truppenbereitstellungen und rueckwaertige Verbindungen des Feindes.

Jagdverbaende schossen in fuenf Tagen suedlich des Ladogasees 97 Sowjetische Flugzeuge bei nur einem eigenen Verlust ab.

In Nordafrika nur Spaehtrupptaetigkeit. Schnelle deutsche Kampfflugzeuge zersprengten in Tunesien motorisierte Abteilungen des Feindes und vernichteten oder beschaedigten auf einem Flugstuetzpunkt eine groessere Anzahl abgestellter Bombenflugzeuge. In den Gewaessern Algiers wurde ein grosses feindliches Transportschiff in Brand geworfen.

Bei Tages- und Nachtvorstoessen in die besetzten Westgebiete verlor der Feind neun Flugzeuge. Einzelne britische Bomber flogen in der vergangenen Nacht unter Verletzung schweizerischen Hoheitsgebietes in Sueddeutschland ein ohne jedoch Bomben zu werfen.

Eine Hafenstadt an der Suedostkueste Englands und eine Ortschaft im Suedosten der Insel wurden am gestrigen Tage mit Bomben schweren Kalibers angegriffen.

Edelweissdivision

Von Oberjaeger Hans Arthur Hirth

gefallen im Kaukasus

Die Sonne senkt, wie jeden Tag, ihre Strahlen erbarmungslos auf die Steppe nieder, durch die unsere Division wie auf brennenden Baendern in endlosen Kolonnen marschiert. Der Wind, der von Osten rauschend über das dürre Gras weht, wird kaum als Abkühlung empfunden. Im Gegenteil! Wir fluchen ihm, denn er entfacht den Brand auf der Strasse, indem er mit jedem Stoss hohe Staubwolken emporwirbelt, die die Marschkolonnen in undurchdringbare Rauchschwaden hüllen. Seit Morgengrauen wird marschiert. Stunde um Stunde verrinnt, aber der Zug durch die Steppe nimmt kein Ende. Noch fehlen die letzten Kilometer an der 40 Kilometer langen Strecke, die an diesem Tag ohne Gnade und Barmherzigkeit bewaeltigt werden muss. Bleischwer fühlen sich die Beine an, die Sohlen in den Bergschuh brennen, als würde man auf glühendem R[illegible] schreiten, die Lungen keuchen, und sc[illegible] weise ruht geht der Atem. Visionen steige[illegible] diesem Marsch durch die endliche E[illegible] sigkeit auf: Ein frischer Bergquell, eine [illegible] sende Schlucht, ein Waldplatz unter [illegible] gen Tannen...

KURZ BERICHTET:

Berlin, 28. Januar. In den Abendstunden des 27. Januar unternahmen einige britische Bomber einen Terrorangriff auf die daenische Hauptstadt wie das Oberkommando der Wehrmacht bekannt gibt. Sie warfen Sprengbomben auf das Stadtgebiet von Kopenhagen, die unter der Bevoelkerung Opfer forderten. Eine der angreifenden Maschinen stuerzt im Flakfeuer brennend ab.

Istanbul, 27. Januar. Im aegyptischen Parlament hat eine stuermische Sitzung stattgefunden. Die Nationalisten vor allem haben darauf gedrungen, dass in Zukunft das Parlament bei allen Angelegenheiten befragt werde. Gesteigerte Erregung herrscht vor allem gegen die englische Einmischung in rein aegyptische Angelegenheiten.

Madrid, 27. Januar. Durch die Indiskretion eines Mitgliedes der englischen Gesandtschaft in Madrid wurde bekannt dass Lord Halifax ein Abschiedsgesuch eingereicht hat. Voran ging ein Streit mit dem amerikanischen Aussenministerium, welches neue Operations-Basen in Britisch-Indien haben wollte.

Stockholm, 27. Januar. Der britische Marineminister Alexander erklaerte dieser Tage in einer Betrachtung ueber die Aussichten des Jahres 1943, dieses Jahr werde eine harte Kraftprobe fuer die alliierte Seemacht bedeuten. Alexander begruendet seine Ansicht mit dem Hinweis darauf, dass der Gegner entschlossen sei, in diesem Jahr sein aeusserstes zu tun. Die Achsenmaechte haetten ihre Taktik geaendert und setzten jetzt Unterseeboote in grosseren und in mehrfach gestaffelten Rudeln ein, die ueberall auf der Lauer liegen.

Lissabon, 27. Januar. In London hat die Polizei eine Razzia durchgefuehrt wobei mehrere tausend Leute festgenommen wurden. Es handelt sich hier um Schwarzhaendler und englisch-amerikanische Deserteure. Die meisten hatten sich in bombenbeschaedigten Haeusern einquartiert.

Der italienische Wehrmachtbericht

Rom, 27. Januar. Das Hauptquartier der italienischen Wehrmacht gibt bekannt:

In Westtripolitanien beschraenkte Gefechtstaetigkeit von motorisierten und Panzereinheiten. Ein von Panzern unterstuetzter Angriff sowie Vorstoesse von Panzerstreitkraeften gegen unsere Stellungen im Abschnitt Tunesien wurden abgeschlagen. Unsere Jaeger zerstoerten ein zweimotoriges amerikanisches Flugzeug im Luftkampf. Weitere vier abgestellte Flugzeuge wurden von deutschen Jaegern bei einem erfolgreichen Angriff auf einen Flugplatz des Gegners in Brand gesetzt. Italienische Kampfflugzeugverbaende griffen zu wiederholten Malen die Anlagen von Bône und Algier an. Im westlichen Mittelmeer erzielte eines unserer Torpedoflugzeuge bei einem kuehnen Nachtangriff Torpedotreffer auf einem im Geleitzug fahrenden Dampfer mittlerer Groesse. Am 26. Januar nachmittags sowie in der vergangenen Nacht versuchten feindliche viermotorige Flugzeuge Einfluege nach Messina. Die Fliegerabwehr verhinderte die Angreifer am Angriff auf die Stadt und zwang sie ihre Bombenlast ins Meer oder in die Umgebung zu werfen. Die Schaeden sind nicht schwer. Zwei der Flugzeuge wurden vom Feuer der Artillerie getroffen und stuerzten ab, das eine oestlich von San Ranieri, das andere westlich von Pellaro. Heute morgen ueberflog kurz vor dem Morgengrauen ein Flugzeug Neapel und warf aus sehr grosser Hoehe einige Bomben, die bei BORRE del DRECO niederfielen. Zwei Bauernhaeuser wurden getroffen, zwei Verletzte unter den Bauernfamilien wurden gemeldet. Eines unserer Flugzeuge ist nicht an seinen Stuetzpunkt zurueckgekehrt.

Friday, January 29, 1943 issue of *Die Karawane.* After new German units arrived in Tunisia in late 1942, the Propaganda Company attached to the 5th Panzer Army quickly established their own field newspaper. First printed on December 12, 1942 *Die Karawane* continued to be printed daily until April 1943. This edition offers a unique commentary from the German perspective of the Casablanca Conference and notable absence of Stalin at this meeting. (David Bunch)

The reverse side of the daily *Die Karaw[ane]* newspaper. As a single page source [of] information, both sides of the paper w[ere] utilized to share local news of interes[t to] the German troops and reports from o[ther] fronts. (David Bunch)

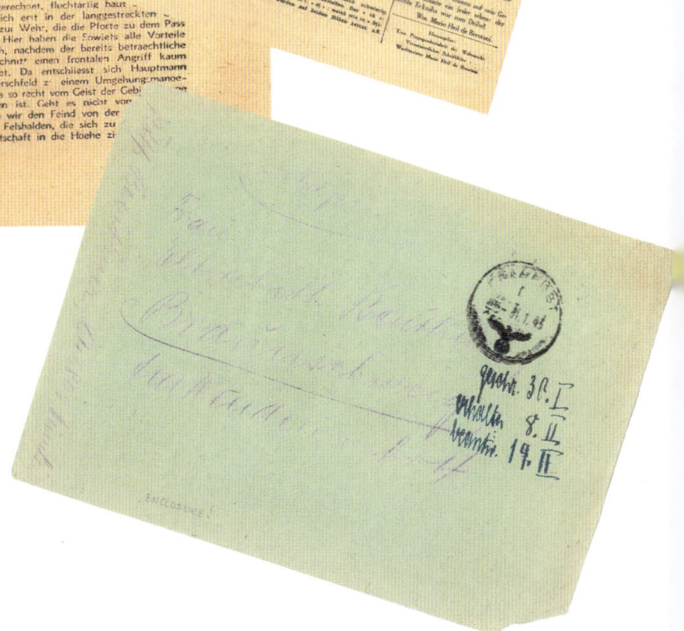

Very few original examples of *Die Karawane* are known to exist today. This particular newspaper was carefully folded into this envelope and successfully mailed back to Germany on January 31, 1943 (note the *feldpost* stamp). (David Bunch)

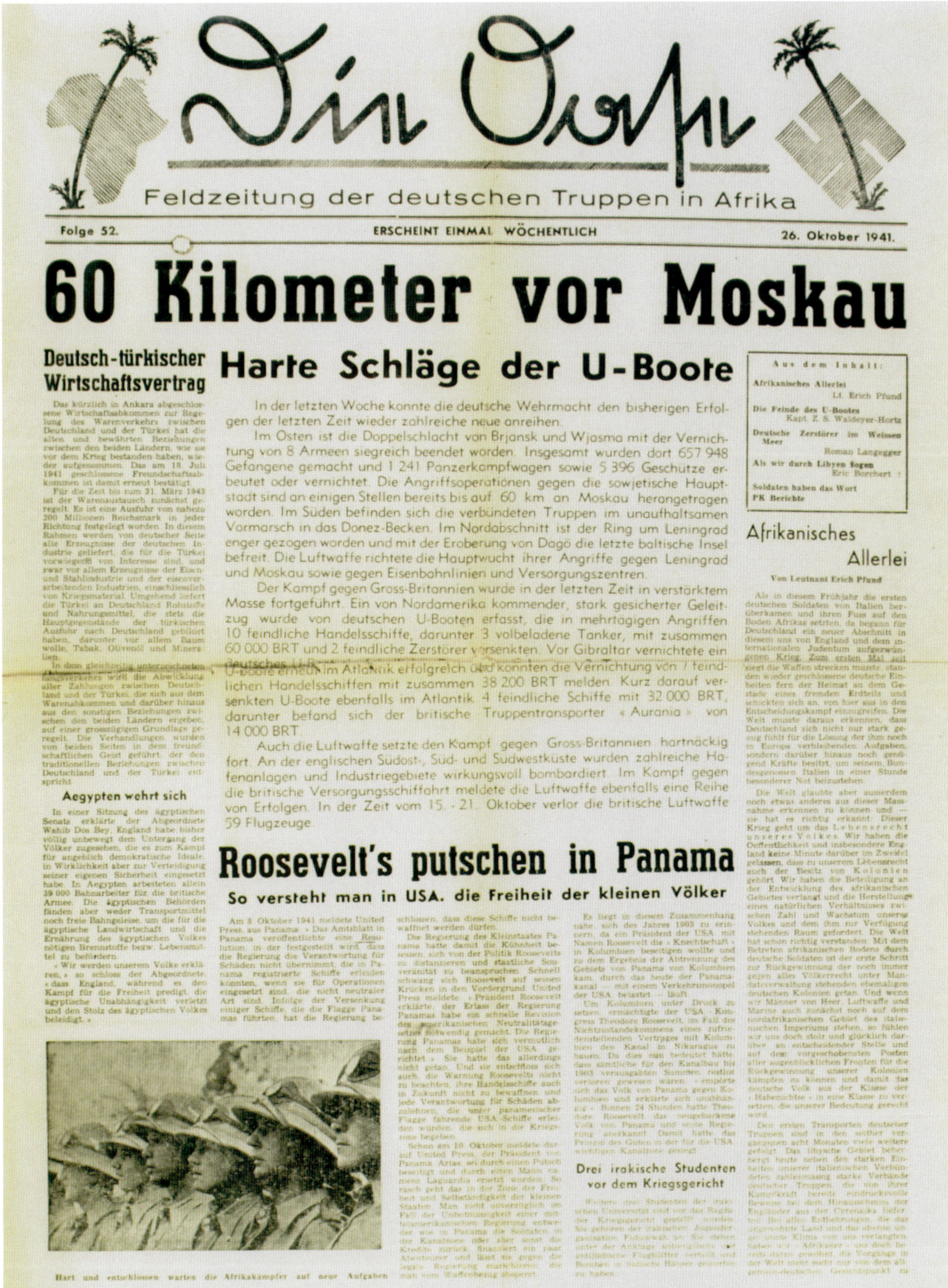

Die Oase

Feldzeitung der deutschen Truppen in Afrika

Folge 52. ERSCHEINT EINMAL WÖCHENTLICH 26. Oktober 1941.

60 Kilometer vor Moskau

Deutsch-türkischer Wirtschaftsvertrag

Harte Schläge der U-Boote

In der letzten Woche konnte die deutsche Wehrmacht den bisherigen Erfolgen der letzten Zeit wieder zahlreiche neue anreihen.

Im Osten ist die Doppelschlacht von Brjansk und Wjasma mit der Vernichtung von 8 Armeen siegreich beendet worden. Insgesamt wurden dort 657 948 Gefangene gemacht und 1 241 Panzerkampfwagen sowie 5 396 Geschütze erbeutet oder vernichtet. Die Angriffsoperationen gegen die sowjetische Hauptstadt sind an einigen Stellen bereits bis auf 60 km an Moskau herangetragen worden. Im Süden befinden sich die verbündeten Truppen im unaufhaltsamen Vormarsch in das Donez-Becken. Im Nordabschnitt ist der Ring um Leningrad enger gezogen worden und mit der Eroberung von Dagö die letzte baltische Insel befreit. Die Luftwaffe richtete die Hauptwucht ihrer Angriffe gegen Leningrad und Moskau sowie gegen Eisenbahnlinien und Versorgungszentren.

Der Kampf gegen Gross-Britannien wurde in der letzten Zeit in verstärktem Masse fortgeführt. Ein von Nordamerika kommender, stark gesicherter Geleitzug wurde von deutschen U-Booten erfasst, die in mehrtägigen Angriffen 10 feindliche Handelsschiffe, darunter 3 volbeladene Tanker, mit zusammen 60 000 BRT und 2 feindliche Zerstörer versenkten. Vor Gibraltar vernichtete ein deutsches U-[illegible] U-Boote erneut im Atlantik erfolgreich und konnten die Vernichtung von 7 feindlichen Handelsschiffen mit zusammen 38 200 BRT melden. Kurz darauf versenkten U-Boote ebenfalls im Atlantik 4 feindliche Schiffe mit 32 000 BRT, darunter befand sich der britische Truppentransporter « Aurania » von 14 000 BRT.

Auch die Luftwaffe setzte den Kampf gegen Gross-Britannien hartnäckig fort. An der englischen Südost-, Süd- und Südwestküste wurden zahlreiche Hafenanlagen und Industriegebiete wirkungsvoll bombardiert. Im Kampf gegen die britische Versorgungsschiffahrt meldete die Luftwaffe ebenfalls eine Reihe von Erfolgen. In der Zeit vom 15. - 21. Oktober verlor die britische Luftwaffe 59 Flugzeuge.

Aus dem Inhalt:

- **Afrikanisches Allerlei** — Lt. Erich Pfund
- **Die Feinde des U-Bootes** — Kapt. Z. S. Waldeyer-Hartz
- **Deutsche Zerstörer im Weissen Meer** — Roman Langegger
- **Als wir durch Libyen fogen** — Eric Borchert
- **Soldaten haben das Wort**
- **PK Berichte**

Afrikanisches Allerlei

Von Leutnant Erich Pfund

Aegypten wehrt sich

Roosevelt's putschen in Panama

So versteht man in USA. die Freiheit der kleinen Völker

Drei irakische Studenten vor dem Kriegsgericht

Hart und entschlossen warten die Afrikakämpfer auf neue Aufgaben

Exceptional edition of the *Die Oase* newspaper headlining German troops are "60 Kilometer from Moscow". This issue was printed on October 24, 1941 and highlights the success of the German troops in Russia as well as other news that would be of interest to an *Afrikakampfer* far away from home. (David Bunch)

A pair of exceptionally rare field-made holiday newsletters prepared by the *Sonderverband 288* field-post unit. These unofficial newspapers were a collection of thoughts and jokes from officers and soldiers in this special unit. They were mimeographed and distributed in conjunction with the Christmas 1941 and Easter 1942 holidays. (David Bunch)

Newspapers from Germany were rare to find, however, this officer has found a copy of *Volkischer Beobachter* which was the official newspaper of the Nazi Party. (David Bunch)

CHAPTER FOUR

Manuals, Calendars, and Postal

Der Johann Janssen
(Vor- und Zuname)
erhält die Erlaubnis, nach bestandener Prüfung ein Kraftfahrzeug mit Antrieb
durch Verbrennungsmaschine
der Klasse -2- zu führen.
O.U., den 27. Febr. 1943
Stempel
Einheit 48248
(Verwaltungsbehörde)
(Unterschrift)
Oberstlt. u. Div.-Ing.
Liste 1943/18

Brustbild entfällt gemäß § 70 Abs. 2 StVZO.
Nur gültig in Verbindung mit dem Soldbuch
(Brustbild des Inhabers ohne Kopfbedeckung von vorn oder schräg vorn) 52 x 74 mm oder 52 x 37 mm
Stempel
Johannes Jansen
(Eigenhändige Unterschrift des Inhabers.)

Afrikakorps military driving license authorizing Johann Janssen to drive Class 2 vehicles which were those powered by internal-combustion engines. Issued on February 27, 1943 *Feldpostnumber* 48248 was associated with *Stab Afrika-Brigade 999*. (David Bunch)

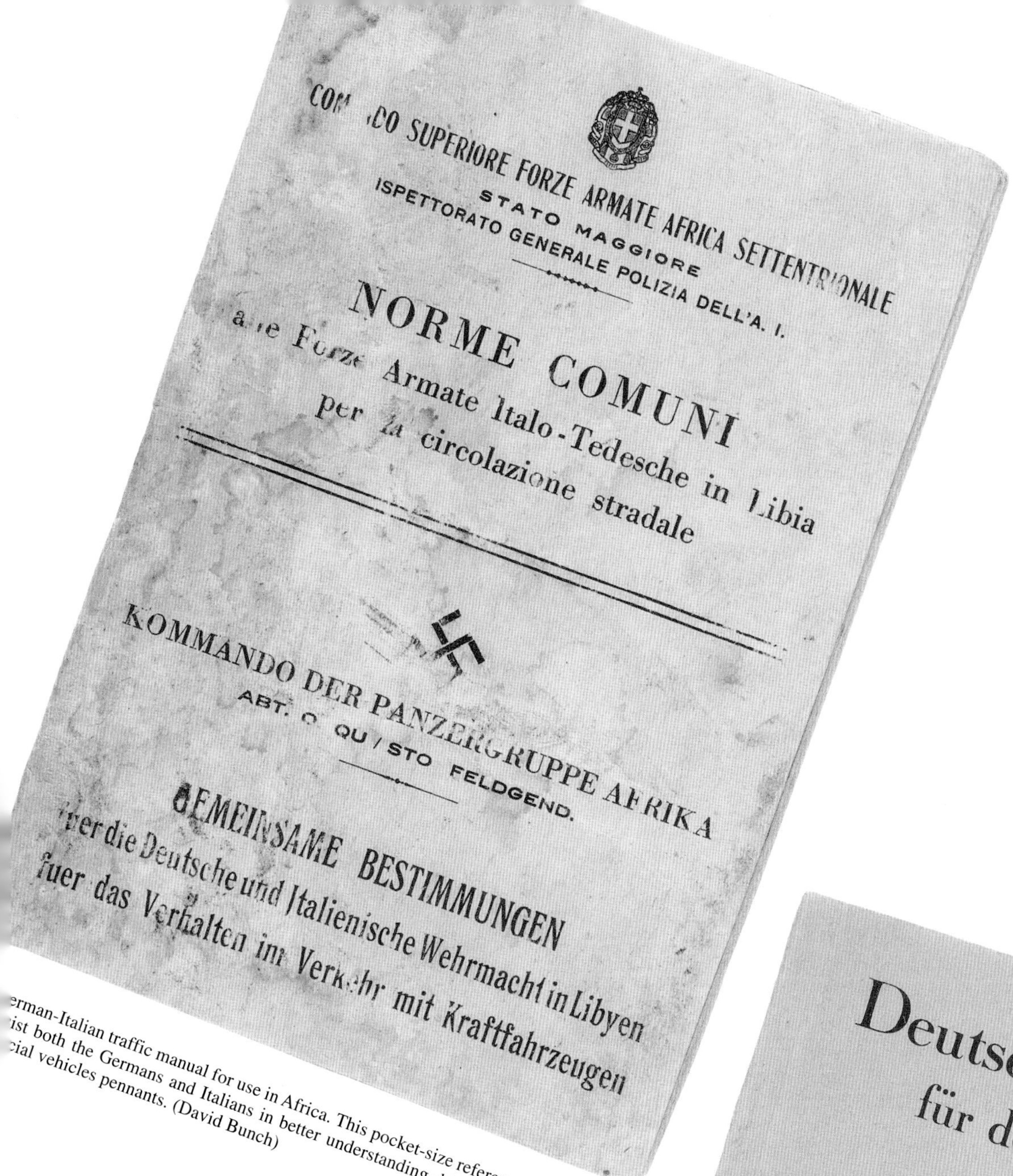

erman-Italian traffic manual for use in Africa. This pocket-size reference was used to ist both the Germans and Italians in better understanding driving regulations and cial vehicles pennants. (David Bunch)

Rare German-Italian dictionary distributed to *Afrikakorps* personnel hen they arrived in Africa. These pocket-size reference guides proved luable to German soldiers when communicating with their Axis tners. This book was printed by the *Propaganda Zug Afrika panie 43402*. (David Bunch)

1942 calendar for *Panzergruppe Afrika*. These calendars were printed by the Propaganda Ministry and distributed to all German forces in Africa in late, 1941. *Panzergruppe Afrika* was later changed to *Panzerarmee Afrika* on January 30, 1942. (David Bunch)

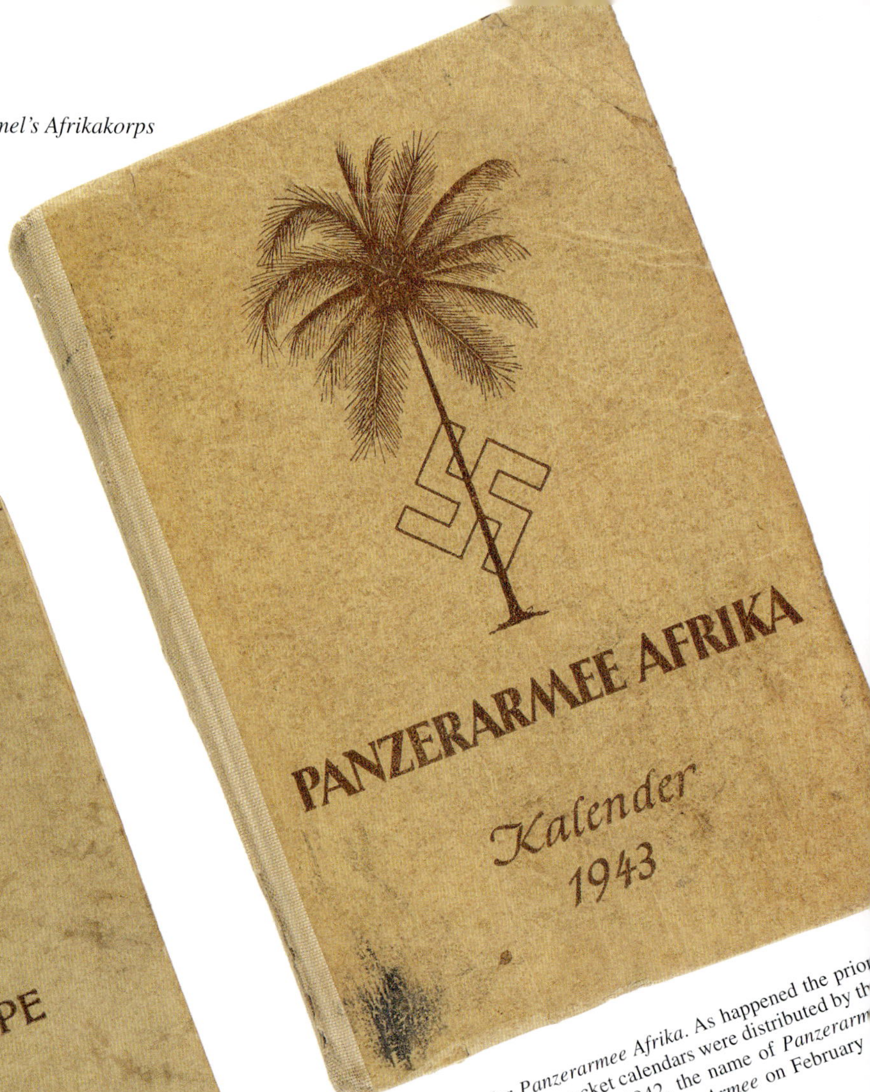

1943 calendar for *Panzerarmee Afrika*. As happened the prio year, by the time these pocket calendars were distributed by th Propaganda Ministry in late 1942, the name of *Panzerarm Afrika* had changed to *1. italienische Armee* on February 1943. (David Bunch)

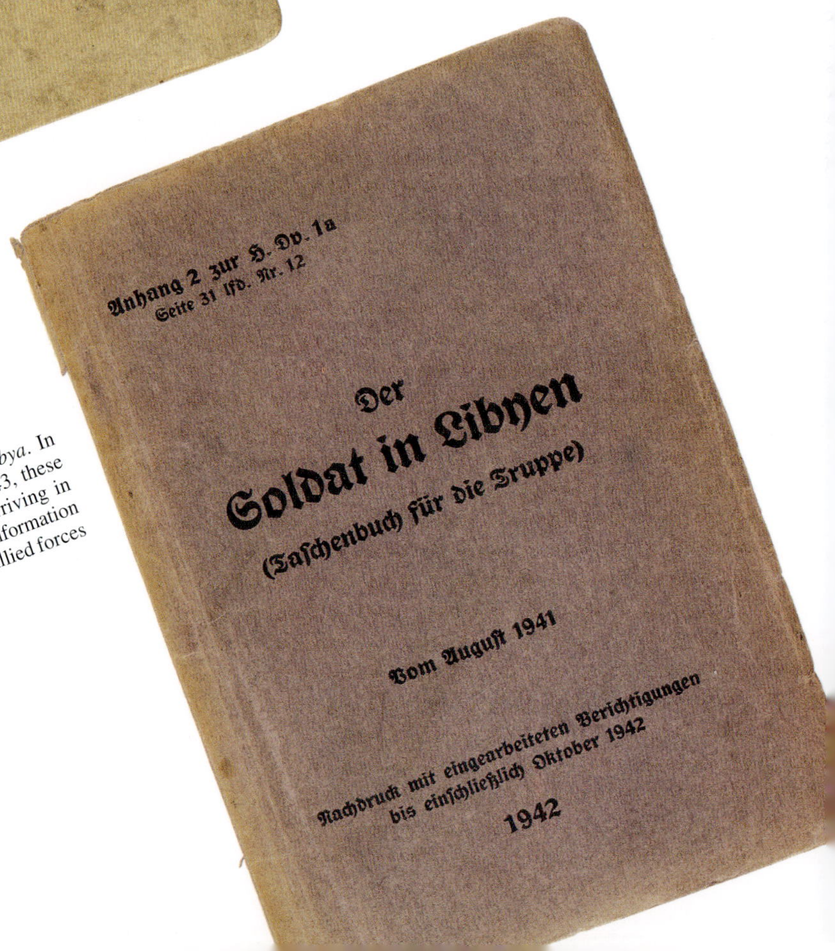

A rare pocket-size reference guide entitled *The Soldier in Libya*. In conjunction with the pocket calendars issued in 1942 and 1943, these small reference guides were issued to all German troops arriving in Africa. This colorful eighty-five page book contained useful information about living in desert conditions as well as how to identify Allied forces on the ground and in the air. (David Bunch)

of a series of letters written by an ...akorps soldier to his mother. He had an ...stic flair with his desert drawing at the ...tom of one of his letters. At the time, he ...d served for seventeen months, been in Naples and was asking his mother how many friends were still alive. He also writes about expecting baked goods! (David Bunch)

Two extremely rare *Afrikakorps* stamps produced by the same company that produced *Die Oase*. These stamps were only produced in March and April 1943. Two minor variations are known to exist. Type "5a" (left) was printed on a yellow hue paper with a light ink, while type "5b" (right) was produced on grainier paper and used a darker ink. The used "5b" stamp (with cancellation markings) is extremely scarce since most mail sent to Germany never made it through the Allied air and sea blockade off North Africa. (David Bunch)

Two-page folded sheet with DAK stamps and cancellations. This "Rommel Souvenir Sheet" was made by the *Afrikakorps Feldpostmaster* as a tribute to "Army Day 1940." Only 2000 were produced of which this is number 1237. The stamps start in France in 1940 and progress through the war in Africa. The item ends with Rommel's facsimile signature stamp. (David Bunch)

CHAPTER FIVE

Remembrance/Death Cards

Remembrance card to a *Luftwaffe* soldier who died on May 3, 1944 in Italy. This card has a very good photograph of the soldier in his full tropical *Luftwaffe* uniform. (David Bunch)

Du warst so jung,
Und wirst so schwer vermißt,
Du warst so lieb und gut,
Daß man dich nie vergißt.

Gebets-Andenken.
Den Heldentod starb
Oberjäger in einem Geb.-Jäg.-Regt.
Kriegsfreiwilliger
Hans Obich
kaufm. Angestellter in Eggenfelden
bei den Kämpfen in Sollum am
9. November 1942 im Alter von
20 Jahren 8 Monaten. Sein Grab
ist im Heldenfriedhof Capuzzo
(Afrika)

Er zog von uns mit schwerem Herzen
Und hoffte auf ein Wiedersehn;
Doch größer sind nun unsere Schmerzen;
Da dieses nicht mehr kann geschehn.
In heißem Kampf im Feindesland,
Traf Dich die Todeswunde,
Die Lieben Dein im Heimatland
Traf schwer die bittre Kunde,
Den Heldentod für's Vaterland
Bist Söhnchen Du gestorben,
Hast mutig Dir mit tapfrer Hand
Den Himmelslohn erworben.

Buchdruck: Konrad Kübler, Eggenfelden / 0477

A very unique *Afrikakorps* remembrance card. Hans Obich was an *Oberjäger* in a *Gebergsjäger Regiment (Sonderverband 288)* killed in Sollum on November 9, 1942 and buried at Fort Capuzzo in Africa. On the back of this card, the family symbolically outlined *Oberjäger* Hans Obich's gravesite memorializing his death in Sollum, Afrika. (David Bunch)

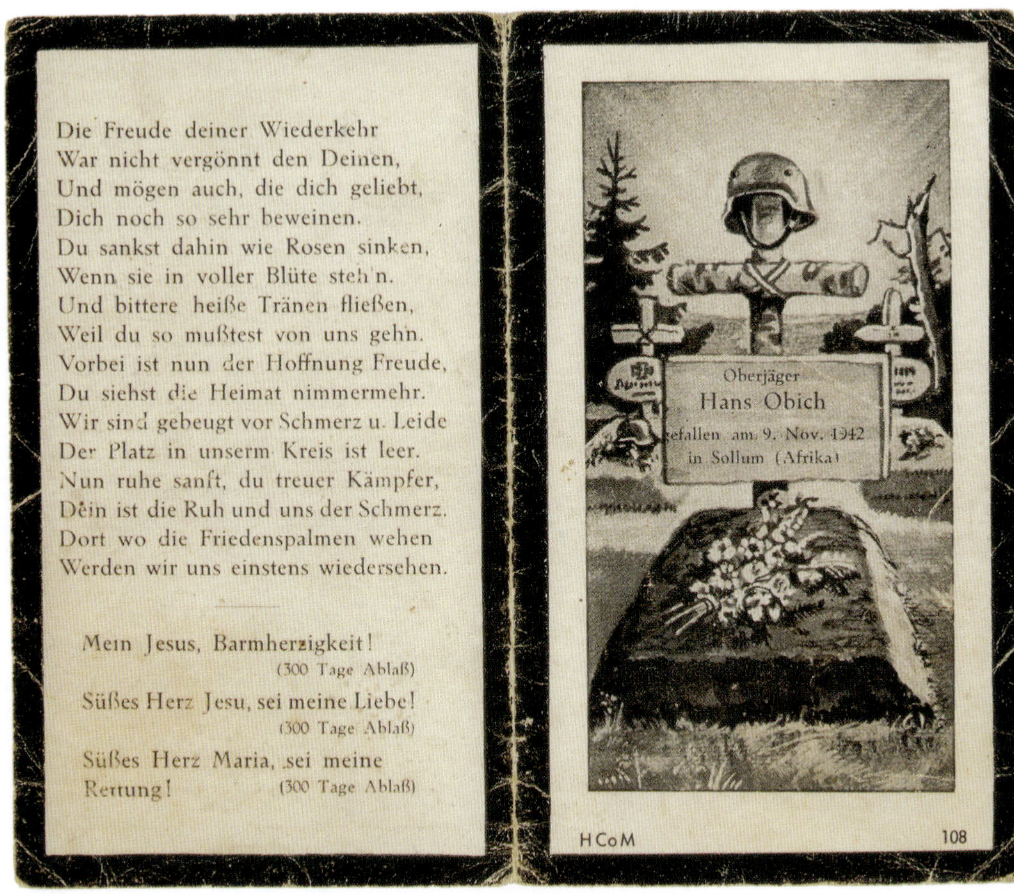

Die Freude deiner Wiederkehr
War nicht vergönnt den Deinen,
Und mögen auch, die dich geliebt,
Dich noch so sehr beweinen.
Du sankst dahin wie Rosen sinken,
Wenn sie in voller Blüte steh'n.
Und bittere heiße Tränen fließen,
Weil du so mußtest von uns gehn.
Vorbei ist nun der Hoffnung Freude,
Du siehst die Heimat nimmermehr.
Wir sind gebeugt vor Schmerz u. Leide
Der Platz in unserm Kreis ist leer.
Nun ruhe sanft, du treuer Kämpfer,
Dein ist die Ruh und uns der Schmerz.
Dort wo die Friedenspalmen wehen
Werden wir uns einstens wiedersehen.

Mein Jesus, Barmherzigkeit!
(300 Tage Ablaß)
Süßes Herz Jesu, sei meine Liebe!
(300 Tage Ablaß)
Süßes Herz Maria, sei meine Rettung! (300 Tage Ablaß)

HCoM 108

Allzufrüh bist du geschieden,
Du starbst fern in fremdem Land;
Trauernd stehen wir hinieden,
Doch umschliesst uns der Liebe Band.
Dein Blick bei deinem Heldentod,
Vergebens sucht er seine Lieben;
Verlassen warst in Todesnot,
In Treue bist du geschieden.
In Liebe werden wir an dich denken,
Wo wir auch immer werden gehen,
Gott möge Trost hier uns schenken,
Bis wir dereinst uns wiedersehen.

Jesus! Maria! Josef!

Herr Dein Wille geschehe,
tut es auch noch so wehe.

Zum frommen Andenken
an unseren herzensguten, unvergeßlichen, einzigen Sohn, unseren lieben Bruder, Schwager, Onkel, Neffen, Vetter und Enkel

Alwin Naumann

Gefr. in einem Spähtrupp des Afrikakorps.

Er starb getreu seinem Gott für Großdeutschland und seine Lieben in der Heimat am 24. Nov. 1941, 24 Stunden nach seiner schweren Verwundung, im fernen Afrika im blühenden Alter von 21 Jahren.

Wir empfehlen die Seele des lieben Verstorbenen dem hl. Meßopfer der Priester und dem frommen Gebete der Gläubigen, auf daß sie

ruhe in Frieden!

In tiefem unfaßbarem Schmerz:
Jakob Naumann u. Frau
geb. Ohlmann
Helene Naumann
Familie Jakob Just
Ww. Naumann, Großmutter
u. die übr. Anverwandten.

Baltersweiler, Bliesen u. z. Zt. im Felde, den 31. 12. 41.

St. Wendeler Buchdruckerei u. Verlag

Afrikakorps remembrance card of *Gefreiter* Alwin Naumann. This *panzer* crewmember was killed on November 24, 1941. Naumann is wearing his black *panzer* uniform with a unique pin attached to his panzer overseas cap. (David Bunch)

Zur frommen Erinnerung
im Gebete an

Martin Attenberger

Uffz. in einem mot. Art.-Rgt.
Inh. des Kriegsverdienstkreuzes 2. Kl.
mit Schwertern und des EK II
Bauersohn von Feldkirchen
geboren am 27. Juli 1916
gefallen am 17. Juli 1942 in Nordafrika.

Mein lieber Sohn, wo ist Dein Grab?
Sag an, daß ich es suchen kann.
„Mein Grab ist ein Hügel im weiten Feld,
Fern von der Heimat in weiter Welt"
Fern von den Deinen, verlassen allein,
Mein Guter, es wird Dir wohl bange sein,
Kein Röslein blüht auf Deinem Grab,
Kein Blümlein, das die Liebe Dir gab!
O Eltern, ihr Lieben, schöner als Blumenzier
Dünkt Euer frommes Gedenken mir.

„Mein Jesus Barmherzigkeit!"
100 Tage Ablaß.

M. Wälischmiller, Dingolfing

Afrikakorps remembrance card for Martin Attenberger, *Unteroffizier* in a Motorized Artillery-Regiment, holder of the Iron Cross 2nd Class, War Merit Cross 2nd Class with Swords and several other decorations was killed in action in North Africa on July 17, 1942. The photo is classic *Afrikakorps* in full tropical uniform and pith helmet. Note that his Iron Cross and War Merit Cross awards were superimposed in the photo through the buttonhole – it can safely be assumed that they were not yet awarded when this photo was taken. (David Bunch)

Dem Heldengedenken
meines lieben, unvergeßlichen Mannes, unseres Bruders, Onkels, Schwagers und Neffen
Klaus Schöpf
Hauptmann einer Panzer-Nachr.-Abteilung
Träger des Eisernen Kreuzes 1. und 2. Kl. und des Panzer-Sturmabzeichens
welcher am 19. März 1943 in Afrika, im 35. Lebensjahre, den Heldentod fand.
Ruhe in Frieden!
In weiter, fremder Erde
Deckt dich ein stilles Grab,
Doch aus dem Reich der Sterne
Schaust du auf uns herab.
Du siehst wohl, wie die Tränen
Uns oft im Auge steh'n,
Du weißt, wie wir uns sehnen
Nach einem Wiederseh'n.
Du kehrst wohl zu den Deinen
Auf Erden nicht zurück,
Doch Gott wird uns vereinen
Mit dir zum ewigen Glück.
D/0109 - 50 - 10. 44 - 2347

Very rare *Afrikakorps* officer remembrance card of Klaus Schopf, *Hauptmann* in a *Panzer Nachrichten-Abteilung* (Captain of an armored communication unit). Before his death, this officer was awarded the Iron Cross First and Second Class and Panzer Assault badge. He was killed in action in Africa on March 19, 1943. (David Bunch)

Auf dem Kampffeld in Afrika starb
fern der Heimat und seinen Lieben
Josef Kronschnabl
Bauers-Sohn von Langbruck
Gefreiter bei einer M.-G.-Komp.,
gefallen am 16. Dez. 1941 vor To-
bruck im Alter von 22 Jahren.

Du zogst von uns mit schwerem Herzen
Und hofftest auf ein Wiederseh'n
Doch größer sind nun unsere Schmerzen,
Da dieses nicht mehr kann geschehn.
So schlaf denn wohl in fremder Erde
Von uns sollst du nicht vergessen werden,
Du warst so gut, starbst viel zu früh
Solch braves Herz vergißt man nie.
Druckerei A. Lackerbauer, Regen Tel. 78

Afrikakorps remembrance card of *Gefreiter* Josef Kronschnabl. This soldier was part of a Machine Gun Company and killed at Tobruk on December 16, 1941. (David Bunch)

Zum Gedenken im Gebete an
IGNAZ ERNST
Hauptwachtm. in einem Panz. Art. Rgt., zuletzt Führer eines Panzer-Spähtrupps im Deutschen Afrikakorps. – Inh. des EK. II, Verwundeten-Abzeichens, versch. anderer Auszeichnungen.
geb. 13. April 1914, gest. nach 2 tägiger Krankheit in einem Feldlazarett am 21. August 1941. Er ruht auf dem Ehrenfriedhof in Derna (Cyrenaika).
R. I. P.

Afrikakorps Remembrance Card of Ignaz Ernst, *Hauptwachmeister* in a Panzer Artillery Regiment and leader of an armored reconnaissance squad. Holder of the Iron Cross Second Class. Wound badge and several othe decorations, Ernst died in a field hospi in Cyrenaika and was buried in Der The photo shows Ernst wearing tropical Dutch pith helmet and tro shirt. (David Bunch)

Unsere sehnenden Gedanken zieh'n um ein Soldatengrab.
Unsrer Liebe Blüten tanken zu dem Toten sich hinab.
Und wir hören liebe Worte in der dunklen Nacht verweh'n:
Seid getrost! Am sel'gen Orte werden wir uns wiederseh'n!

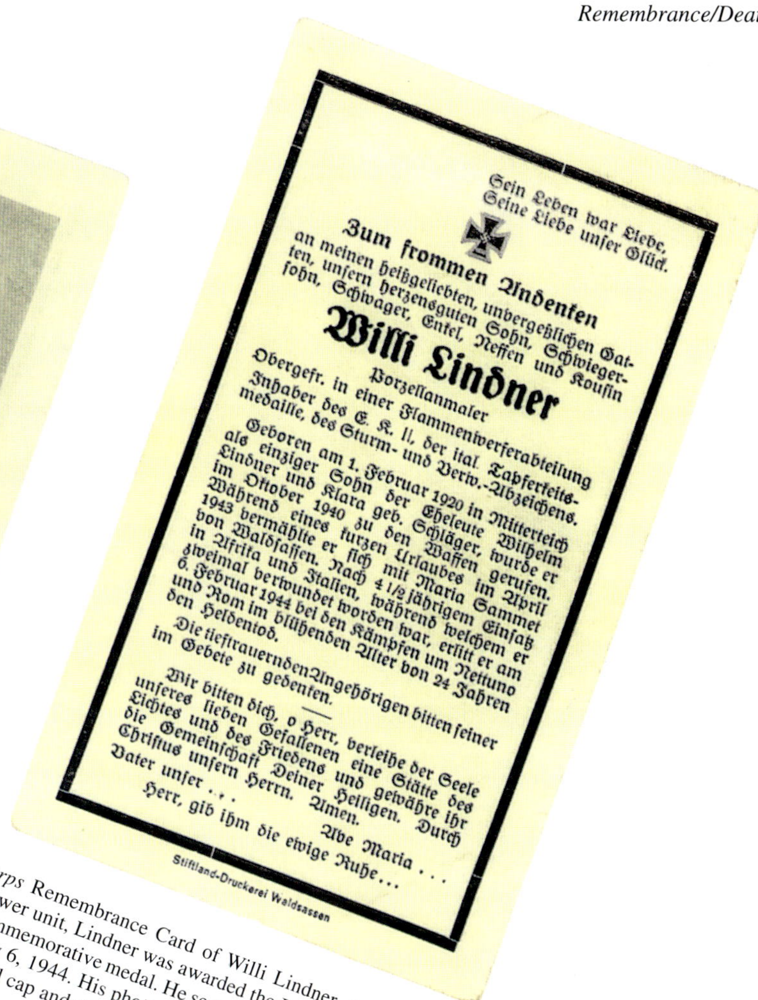

Sein Leben war Liebe,
Seine Liebe unser Glück.

Zum frommen Andenken

an meinen heißgeliebten, unvergeßlichen Gatten, unsern herzensguten Sohn, Schwiegersohn, Schwager, Enkel, Neffen und Cousin

Willi Lindner

Porzellanmaler

Obergefr. in einer Flammenwerferabteilung
Inhaber des E. K. II, der ital. Tapferkeitsmedaille, des Sturm- und Verw.-Abzeichens.

Geboren am 1. Februar 1920 in Mitterteich als einziger Sohn der Eheleute Wilhelm Lindner und Klara geb. Schläger, wurde er im Oktober 1940 zu den Waffen gerufen. Während eines kurzen Urlaubes im April 1943 vermählte er sich mit Maria Sammet von Waldsassen. Nach 4 1/2 jährigem Einsatz in Afrika und Italien, während welchem er zweimal verwundet worden war, erlitt er am 6. Februar 1944 bei den Kämpfen um Nettuno und Rom im blühenden Alter von 24 Jahren den Heldentod.

Die tieftrauernden Angehörigen bitten seiner im Gebete zu gedenken.

Wir bitten dich, o Herr, verleihe der Seele unseres lieben Gefallenen eine Stätte des Lichtes und des Friedens und gewähre ihr die Gemeinschaft Deiner Heiligen. Durch Christus unsern Herrn. Amen.

Vater unser . . . Ave Maria . . .
Herr, gib ihm die ewige Ruhe . . .

Stiftland-Druckerei Waldsassen

Afrikakorps Remembrance Card of Willi Lindner. An *Obergefreiter* in a flamethrower unit, Lindner was awarded the Iron Cross (Second Class) and Italian Commemorative medal. He served in Africa & died in Italy (Nettuno) on February 6, 1944. His photograph reflects the bleached out condition of both his field cap and shoulder straps! (David Bunch)

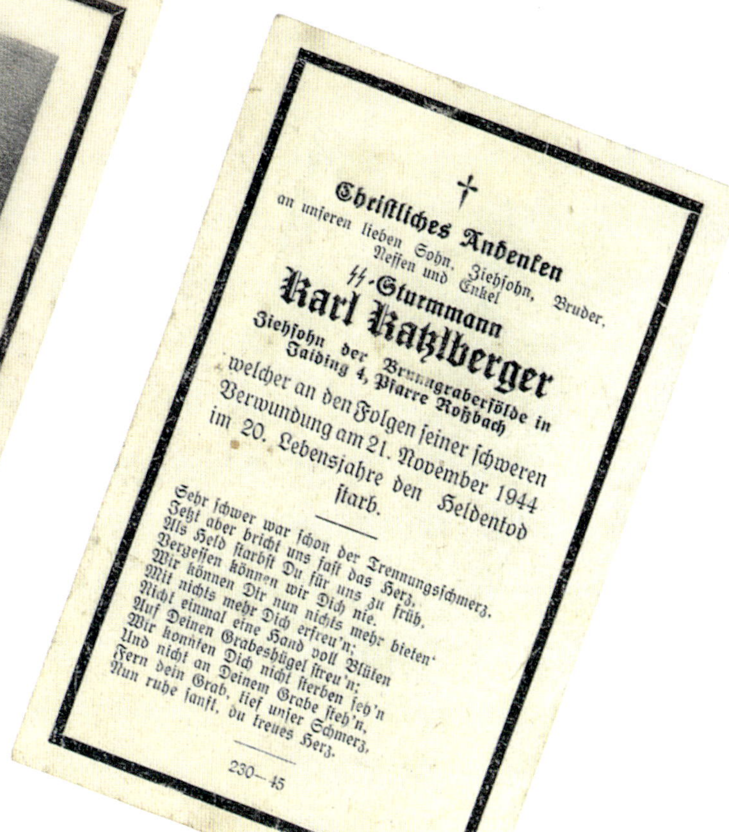

Christliches Andenken

an unseren lieben Sohn, Ziehsohn, Bruder, Neffen und Enkel

SS-Sturmmann

Karl Katzlberger

Ziehsohn der Brunngraberfölde in Saiding 4, Pfarre Roßbach

welcher an den Folgen seiner schweren Verwundung am 21. November 1944 im 20. Lebensjahre den Heldentod starb.

Sehr schwer war schon der Trennungsschmerz,
Jetzt aber bricht uns fast das Herz.
Als Held starbst Du für uns zu früh,
Vergessen können wir Dich nie.
Wir können Dir nun nichts mehr bieten,
Mit nichts mehr Dich erfreu'n;
Nicht einmal eine Hand voll Blüten
Auf Deinem Grabeshügel streu'n;
Wir konnten Dich nicht sterben seh'n
Und nicht an Deinem Grabe steh'n,
Fern dein Grab, tief unser Schmerz,
Nun ruhe sanft, du treues Herz.

230—45

Remembrance Card of *SS-Sturmmann* Karl Katzlberger in his full tropical uniform. Photos of *Waffen-SS* in tropical uniform are rare given their limited action in areas that would have required such attire. (Gary Schaefer)

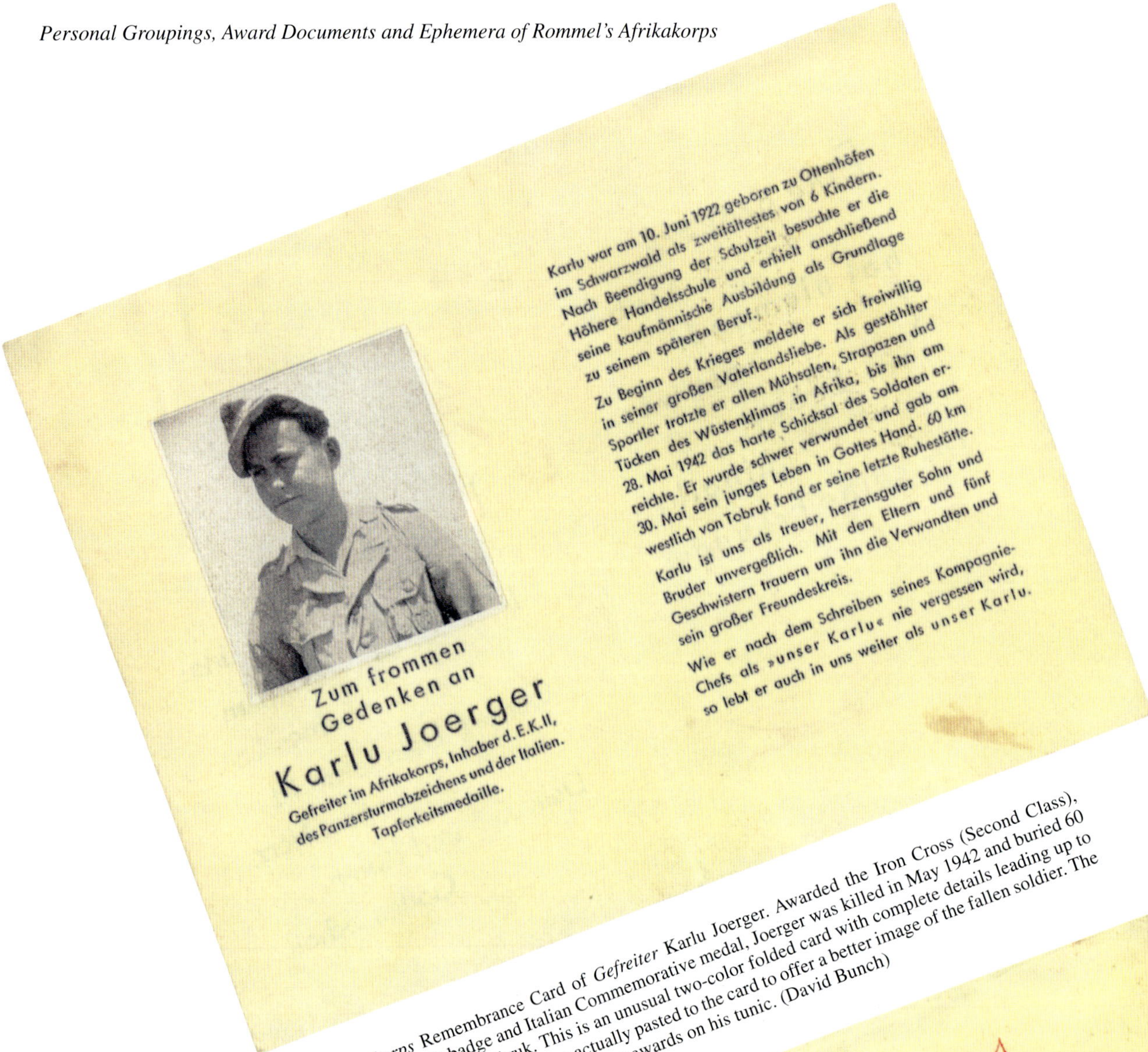

Afrikakorps Remembrance Card of *Gefreiter* Karlu Joerger. Awarded the Iron Cross (Second Class), *Panzer* Assault badge and Italian Commemorative medal, Joerger was killed in May 1942 and buried 60 kilometers west of Tobruk. This is an unusual two-color folded card with complete details leading up to his death. This photograph was actually pasted to the card to offer a better image of the fallen soldier. The photo is so clear you can see all three awards on his tunic. (David Bunch)

Personal identity disk and photograph of a member of the *Hermann Göring Division* in Africa. This soldier had blood type O and by referencing the unit numbers on his *erkennnungsmarke*, he was in the headquarters of *1st Regiment, Hermann Göring Division* in Tunis. (David Bunch)

CHAPTER FIVE

Propaganda Leaflets

***Afrikakorps* propaganda leaflets are extremely rare and highly sought after by collectors. Unlike some other leaflets, the only ones existing today are those that were actually dropped over the Allied front lines in Africa. There were no propaganda leaflet records, including pristine file copies of leaflets, kept by the Germans. Generally the leaflets were not meant to last and were printed on poor quality paper – a fact that has not helped their survival rate. To some extent only the leaflets have survived to tell the tale, supplemented by the time-clouded memories of those who picked them up on the battlefield.** (All leaflets, David Bunch)

British propaganda leaflet. This leaflet was dropped over the Afrikakorps in 1942:

Soldiers of the German Africa Corps:

Consider the following:

Do you know that while you are fighting in the desert against the steadily growing might of the British Empire, which is receiving considerable support from the American arms industry, the convoys that are destined for you are being sent to the bottom by the English navy?

Do you know that the Royal Air Force, with ever increasing strength, is destroying military and economic targets in the hearts of your cities?

Your homes, your loved ones and friends, are at the mercy of Sterling heavy bombers and the new Flying Fortresses flown in from America, which carry new English bombs with much greater destructive power compared to earlier bombs!

You have your Führer to thank for this!

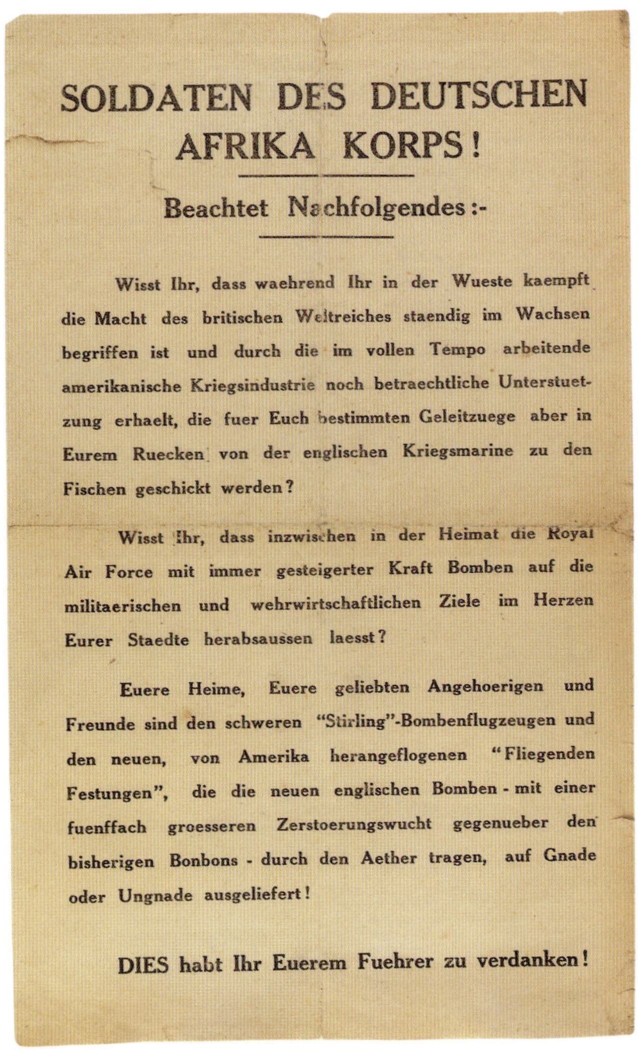

SOLDATEN DES DEUTSCHEN AFRIKA KORPS!

Beachtet Nachfolgendes:-

Wisst Ihr, dass waehrend Ihr in der Wueste kaempft die Macht des britischen Weltreiches staendig im Wachsen begriffen ist und durch die im vollen Tempo arbeitende amerikanische Kriegsindustrie noch betraechtliche Unterstuetzung erhaelt, die fuer Euch bestimmten Geleitzuege aber in Eurem Ruecken von der englischen Kriegsmarine zu den Fischen geschickt werden?

Wisst Ihr, dass inzwischen in der Heimat die Royal Air Force mit immer gesteigerter Kraft Bomben auf die militaerischen und wehrwirtschaftlichen Ziele im Herzen Eurer Staedte herabsaussen laesst?

Euere Heime, Euere geliebten Angehoerigen und Freunde sind den schweren "Stirling"-Bombenflugzeugen und den neuen, von Amerika herangeflogenen "Fliegenden Festungen", die die neuen englischen Bomben - mit einer fuenffach groesseren Zerstoerungswucht gegenueber den bisherigen Bonbons - durch den Aether tragen, auf Gnade oder Ungnade ausgeliefert!

DIES habt Ihr Euerem Fuehrer zu verdanken!

ied propaganda leaflet dropped on German positions in Tunisia 1943:

mmel Has Fled!

ld Marshall Rommel and the best members of his staff have fled to Italy! The OKH given up hope of holding the Tunisian bridgehead. But you, German soldier,

u have been left in the lurch!

u are expected to defend the bridgehead to cover the flight of officers and specialists. u are being sacrificed so that the upper echelon may survive.

u have no air cover – for the upper echelon need air cover for their flight. There are heavy weapons behind you – for they are too precious to be wasted for common diers.

s is your last chance

ur transport aircraft are being shot down. Your transport ships are being sunk!

ur only choice is death or captivity. Why die for a lost cause? Why do you want do down your life while the staffs get to safety?

e yourselves

you there is only one way out of Tunisgrad. It is the only that will lead you to peace rest – and a reunion with your family.

you there is only one way home: by becoming a prisoner of war!

ROMMEL GEFLOHEN!

Feldmarschall Rommel ist mit den besten Leuten seines Stabs nach Italien geflohen ! Das OKW hat die Hoffnung aufgegeben, den Tunesien-Brueckenkopf zu Halten.
Aber Du, Landser, —

DU WIRST IM STICH GELASSEN

Du sollst den Brueckenkopf ohne Bruecke verteidigen, um die Flucht der Offiziere und Spezialisten zu decken. Du wirst geopfert, damit die Etappenhengste leben koennen.
Du kriegst keinen Fliegerschutz, — denn die Etappenhengste brauchen ja Fliegerschutz fuer die Flucht. Hinter Dir stehen keine schweren Waffen, — denn die sind ja zu kostbar, um fuer Landser verschwendet zu werden.

JETZT KOMMT DEINE LETZTE CHANCE

Eure Transportflugzeuge werden abgeschossen. Eure Transportschiffe werden versenkt !
Du hast nur die Wahl zwischen Tod und Gefangenschaft. Warum sterben fuer eine aussichtslose Sache ? Warum willst Du Dein Leben hergeben, wenn die Staebe sich in Sicherheit bringen ?

BRING AUCH DU DICH IN SICHERHEIT

Fuer Dich gibt es nur einen Ausweg aus Tunisgrad. Es ist der einzige Weg, der Dir Ruhe und Frieden, — und ein Wiedersehen mit Deiner Familie bringt.

FUER DICH GIBT ES
NUR EINEN WEG NACH HAUSE :
UEBER DIE GEFANGENSCHAFT !

ed leaflet directed towards the Italians in 1943.

Soldati italiani!

Il Mare è il vostro nemico

La potenza dell'Impero Britannico e dei suoi alleati sta di fronte a voi.

Dietro a voi sta il Mare ostile ed insaziabile

Le grigie e minacciose navi della Flotta Britannica montano la guardia.
I vostri convogli che recano rinforzi in uomini e materiale sono costretti ad uscire di nascosto dai porti. Piu' della metà dei valorosi soldati italiani che salpano verso l'Africa trovano nel mare infido la loro tomba.

La Flotta britannica è padrona dei Mari

Il Mediterraneo vi separa, combattenti della Marmarica, dalle vostre case e dalle vostre famiglie; insaziabile, esso inghiottisce i rinforzi che dovrebbero giungervi.

Non potete combattere senza armi e senza rifornimenti!

Noi sappiamo che avete combattuto valorosamente con armi inadeguate e insufficienti. Ma la vostra situazione è ora disperata. Non potrete sostenere un'altra lotta contro la forza dell'Impero Britannico.

Soldati Italiani ! Non dimenticate che il mare inghiottisce ogni vostra speranza di vincere questa lotta

Published by the British to help undermine the morale of the German troops in Africa, this leaflet states the following message:

What does Roosevelt's victory mean?

On 5 November 1940 Franklin Delano Roosevelt was elected President of the United States.

Who is this man, the first in American history to receive the honor of being elected to a third term as president of the freest republic in the world?

Roosevelt has denounced the dictators in numerous speeches, revealed their true objectives and decried their methods.

Roosevelt has ensured from the beginning of the war that American aid has flowed to Great Britain, even more so since the collapse of France.

Roosevelt has the entire American people behind him in his decision to fight the dictators. During the election campaign Republican candidate Wendell Willkie raised only one criticism of his opponent's foreign policy: that Great Britain was not yet receiving sufficient aid. After the election Willkie promised his unconditional support in all measures to increase aid to Great Britain. Great Britain is now receiving half of all American war production.

The reelection of President Roosevelt means:

130 million in the USA are united against Hitler!

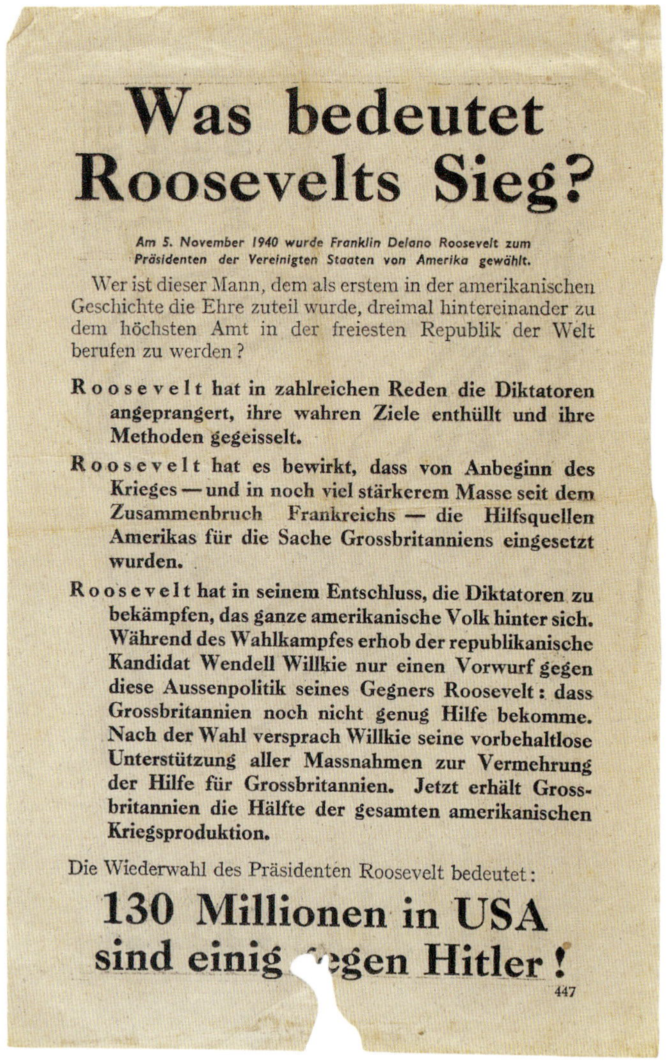

Was bedeutet Roosevelts Sieg?

Am 5. November 1940 wurde Franklin Delano Roosevelt zum Präsidenten der Vereinigten Staaten von Amerika gewählt.

Wer ist dieser Mann, dem als erstem in der amerikanischen Geschichte die Ehre zuteil wurde, dreimal hintereinander zu dem höchsten Amt in der freiesten Republik der Welt berufen zu werden?

Roosevelt hat in zahlreichen Reden die Diktatoren angeprangert, ihre wahren Ziele enthüllt und ihre Methoden gegeisselt.

Roosevelt hat es bewirkt, dass von Anbeginn des Krieges — und in noch viel stärkerem Masse seit dem Zusammenbruch Frankreichs — die Hilfsquellen Amerikas für die Sache Grossbritanniens eingesetzt wurden.

Roosevelt hat in seinem Entschluss, die Diktatoren zu bekämpfen, das ganze amerikanische Volk hinter sich. Während des Wahlkampfes erhob der republikanische Kandidat Wendell Willkie nur einen Vorwurf gegen diese Aussenpolitik seines Gegners Roosevelt: dass Grossbritannien noch nicht genug Hilfe bekomme. Nach der Wahl versprach Willkie seine vorbehaltlose Unterstützung aller Massnahmen zur Vermehrung der Hilfe für Grossbritannien. Jetzt erhält Grossbritannien die Hälfte der gesamten amerikanischen Kriegsproduktion.

Die Wiederwahl des Präsidenten Roosevelt bedeutet:

130 Millionen in USA sind einig gegen Hitler!

447

Below

The backside of the same leaflet has a very simple diagram depicting Canada, United States and South America shipping their products to Britain to supply the war effort.

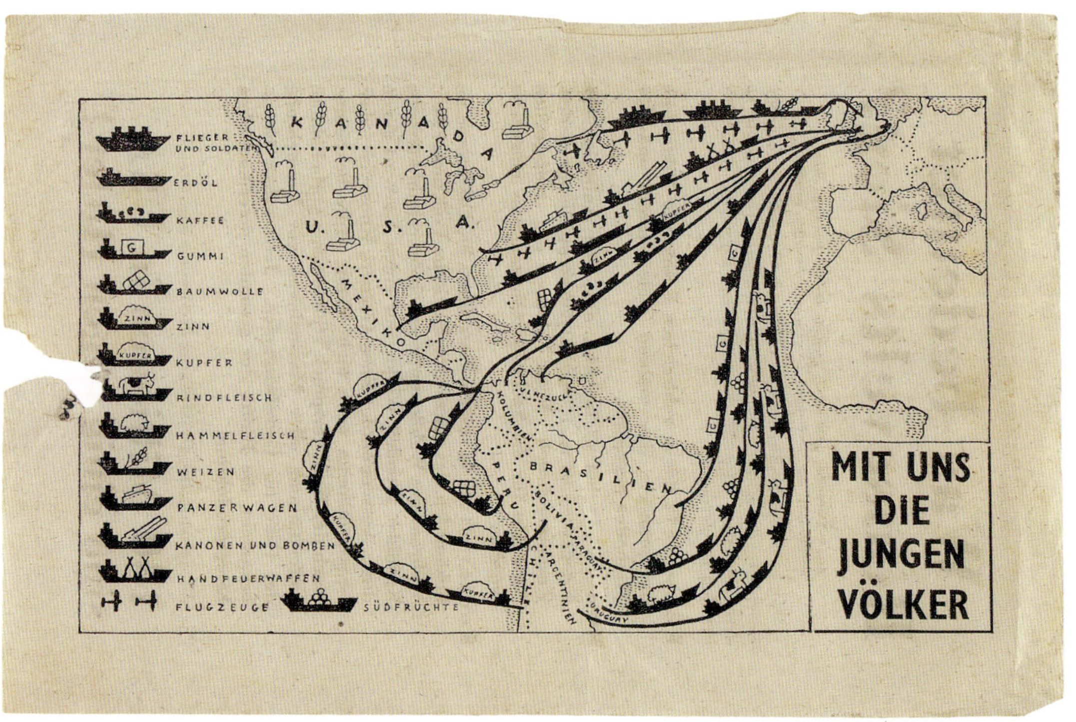

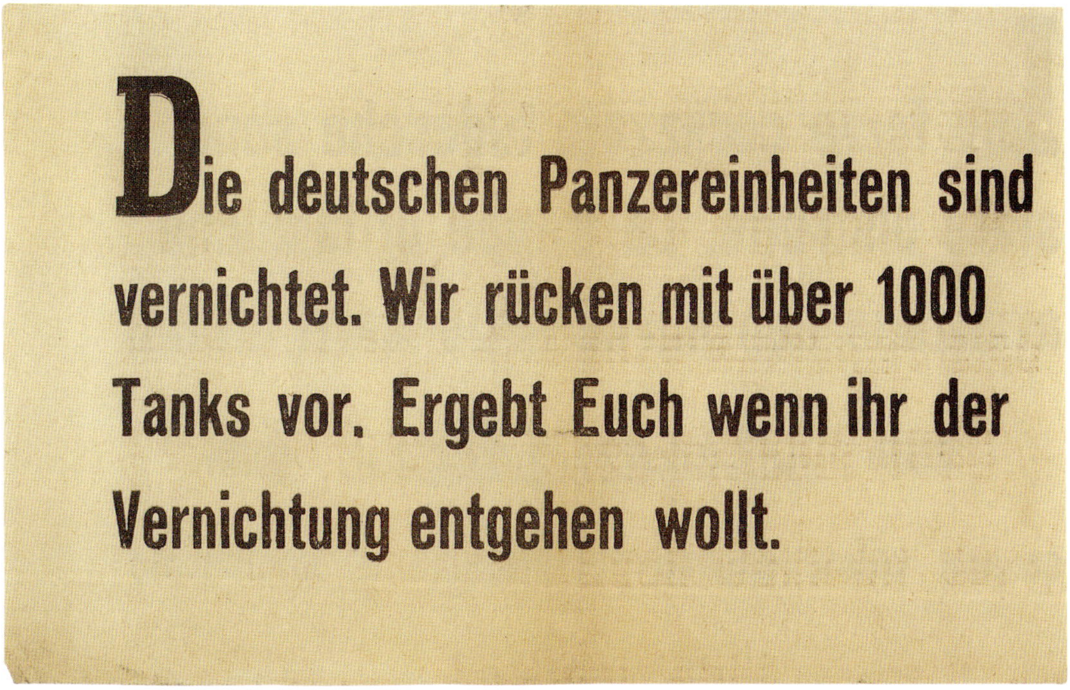

Die deutschen Panzereinheiten sind vernichtet. Wir rücken mit über 1000 Tanks vor. Ergebt Euch wenn ihr der Vernichtung entgehen wollt.

Allied Propaganda Leaflet

The German panzer units have been destroyed. We are advancing with more than 1,000 tanks. Surrender if you wish to avoid destruction.

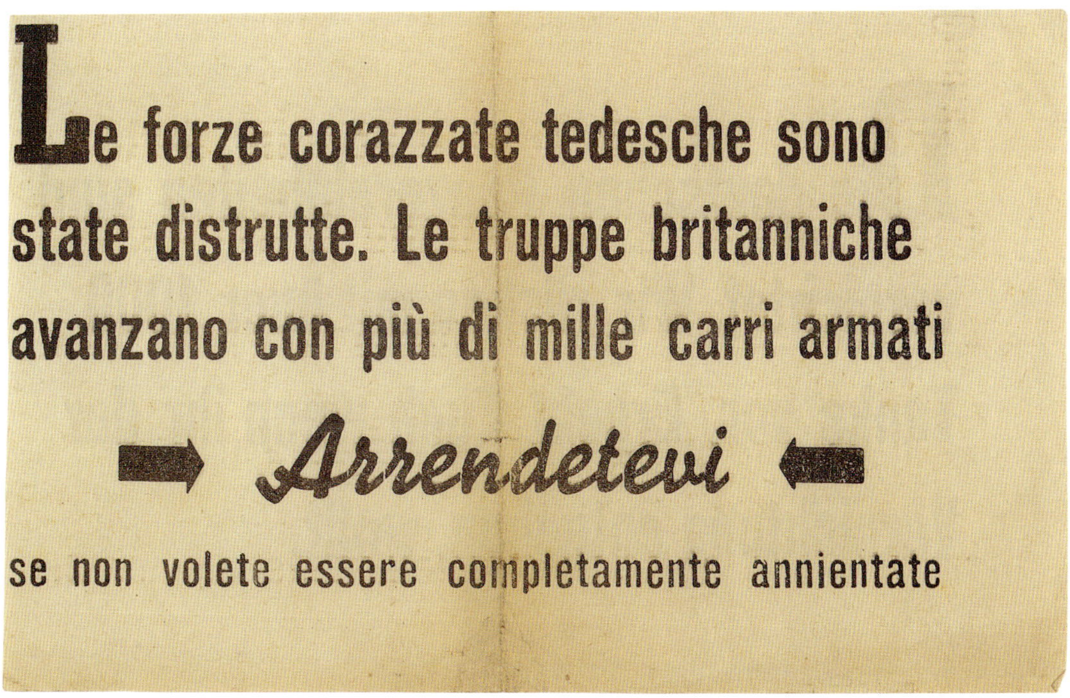

Le forze corazzate tedesche sono state distrutte. Le truppe britanniche avanzano con più di mille carri armati

→ Arrendetevi ←

se non volete essere completamente annientate

The reverse side of the above leaflet directed towards the Italians.

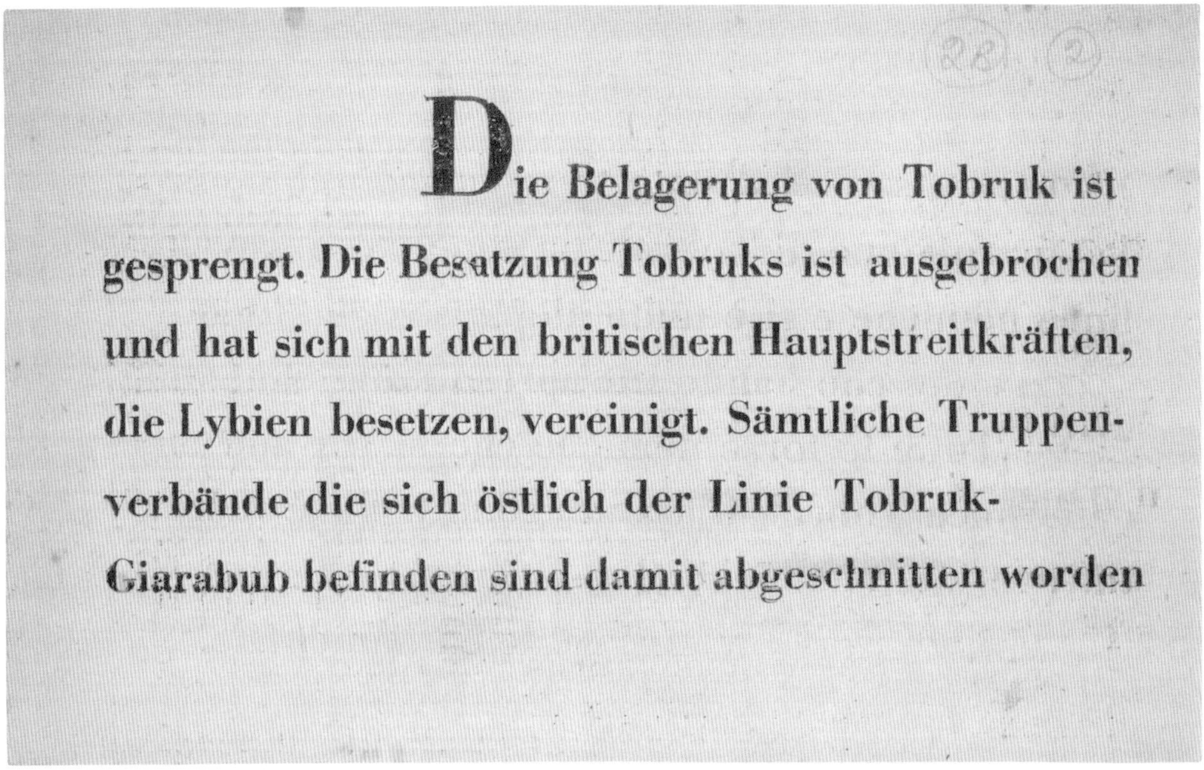

Die Belagerung von Tobruk ist gesprengt. Die Besatzung Tobruks ist ausgebrochen und hat sich mit den britischen Hauptstreitkräften, die Lybien besetzen, vereinigt. Sämtliche Truppenverbände die sich östlich der Linie Tobruk-Giarabub befinden sind damit abgeschnitten worden

Allied Propaganda Leaflet

The siege of Tobruk is broken. The garrison of Tobruk has broken out and linked up with the main British forces occupying Libya. All units east of the line Tobruk-Giarabub have thus been cut off.

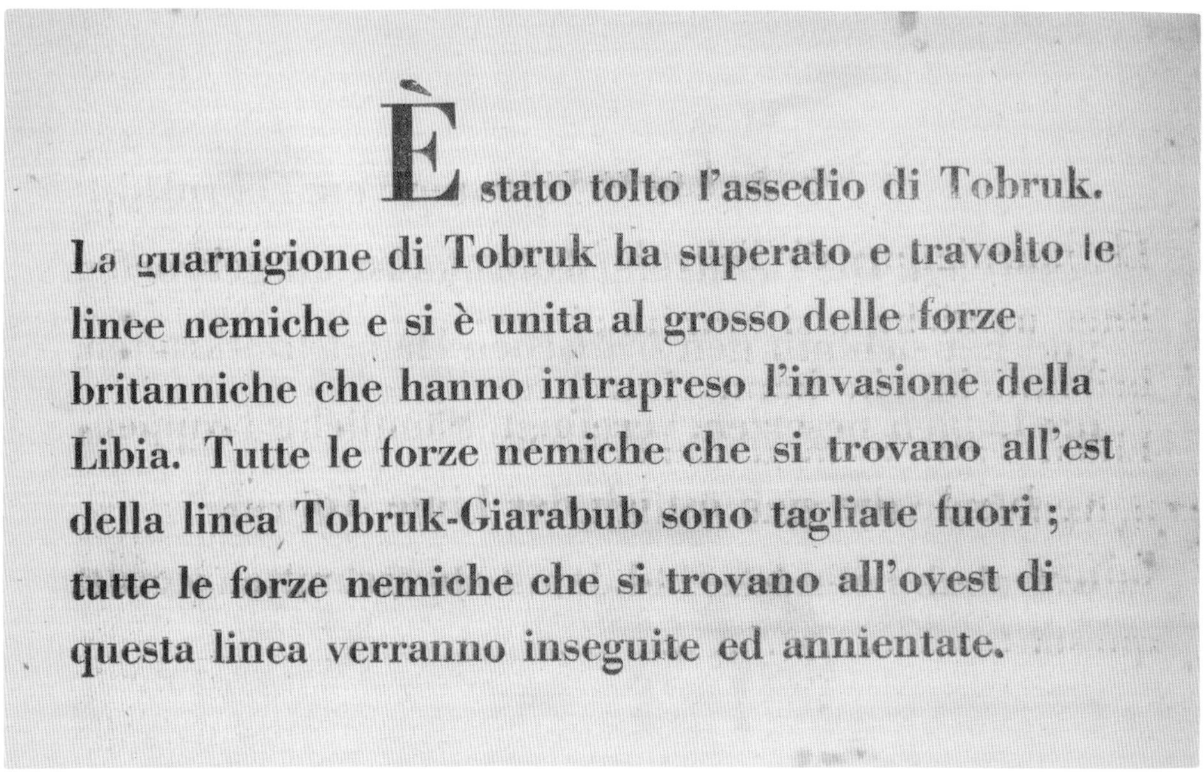

È stato tolto l'assedio di Tobruk. La guarnigione di Tobruk ha superato e travolto le linee nemiche e si è unita al grosso delle forze britanniche che hanno intrapreso l'invasione della Libia. Tutte le forze nemiche che si trovano all'est della linea Tobruk-Giarabub sono tagliate fuori; tutte le forze nemiche che si trovano all'ovest di questa linea verranno inseguite ed annientate.

Wanting to send the same propaganda message to the Italians, the Allies used the reverse side of the leaflets to write a similar message in Italian.

'ed Propaganda Leaflet

nk of the Sea!

ore you the advancing forces of the British Empire and its allies.

ind you the hostile, voracious sea!

ferocious gray ships of the Royal Navy stand watch!
convoys bringing you reinforcements are forced to sneak out of their ports! The
hty battleships and cruisers of the Royal Navy are always ready – they are waiting;
the sea becomes a grave for more than half of the bold German soldiers trying to
h Africa. The German Armed Services are mighty. They would be the pride of any
on.

the British are the masters of the sea!

sea stands between you and your home.
sea stands between you and the needed reinforcements.
sea stands between you and your supplies.

army can continue to fight without reinforcements!

bear no grudge against soldiers who fight like men despite pitiful material. But we
continue to fight without mercy until this war that has devastated Europe and spread
frica is over and all people can once again live in peace and dignity.

have no desire to destroy you!

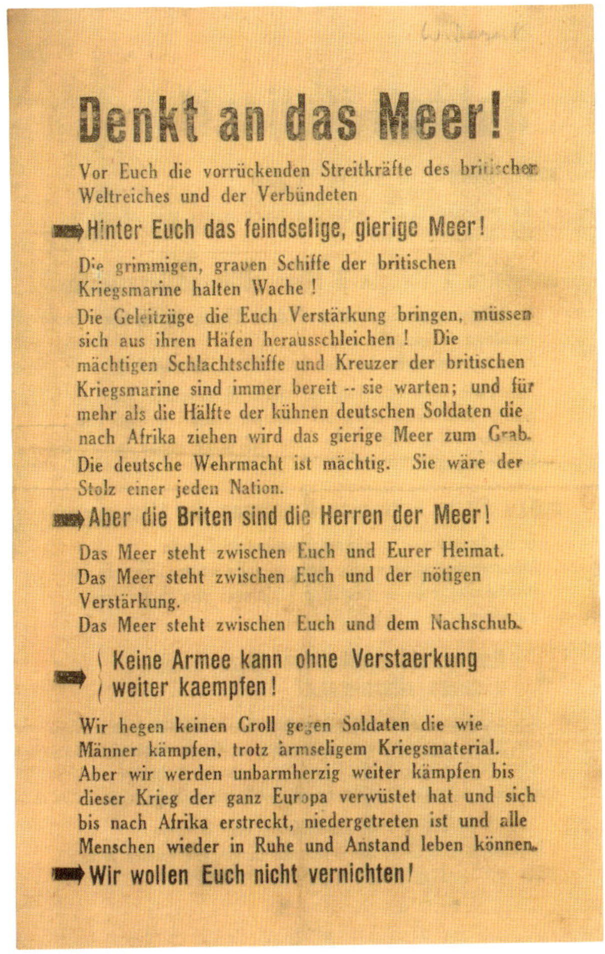

Denkt an das Meer!

Vor Euch die vorrückenden Streitkräfte des britischen Weltreiches und der Verbündeten

Hinter Euch das feindselige, gierige Meer!

Die grimmigen, grauen Schiffe der britischen Kriegsmarine halten Wache !
Die Geleitzüge die Euch Verstärkung bringen, müssen sich aus ihren Häfen herausschleichen ! Die mächtigen Schlachtschiffe und Kreuzer der britischen Kriegsmarine sind immer bereit -- sie warten; und für mehr als die Hälfte der kühnen deutschen Soldaten die nach Afrika ziehen wird das gierige Meer zum Grab.
Die deutsche Wehrmacht ist mächtig. Sie wäre der Stolz einer jeden Nation.

Aber die Briten sind die Herren der Meer!

Das Meer steht zwischen Euch und Eurer Heimat.
Das Meer steht zwischen Euch und der nötigen Verstärkung.
Das Meer steht zwischen Euch und dem Nachschub.

Keine Armee kann ohne Verstaerkung weiter kaempfen!

Wir hegen keinen Groll gegen Soldaten die wie Männer kämpfen, trotz ärmseligem Kriegsmaterial. Aber wir werden unbarmherzig weiter kämpfen bis dieser Krieg der ganz Europa verwüstet hat und sich bis nach Afrika erstreckt, niedergetreten ist und alle Menschen wieder in Ruhe und Anstand leben können.

Wir wollen Euch nicht vernichten!

ed Propaganda Leaflet *(reverse of above)*

in, sending the same message to the Italians was important to maximize the impact
e propaganda campaign.

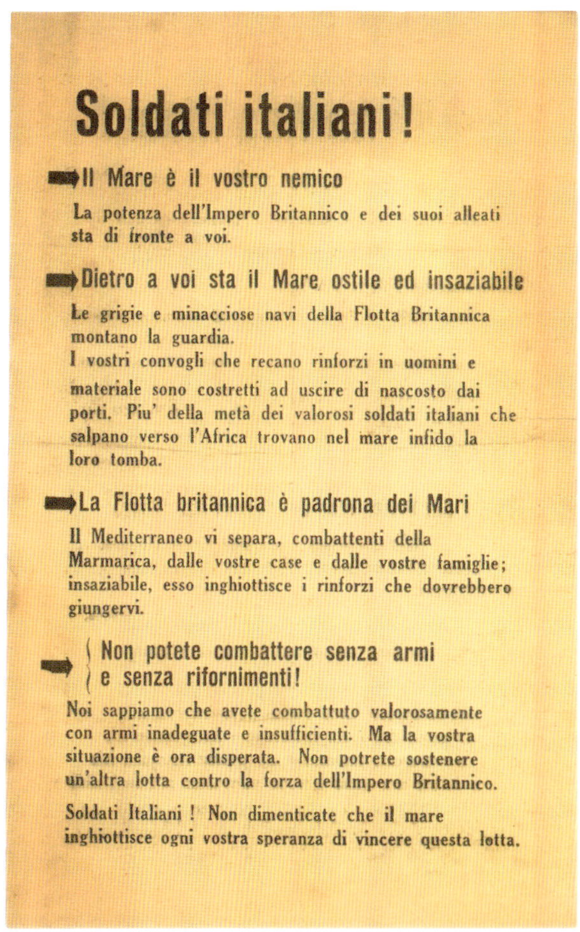

Soldati italiani!

Il Mare è il vostro nemico

La potenza dell'Impero Britannico e dei suoi alleati sta di fronte a voi.

Dietro a voi sta il Mare ostile ed insaziabile

Le grigie e minacciose navi della Flotta Britannica montano la guardia.
I vostri convogli che recano rinforzi in uomini e materiale sono costretti ad uscire di nascosto dai porti. Piu' della metà dei valorosi soldati italiani che salpano verso l'Africa trovano nel mare infido la loro tomba.

La Flotta britannica è padrona dei Mari

Il Mediterraneo vi separa, combattenti della Marmarica, dalle vostre case e dalle vostre famiglie; insaziabile, esso inghiottisce i rinforzi che dovrebbero giungervi.

Non potete combattere senza armi e senza rifornimenti!

Noi sappiamo che avete combattuto valorosamente con armi inadeguate e insufficienti. Ma la vostra situazione è ora disperata. Non potrete sostenere un'altra lotta contro la forza dell'Impero Britannico.

Soldati Italiani ! Non dimenticate che il mare inghiottisce ogni vostra speranza di vincere questa lotta.

Allied Propaganda Leaflet

German Soldiers in Africa!

General Rommel has called it quits and has pulled back.

Three-quarters of all the tanks of the German Africa Corps have been lost – destroyed.

Today General Rommel is west of Acroma. Tomorrow he will be even further west!

The siege of Tobruk has been lifted – the heroic garrison army is now attacking with its mighty force of tanks and artillery!

The British are superior to you in everything!

There will be no reinforcements or resupply!

Soldiers of Bardia, Halfaya, Sollum!

Surrender now, or else you will starve to death or be killed in the desert sands of Libya!

Think of your homes, your families!

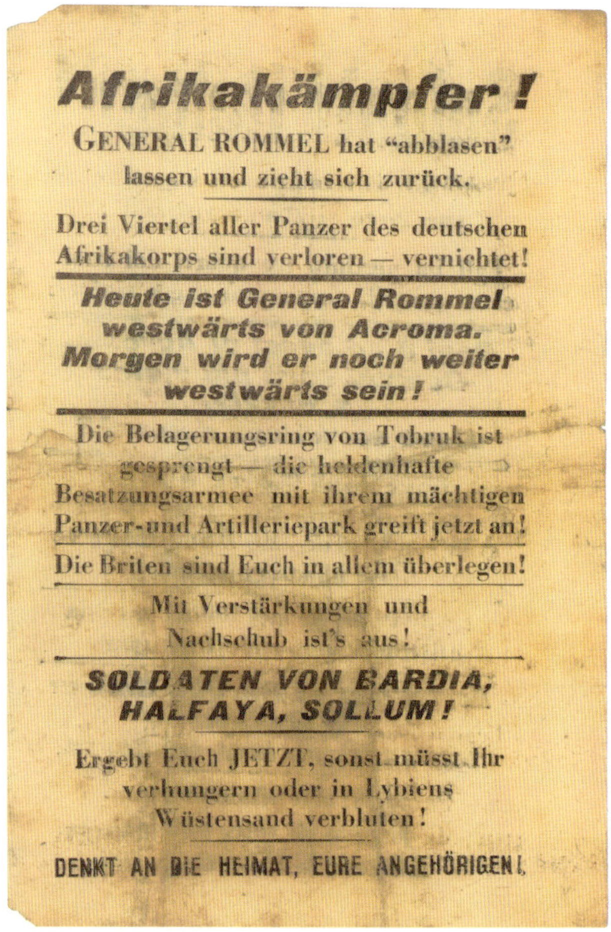

Afrikakämpfer!

GENERAL ROMMEL hat "abblasen" lassen und zieht sich zurück.

Drei Viertel aller Panzer des deutschen Afrikakorps sind verloren — vernichtet!

Heute ist General Rommel westwärts von Acroma. Morgen wird er noch weiter westwärts sein!

Die Belagerungsring von Tobruk ist gesprengt — die heldenhafte Besatzungsarmee mit ihrem mächtigen Panzer-und Artilleriepark greift jetzt an!

Die Briten sind Euch in allem überlegen!

Mit Verstärkungen und Nachschub ist's aus!

SOLDATEN VON BARDIA, HALFAYA, SOLLUM!

Ergebt Euch JETZT, sonst müsst Ihr verhungern oder in Lybiens Wüstensand verbluten!

DENKT AN DIE HEIMAT, EURE ANGEHÖRIGEN!

Allied Propaganda Leaflet *(reverse of above)*

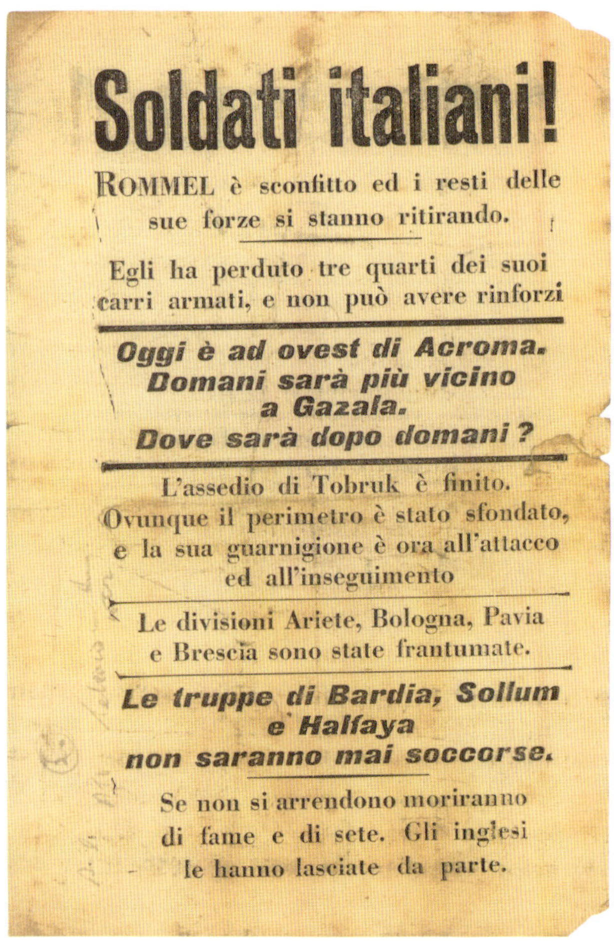

Soldati italiani!

ROMMEL è sconfitto ed i resti delle sue forze si stanno ritirando.

Egli ha perduto tre quarti dei suoi carri armati, e non può avere rinforzi

Oggi è ad ovest di Acroma. Domani sarà più vicino a Gazala. Dove sarà dopo domani?

L'assedio di Tobruk è finito. Ovunque il perimetro è stato sfondato, e la sua guarnigione è ora all'attacco ed all'inseguimento

Le divisioni Ariete, Bologna, Pavia e Brescia sono state frantumate.

Le truppe di Bardia, Sollum e Halfaya non saranno mai soccorse.

Se non si arrendono moriranno di fame e di sete. Gli inglesi le hanno lasciate da parte.

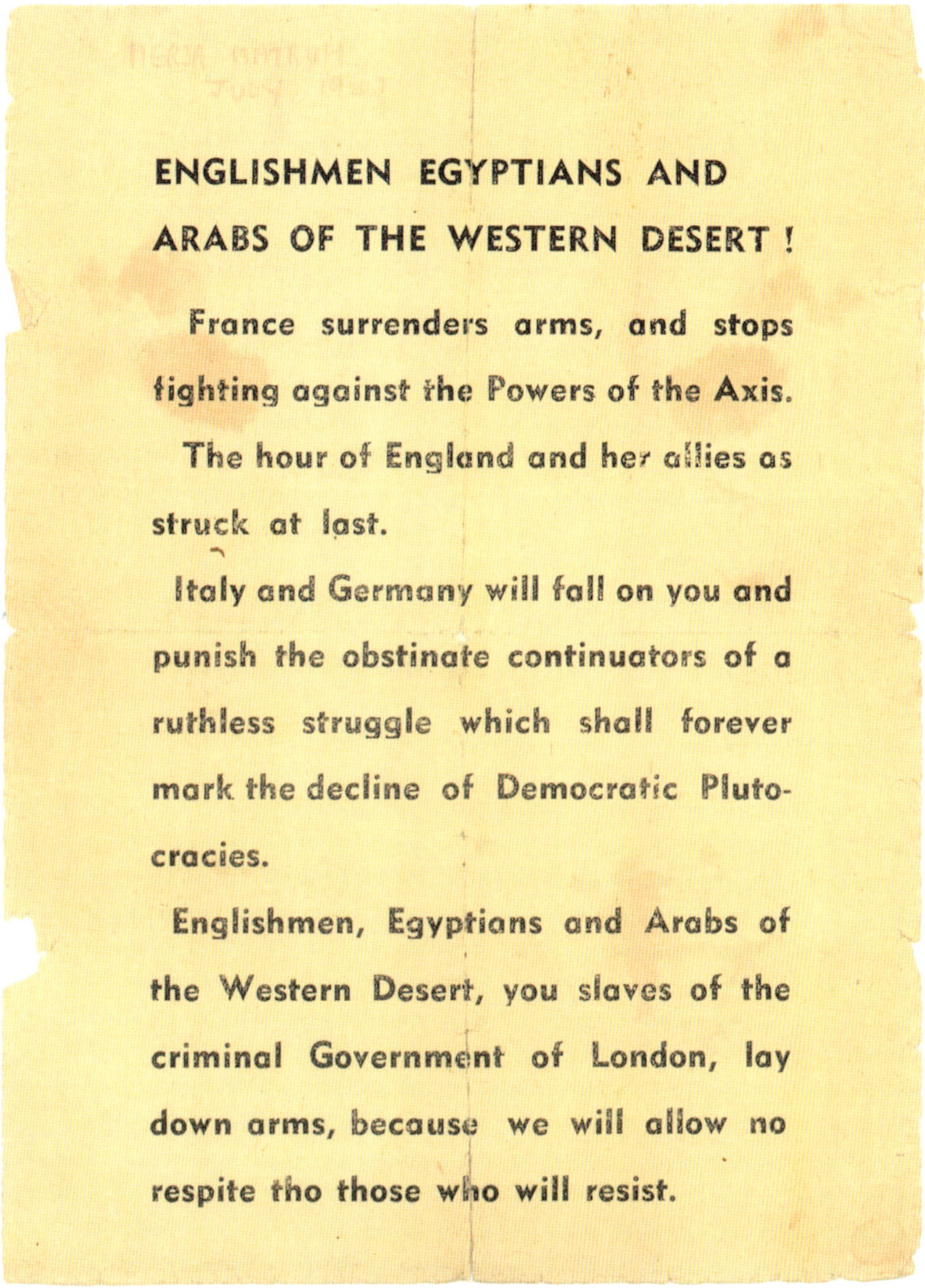

ENGLISHMEN EGYPTIANS AND ARABS OF THE WESTERN DESERT !

France surrenders arms, and stops fighting against the Powers of the Axis.

The hour of England and her allies as struck at last.

Italy and Germany will fall on you and punish the obstinate continuators of a ruthless struggle which shall forever mark the decline of Democratic Pluto-cracies.

Englishmen, Egyptians and Arabs of the Western Desert, you slaves of the criminal Government of London, lay down arms, because we will allow no respite tho those who will resist.

Axis propaganda leaflet dropped over the British, Egyptians and Arabs in the western desert. This leaflet has a handwritten note indicating it was picked up at Mersa Matruh, Egypt.

A very rare *Afrikakorps* propaganda postcard in Arabic showing a British Tommy holding a rifle with bayonet sitting on dead Arabs. It reads, "Wherever you find the English you will not escape from death and calamity."

Afrikakorps propaganda postcard in Arabic showing a British soldier with dead Arab hanging from his bayonet. The back of the leaflet is handwritten, "German propagan Western Desert."

Afrikakorps propaganda leaflet in Arabic with a British snake wrapped around an Arab reads, "The British Empire is strangling the nation of Palestinian Arabs."

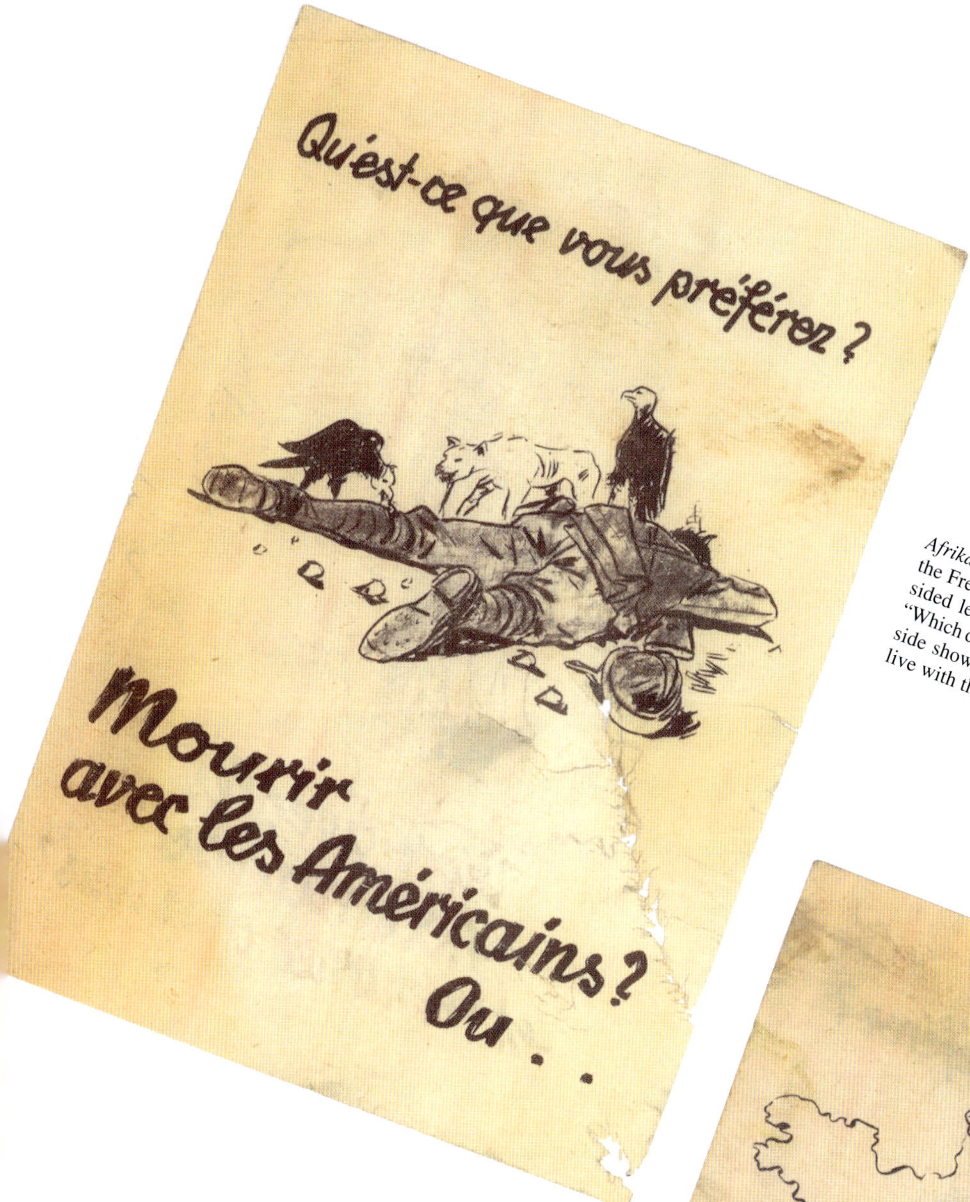

Afrikakorps propaganda leaflet written in French and directed toward the Free French soldiers in French Algiers and Morocco. This two-sided leaflet shows a dead French soldier on one side and reads, "Which do you prefer? To die with the Americans? Or..." The opposite side shows a Free French soldier kissing a woman and reads, "To live with the Germans and return home?"

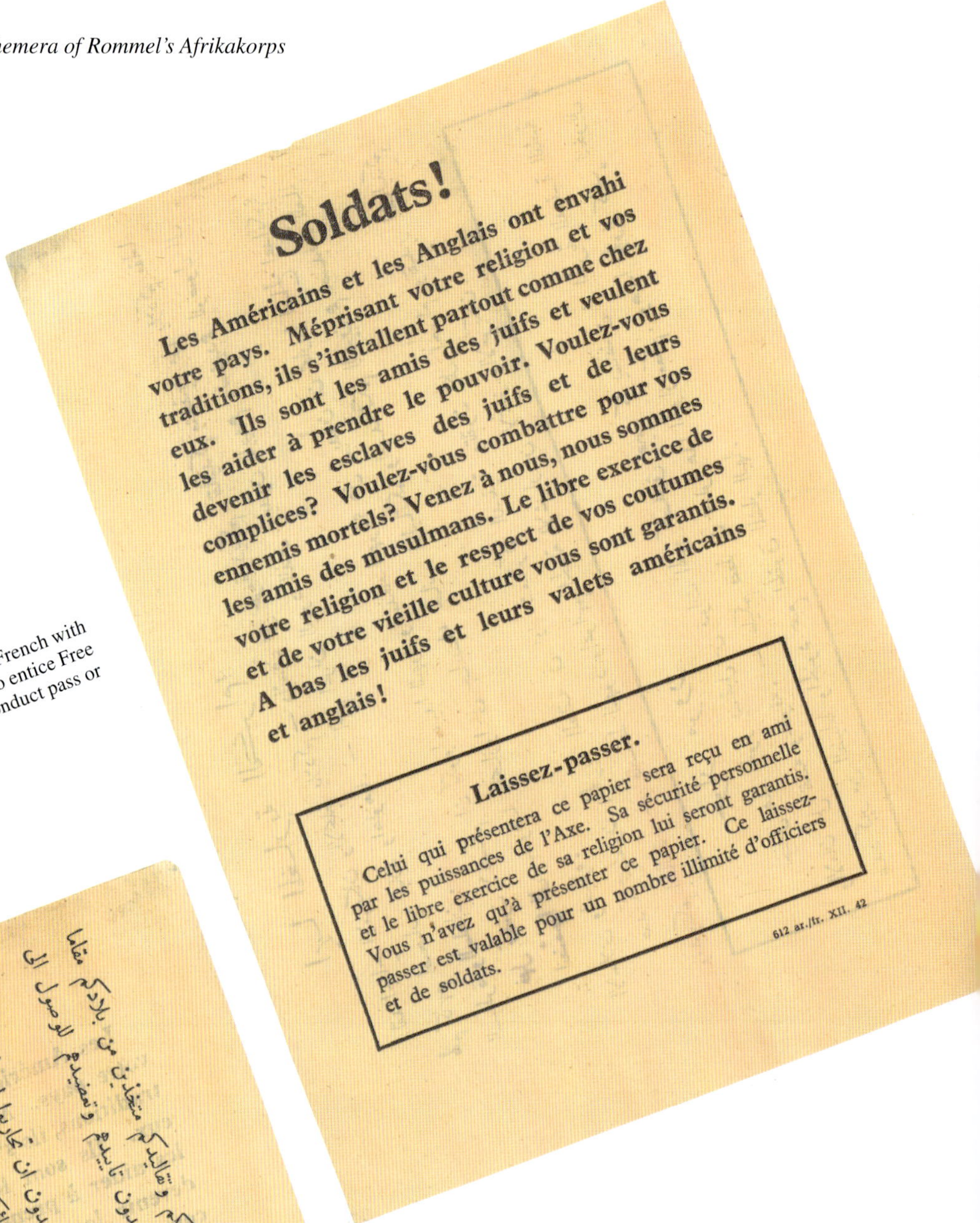

Soldats!

Les Américains et les Anglais ont envahi votre pays. Méprisant votre religion et vos traditions, ils s'installent partout comme chez eux. Ils sont les amis des juifs et veulent les aider à prendre le pouvoir. Voulez-vous devenir les esclaves des juifs et de leurs complices? Voulez-vous combattre pour vos ennemis mortels? Venez à nous, nous sommes les amis des musulmans. Le libre exercice de votre religion et le respect de vos coutumes et de votre vieille culture vous sont garantis. A bas les juifs et leurs valets américains et anglais!

Laissez-passer.

Celui qui présentera ce papier sera reçu en ami par les puissances de l'Axe. Sa sécurité personnelle et le libre exercice de sa religion lui seront garantis. Vous n'avez qu'à présenter ce papier. Ce laissez-passer est valable pour un nombre illimité d'officiers et de soldats.

612 ar./fr. XII. 42

A 1942-dated *Afrikakorps* propaganda leaflet written in French with repeated Arabic text on the reverse. The intention was to entice Free French and Arab soldiers to use this leaflet as a safe conduct pass or "Laissez-passer" and surrender to the Germans.

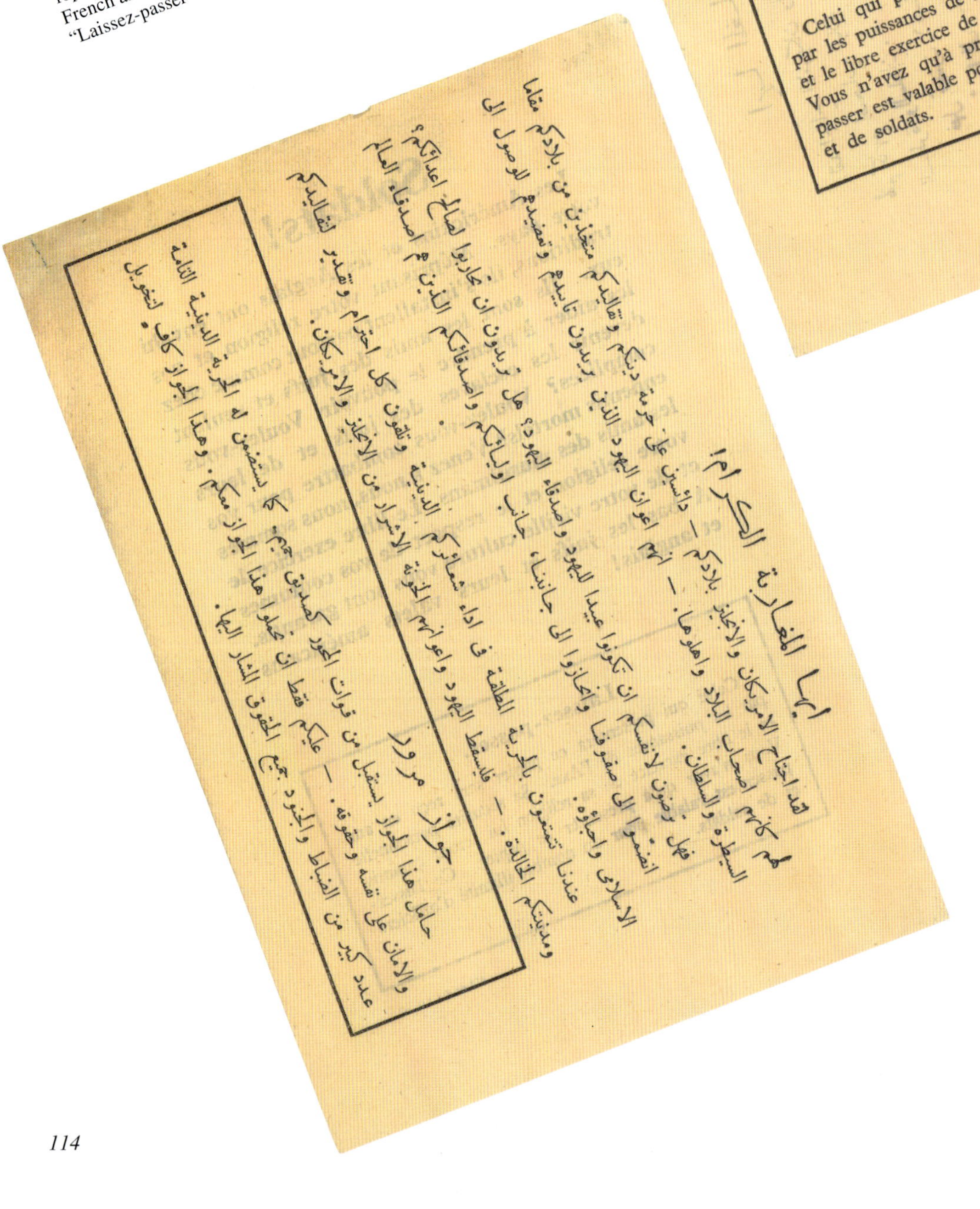

ايها المغاربة الكرام!

قد اجتاح الامريكان والانجليز بلادكم - دائسين على حرمة دينكم وتقاليدكم متخذين من بلادكم مقاما لهم كأنهم اصحاب البلاد واهلها. - انهم اخوان اليهود الذين يريدون تأييدهم وتعضيدهم للوصول الى السيطرة والسلطان.

فهل ترضون لانفسكم ان تكونوا عبيدا لليهود واصدقاء اليهود؟ هل تريدون ان تحاربوا لصالح اعدائكم؟ انضموا الى صفوفنا وانحازوا الى جانبنا، جانب اوليائكم واصدقائكم الذين هم اصدقاء العالم الاسلامي وحماته.

عندنا تتمتعون بالحرية المطلقة فى اداء شعائركم الدينية وتلقون كل احترام وتقدير لتقاليدكم ومدنيتكم التالدة. - فليسقط اليهود واعوانهم الخونة الاشرار من الانجليز والامريكان.

جواز مرور

حامل هذا الجواز يستقبل من قوات المحور كصديق حميم ويضمن له الحرية الدينية التامة والامان على نفسه وحقوقه. - عليكم فقط ان تحملوا هذا الجواز معكم. وهذا الجواز كاف لتحويل عدد كبير من الضباط والجنود من جميع الطبقات الى البلد.

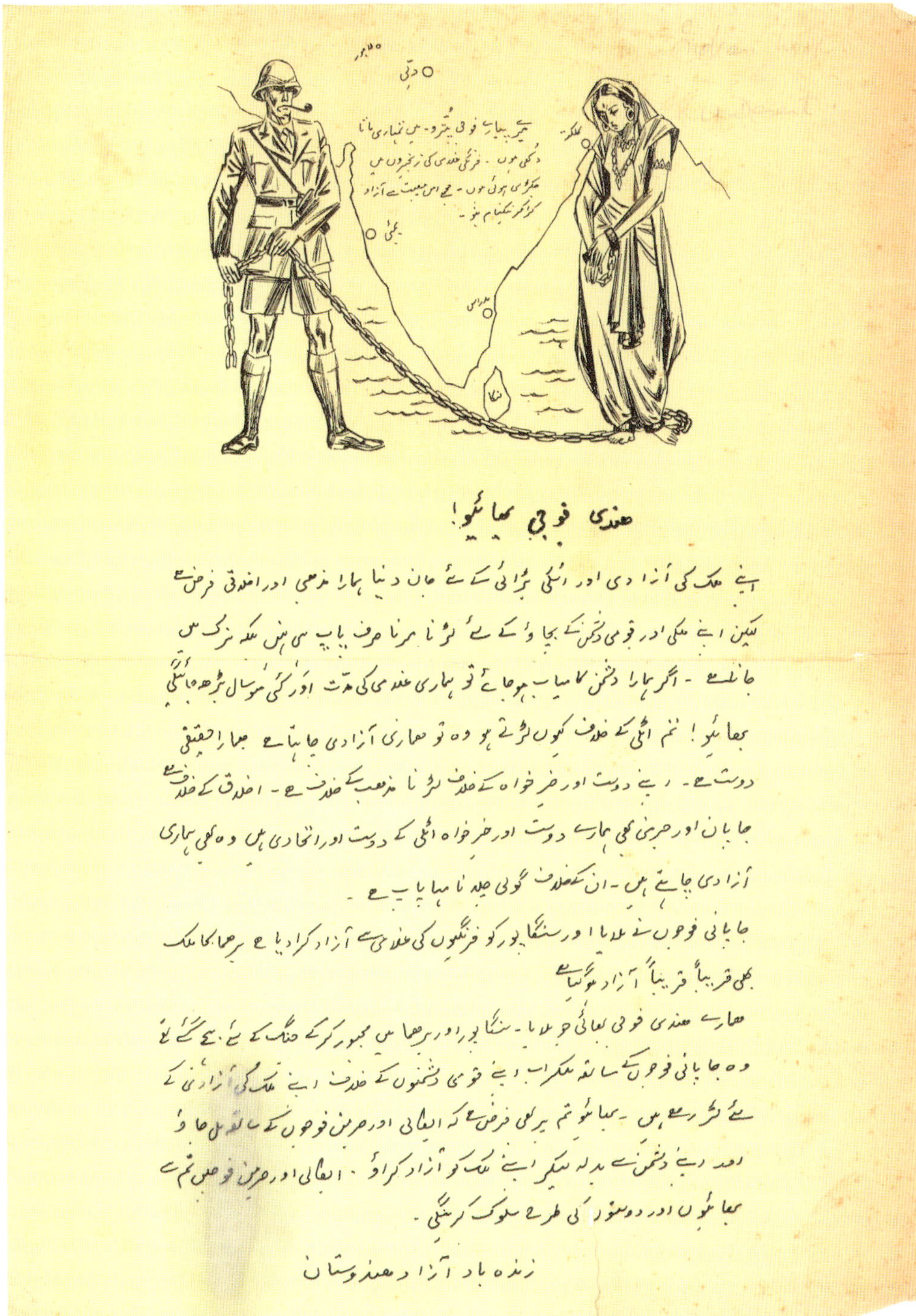

Axis propaganda leaflet in an Indian language showing a British officer holding an Indian woman in chains. This leaflet was obviously targeted towards the Indian troops fighting for the British and reads:

"Men of India

I am trapped by these people. Please save me and you will be thanked by God. I am your mother who is very severely harassed.

Brothers – It is our duty to die for our country. It is not a sin to wage war if it is done for good reasons. If we do not fight for our rights then we can be ill-treated for longer periods of time. Brothers! Why do you fight against Italy? Italy wants us to be a free nation and Italy is our friend. It is against our religion to fight a friend. It is wrong to fight in friendship. Japan and Germany are also our friends, we are all united. They also want freedom for us. To shoot them is a very big sin.

Malaya and Singapore were helped by the Japanese Army and who freed them? The Hindu troops (from Singapore, Burma and Malaya) were sent to war together with the Japanese troops – now they are all fighting for our country's freedom.

Brothers, it is your duty to join Italian and German soldiers and fight the enemies to free our country. Italian and German soldiers will treat you as their brothers and sisters … LONG LIVE A FREE INDIA"

Allied Propaganda Leaflet

The dead will not come home.

But the prisoner of war stays alive and lives to see his home again.

Africa 1943 or Germany 1944

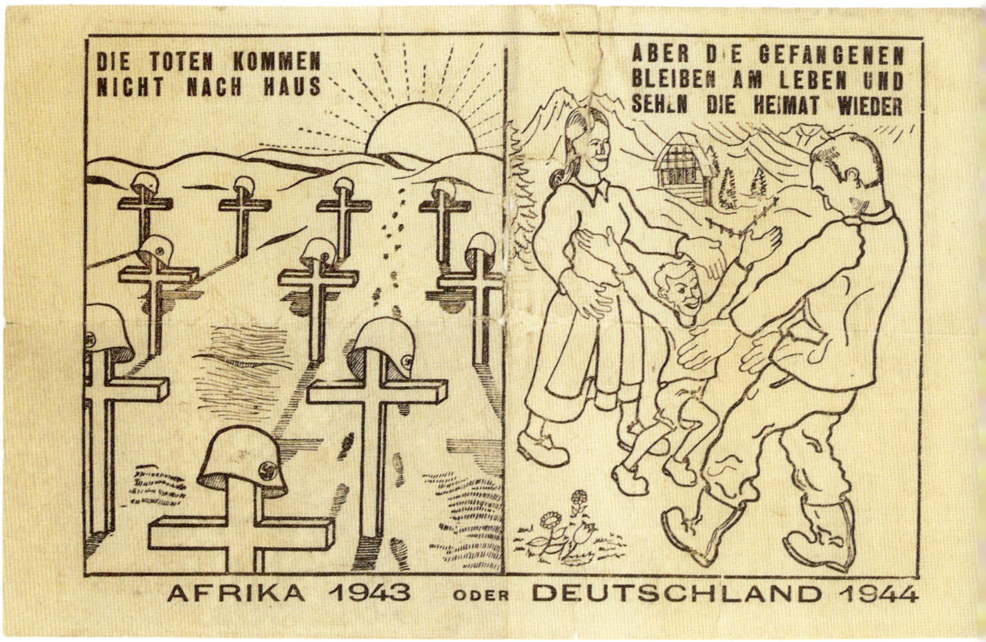

Allied Propaganda Leaflet

Surrounded

These were the German soldiers at Stalingrad. They fought bravely. More than 200,000 of them are dead. Half this number, including Field Marshall von Paulus and 21 generals, surrendered.

Who gained by the heroic deaths of so many?

Not Germany. Germany, which now faces an entire world under arms, has as good as lost the war. And it could have used those men in the peaceful task of rebuilding in the future.

The wives and mothers? No words are necessary.

The soldiers themselves? According to Hitler's words it was their duty to die. But the German people's order to every young German is: live for our future!

Surrounded !

So are you too in Tunisia. Tunisia has become a trap for you. And the more German soldiers that are lured into the trap, the more satisfied we are. For one day the trap will snap shut. What General von Arnim recently said applies to you: "No retreat!"

What will become of you?

Do you want to go home? The dead will not go home. Do you want to see your loved ones again? No one loves a cripple.

Prisoners, however, will stay alive and see their homes again. And the sooner the war is over, the sooner you will see home again.

For you, therefore,

There is only one way out!

Surrender!

This paper will allow you to pass safely through our lines. You will be well received and treated. After the war you will return to Germany.

This paper represents your best chance of seeing your loved ones again.

Make use of this paper. You will surely not be the first. For if you wish to avoid the fate of those lost at Stalingrad, there is only one way out of the Tunisian trap!

EINGEKESSELT !

Das waren die deutschen Truppen vor Stalingrad. Sie schlugen sich tapfer. Mehr als 200.000 von ihnen sind tot. Die Haelfte dieser Zahl, darunter Generalfeldmarschall Paulus und 21 Generaele, haben sich ergeben.

Wem hat der Heldentot so vieler genutzt ?

Deutschland nichts. Deutschland, das jetzt gegen eine ganze Welt in Waffen kaempft, haette den Krieg so wie so verloren. Und es haette in Zukunft diese jungen Maenner fuer die friedliche Arbeit des Wiederaufbaus so gut gebrauchen koennen.

Den Frauen und Muettern ? Es eruebrigt sich darueber jedes Wort.

Den Soldaten selbst ? Zu sterben war — laut Hitler — ihre Pflicht. Aber das Gebot des deutschen Volkes an jeden jungen Deutschen lautet : Lebt fuer unsere Zukunft !

EINGEKESSELT !

Das seid Ihr in Tunesien auch. Tunesien ist fuer Euch zur Falle geworden. Und je mehr deutsche Soldaten in die Falle gelockt werden, desto zufriedener werden wir sein. Denn eines Tages klappt die Falle zu. Wie Generaloberst von Arnim kuerzlich sagte, gibt es fuer Euch « Kein Zurueck mehr ».

WAS WIRD AUS EUCH ?

Wollt Ihr nach Hause kommen ? Die Toten kommen nicht nach Haus. Wollt Ihr Eure Geliebte wiedersehen ? Die Krueppel bleiben ungeliebt.

Die Gefangenen aber bleiben am Leben und sehen die Heimat wieder. Und je frueher der Krieg aus ist, [illegible] weniger [illegible] die Heimat.

Es gibt also fuer Euch —

NUR EINEN AUSWEG !

Gebt Euch gefangen !

Dieses Blatt erlaubt Euch, unversehrt durch unsere Linien zu gehen. Ihr werdet gut empfangen und behandelt werden. Nach Ende des Krieges kehrt Ihr nach Deutschland zurueck.

Dieses Blatt stellt ja Eure beste Hoffnung dar, dass Ihr doch Eure Lieben wiederseht.

Macht von diesem Blatt Gebrauch ! Ihr werdet bei Weitem nicht die Ersten sein. Denn fuer Euch, wenn Ihr nicht das Schicksal der eingekesselten Armeen von Stalingrad teilen wollt, gibt es aus der tunesischen Falle —

NUR EINEN AUSWEG !

PASSIERSCHEIN

To British and American Outposts : Any German soldier presenting this safe-conduct is to be disarmed and made prisoner.

Aux Avant-postes français : Tout soldat allemand qui présentera ce laissez-passer, sera désarmé, fait prisonnier et envoyé à l'arrière.

FRANÇAIS DE TUNISIE: Ceci est destiné aux soldats allemands. Faites qu'ils le reçoivent !

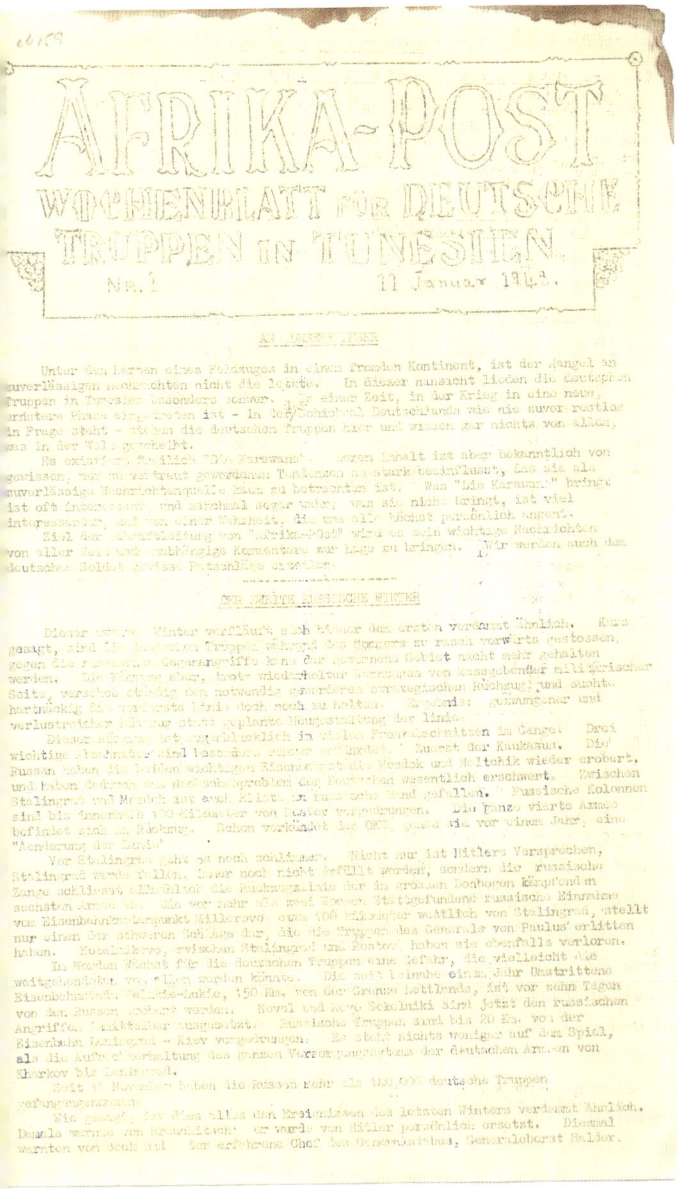

AFRIKA-POST

WOCHENBLATT FÜR DEUTSCHE TRUPPEN IN TUNESIEN

Nr. 1 11 Januar 1943.

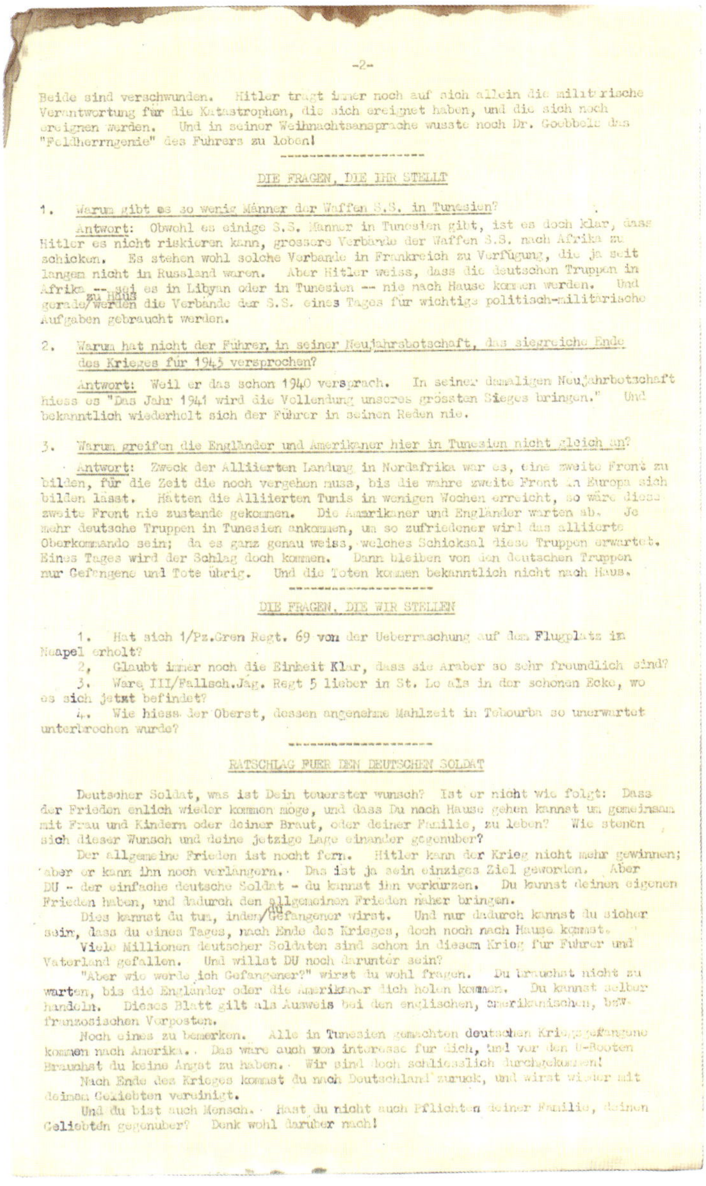

-2-

Beide sind verschwunden. Hitler trägt immer noch auf sich allein die militärische Verantwortung für die Katastrophen, die sich ereignet haben, und die sich noch ereignen werden. Und in seiner Weihnachtsansprache wusste noch Dr. Goebbels das "Feldherrngenie" des Führers zu loben!

DIE FRAGEN, DIE IHR STELLT

1. Warum gibt es so wenig Männer der Waffen S.S. in Tunesien?

Antwort: Obwohl es einige S.S. Männer in Tunesien gibt, ist es doch klar, dass Hitler es nicht riskieren kann, grossere Verbände der Waffen S.S. nach Afrika zu schicken. Es stehen wohl solche Verbände in Frankreich zu Verfügung, die ja seit langem nicht in Russland waren. Aber Hitler weiss, dass die deutschen Truppen in Afrika -- sei es in Libyen oder in Tunesien -- nie nach Hause kommen werden. Und gerade zu Haus werden die Verbände der S.S. eines Tages für wichtige politisch-militärische Aufgaben gebraucht werden.

2. Warum hat nicht der Führer, in seiner Neujahrsbotschaft, das siegreiche Ende des Krieges für 1943 versprochen?

Antwort: Weil er das schon 1940 versprach. In seiner damaligen Neujahrbotschaft hiess es "Das Jahr 1941 wird die Vollendung unseres grössten Sieges bringen." Und bekanntlich wiederholt sich der Führer in seinen Reden nie.

3. Warum greifen die Engländer und Amerikaner hier in Tunesien nicht gleich an?

Antwort: Zweck der Alliierten Landung in Nordafrika war es, eine zweite Front zu bilden, für die Zeit die noch vergehen muss, bis die wahre zweite Front in Europa sich bilden lässt. Hätten die Alliierten Tunis in wenigen Wochen erreicht, so wäre diese zweite Front nie zustande gekommen. Die Amerikaner und Engländer warten ab. Je mehr deutsche Truppen in Tunesien ankommen, um so zufriedener wird das alliierte Oberkommando sein; da es ganz genau weiss, welches Schicksal diese Truppen erwartet. Eines Tages wird der Schlag doch kommen. Dann bleiben von den deutschen Truppen nur Gefangene und Tote übrig. Und die Toten kommen bekanntlich nicht nach Haus.

DIE FRAGEN, DIE WIR STELLEN

1. Hat sich 1/Pz.Gren Regt. 69 von der Ueberraschung auf dem Flugplatz in Neapel erholt?

2. Glaubt immer noch die Einheit Klar, dass sie Araber so sehr freundlich sind?

3. Ware III/Fallsch.Jäg. Regt 5 lieber in St. Lo als in der schonen Ecke, wo es sich jetzt befindet?

4. Wie hiess der Oberst, dessen angenehme Mahlzeit in Tebourba so unerwartet unterbrochen wurde?

RATSCHLAG FUER DEN DEUTSCHEN SOLDAT

Deutscher Soldat, was ist Dein teuerster wunsch? Ist er nicht wie folgt: Dass der Frieden enlich wieder kommen möge, und dass Du nach Hause gehen kannst um gemeinsam mit Frau und Kindern oder deiner Braut, oder deiner Familie, zu leben? Wie stehen sich dieser Wunsch und deine jetzige Lage einander gegenuber?

Der allgemeine Frieden ist nocht fern. Hitler kann der Krieg nicht mehr gewinnen; aber er kann ihn noch verlängern. Das ist ja sein einziges Ziel geworden. Aber DU - der einfache deutsche Soldat - du kannst ihn verkürzen. Du kannst deinen eigenen Frieden haben, und dadurch den allgemeinen Frieden näher bringen.

Dies kannst du tun, indem du Gefangener wirst. Und nur dadurch kannst du sicher sein, dass du eines Tages, nach Ende des Krieges, doch noch nach Hause kommst.

Viele Millionen deutscher Soldaten sind schon in diesem Krieg für Führer und Vaterland gefallen. Und willst DU noch darunter sein?

"Aber wie werde ich Gefangener?" wirst du wohl fragen. Du brauchst nicht zu warten, bis die Engländer oder die Amerikaner dich holen kommen. Du kannst selber handeln. Dieses Blatt gilt als Ausweis bei den englischen, amerikanischen, bzw. französischen Vorposten.

Noch eines zu bemerken. Alle in Tunesien gemachten deutschen Kriegsgefangene kommen nach Amerika. Das wäre auch von interesse für dich, und vor den U-Booten Brauchst du keine Angst zu haben. Wir sind doch schliesslich durchgekommen!

Nach Ende des Krieges kommst du nach Deutschland zurück, und wirst wieder mit deinem Geliebten vereinigt.

Und du bist auch Mensch. Hast du nicht auch Pflichten deiner Familie, deinen Gelíebtén gegenuber? Denk wohl daruber nach!

A young British captain by the name of Con O'Neill was one of the most brilliant scholars of his generation, taking a double first at Oxford. After working for the British Diplomatic Service, he joined the Army at the outbreak of war in 1940 and entered Intelligence. In 1943, he joined the headquarters of the British 5th Army Corps in Tunisia and decided to "make a little propaganda." His first effort was "Afrika-Post Nr.1" which he personally wrote, had lithographed locally and packed into leaflet shells. Four leaflet shells were then fired over the German lines. "Afrika-Post Nr.2" was also duplicated. Due to the success of these two leaflets, they were followed by numbers 3 through 6 and were all typeset and produced in much larger quantities. This is a very rare "Afrika-Post Nr.1", the heading translating as "Weekly News for German Troops in Tunisia" dated January 11, 1943.

AFRIKA-POST

NACHRICHTENBLATT FUER DEUTSCHE TRUPPEN IN TUNESIEN

Nr 6 — den 8 April 1943

EINGEKESSELT !

8 April: So viel hattet ihr noch!

Studiert die Karte! So viel habt Ihr noch von Tunesien — oder so viel hattet Ihr am 8. April. Bis Ihr diese Zeilen lest, wird der Raum noch enger geworden sein. Schon greifen die Alliierten wieder an!

Die Mareth-Linie, die Rommel bis ins letzte verteidigen wollte, ist vor 2 Wochen von der britischen 8ten Armee genommen worden. Rommel zieht jetzt das Gros seiner Armee so schnell wie moeglich in den Brueckenkopf von Nordtunesien zurueck. Ihr muesst also einen Brueckenkopf ohne Bruecke verteidigen.

Ihr seid hier eingekesselt, wie es die 6te Armee vor Stalingrad war. Zwei Drittel der Maenner von jener Armee sind tot 100,000 — darunter ein Generalfeldmarschall, 23 Generaele und 2.500 andere Offiziere — haben sich ergeben.

Euch droht dasselbe Schicksal. Vor Euch steht dieselbe Wahl. Was nutzt euren Lieben zu Hause eine Verlaengerung des Widerstandes in Afrika, wenn Ihr dabei zugrunde geht?

VOR STALINGRAD VERLOREN

Viele von Euch haben in Russland gedient. Und da wart Ihr in den verschiedensten Einheiten und Divisionen. Es sollte fuer manche von Interesse sein, zu wissen, welche deutsche Divisionen in jenen dunklen Tagen eingekesselt und aufgerieben wurden. Wir geben hier die Liste:

Panzer Divisionen: 14, 16, 23, 24.
Motorisierte Divisionen: 3, 29, 60.
Leichte Division: 100.
Infanterie Divisionen: 1, 44, 71, 76, 94, 113, 295, 297, 305, 371, 376, 384, 389.

DIE FRAGEN, DIE WIR STELLEN

1. Wie viele Maenner des Feldbataillons T 3 sind an die Stellungen am Klingenberg zurueckgekehrt, die sie vier Wochen frueher verliessen?
2. Was ist aus dem Bataillon A 24 geworden? Oblt. Helmcke, der es fuehrte, hat das E.K.I. bekommen: aber sind a l l e seine Maenner tot?
3. Warum kriegen die Fallschirmjaeger hier in Tunesien so viele Ritterkreuze, obwohl die gewoehnlichen Grenadiere immer die schwersten Verluste erleiden?
4. Warum fuehlt sich der Hauptmann Kindler, Fuehrer des Pi. Zuges des Regt. Barenthin, immer krank, wenn eine Schlacht bevorsteht?
5. Wievele Generaele werden in Tunesien bleiben, und Eure Gefangenschaft teilen? Und wieviele werden gesund und munter mit Sonderflugzeugen nach Hause fliegen?
6. Glauben die Hermann Goering Grenadiere, sie werden lang genug in Tunesien bleiben koennen, um die Italienisch - Deutsche Erinnerungsmedaille tragen zu duerfen?
7. Sehnt sich der Lt. Jakobi, von 3/T3, nach dem wasserdichten Bunker, den er extra fuer sich hat bauen lassen, da vorn am Brocken?
8. Wirst DU, der diese Zeilen liest, Deinen Aufenthalt in Tunesien als Kriegsgefangener oder als Leichnam beenden?

AN DIE OESTERREICHER !

Folgende Zeilen wurden von einem Oesterreicher geschrieben, der fuer die Freiheit seines Vaterlandes in der englischen Armee hier in Tunesien kaempft :—

Ich liebe Oesterreich. Du, der Du von Goisern oder von Kindsberg, Schloeglmuehl oder Hinterstoder bist, wirst deine Heimat eben so sehr lieben. Warum erfuellst Du deine Pflicht nicht gegen das Land, das Deine Mutter geboren hat? Die Heimat ruft, die Heimat wartet. Wartet auf Dich. Deine Frau, dein Maedel, die warten auch dass Du gesund Zurueckkommst. Heute bist Du noch gesund, wer weiss was Morgen ist? Komme zu uns, und Du wirst die Deinen wiedersehen. Erfuelle Deine

AFRIKA-POST

Pflicht gegenueber der Heimat, bleibe am Leben, um Dein Land wieder aufzubauen. Zoegere nicht, heute hast Du noch die Moeglichkeit. Denke daran: Die Heimat, die Frau, die Mutter, das Maedel — sie warten. Sie warten fuer den Lebenden. Entscheide Dich.

WICHTIGE BEMERKUNG !

Einige deutschen Gefangenen haben erklaert, dass die Kameraden den Eindruck bekommen haben, sie duerfen erst dann zu uns ueberkommen, wenn sie einen Flugzettel als Passierschein haben.

Dieser Eindruck ist falsch! Jeder deutsche Soldat kann zu jeder Stunde zu uns kommen, ohne Passierschein. Jeder wird gut empfangen und behandelt werden. Es gibt keine Gefahr! Wir schiessen auf Euch nicht! Aber kommt unbewaffnet, und kommt wenn moeglich bei Tage an! Es ist nicht noetig, allein zu kommen. Je mehr, desto besser!

DUENKIRCHEN ?

Es gibt schon Zeichen genug, die deutlich erkennen lassen, dass das deutsche Oberkommando die Raeumung Tunesiens eifrig vorbereitet. Und es gibt andere Zeichen, die beweisen, was schon im voraus ganz klar war, dass das Oberkommando nur damit rechnet, einen sehr geringen Prozentsatz der in Tunesien kaempfenden Truppen nach Italien zurueckziehen zu koennen.

Die sehr grosse Mehrzahl von Euch wird also doch hier in Tunesien bleiben muessen. Und die wichtige Frage fuer diese Mehrzahl ist wohl: ob sie tot oder lebendig hier bleibt?

Wer wird gehen koennen, wer wird bleiben muessen? Wie wir annehmen, wird der Versuch gemacht werden, die Flieger, die Hermann Goering Fallschirmjaeger, Grenadiere und Flakleute (nicht aber die gewoehnlichen Flakartilleristen!), einige der Panzermaenner vielleicht und selbstverstaendlich die Generaltabsoffiziere zurueckzuziehen. Aber die gewoehnliche Infanterie, die richtigen Frontkaempfer, die hier in Tunesien am schwersten gelitten haben, und deren Mut und Geduld die deutsche Sache bisher getragen hat — s i e muessen bleiben.

Sie muessen bleiben und den Ring halten, damit die anderen in die Flugzeuge und Kaehne einsteigen koennen. Ihr Maenner, die noch das Ueberbleibsel von T3, T4 oder A30 bilden: Ihr Maenner von Gren. Regt. 47, 754 und 755 und Geb. Jaeg. Regt. 756: ja, Ihr Panzergrenadiere auch von Pz. Gren. Regt. 69 und 86: I h r geht nicht nach Haus! E u r e Aufgabe ist einfach: zu bleiben und zu sterben.

Dass Ihr bleibt, damit sind wir einverstanden. Aber w i r wollen nicht dass Ihr sterbt. Wir wollen unnoetiges Blutvergiessen vermeiden. Denn die Toten kommen nicht nach Haus. Aber die Gefangenen bleiben am Leben, und sehen die Heimat wieder. I h r habt die Wahl!

Ihr deutsche Jugend habt fuer Euer Volk eine andere Aufgabe zu erfuellen, als hier in Afrika zu sterben. Die Heimat braucht sie! Ist nicht der gute Deutsche gerade der, der das unausweichliche Ende des Krieges moeglichst bald herbeizufuehren sucht, um in Zukunft fuer ein besseres Deutschland arbeiten zu koennen?

542,000

Am 21. Maerz sprach Hitler am Heldengedenktag in Berlin. Er sagte, seit Beginn des Krieges seien von Heer, Marine und Luftwaffe insgesamt 542.000 gefallen.

Glaubst Du diese Zahl, deutscher Landser in Tunesien? Mehr als zwei Millionen tote Kameraden glauben sie nicht.

Sie sind fuer Fuehrer und Vaterland gefallen. Das Vaterland, die Heimat — sie wissen es nur zu gut. Aber der Fuehrer ist immer sehr beschaeftigt. E r hat es nicht gemerkt.

LANDSER BLEIB AM LAND !

Wenn die Raeumung Tunesiens so weit geht, dass auch Du an die Reihe kommst, so bedenke Folgendes, bevor Du ins Flugzeug oder in den Kahn einsteigst.

Die alliierte Luftueberlegenheit ist ungeheuer. Das wirst Du schon bis dahin zu spueren bekommen haben. Und die Bomben hoeren nicht, wie etwa das Arie-Feuer, an der Kueste auf. Sie werden Dir folgen. Fuer jedes Schiff, das in Sizilien ankommt, werden wohl 10 Tunesien verlassen haben. Absaufen ist kein schoener Tod.

Jagdflugzeuge koennen auch folgen. Und Du weisst, wie gut sich ein Ju. gegen ein Spitfire verteidigen kann. Auch unsere Flotte steht bereit!

Warum nicht lieber am Land bleiben, wohin schliesslich der Landser gehoert? Die Gefangenschaft ist barmherziger als der Tod.

Und wenn Du doch nach Italien entkommen solltest, wirst Du gleich wieder nach Russland geschickt.

AN DIE FUNKER

Manchmal habt auch Ihr Pause. Wenn das um 1845 Uhr deutsche Sommerzeit geschehen sollte, so schaltet in 34 Meterband an. Jeden Tag um diese Stunde bringt die « Stimme aus Amerika » Nachrichten in deutscher Sprache aus dem alliierten Hauptquartier in Nordafrika.

The sixth and last issue of "Afrika-Post" dated April 8, 1943 anticipating the pending destruction of the *Afrikakorps*.

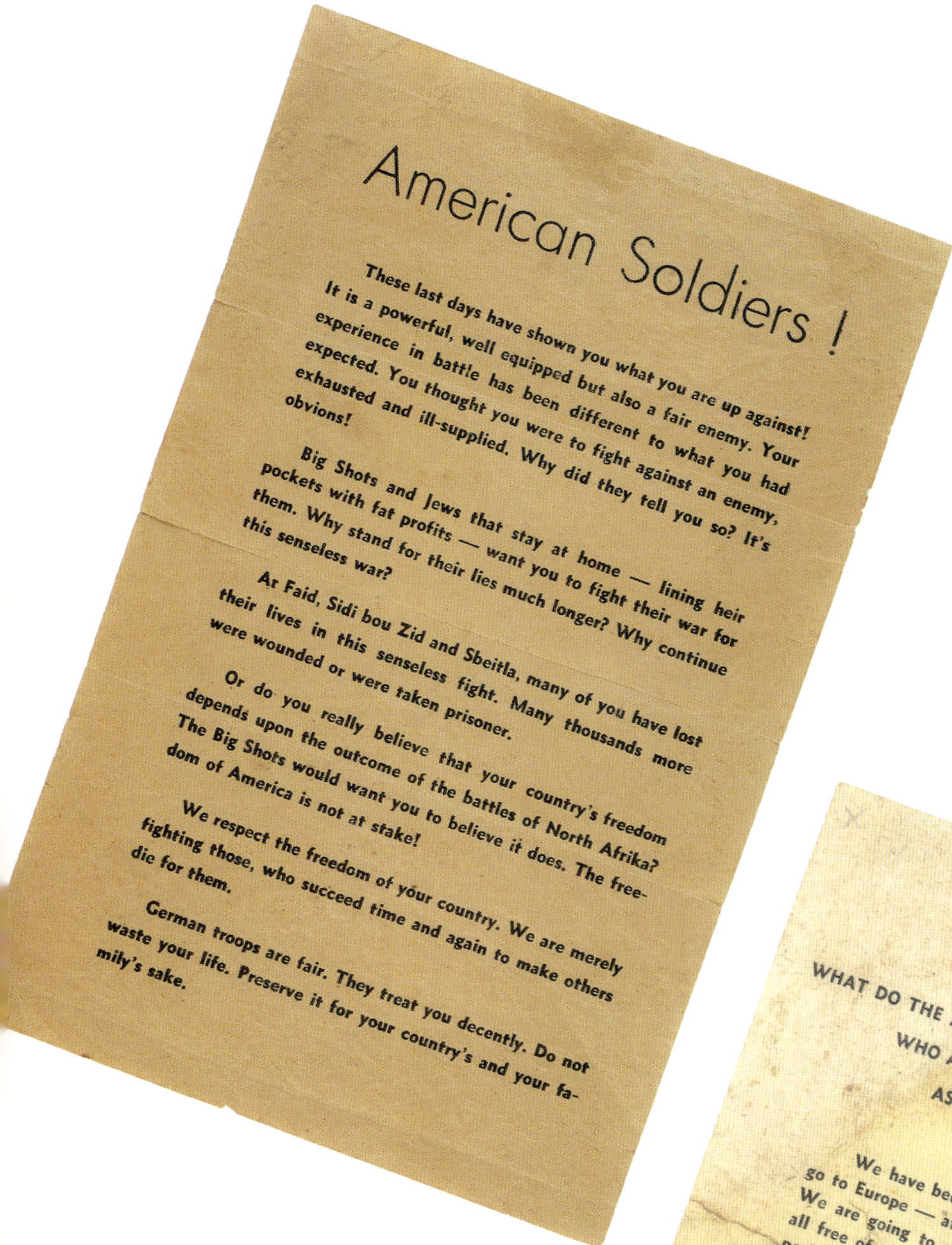

American Soldiers !

These last days have shown you what you are up against! It is a powerful, well equipped but also a fair enemy. Your experience in battle has been different to what you had expected. You thought you were to fight against an enemy, exhausted and ill-supplied. Why did they tell you so? It's obvions!

Big Shots and Jews that stay at home — lining heir pockets with fat profits — want you to fight their war for them. Why stand for their lies much longer? Why continue this senseless war?

Ar Faid, Sidi bou Zid and Sbeitla, many of you have lost their lives in this senseless fight. Many thousands more were wounded or were taken prisoner.

Or do you really believe that your country's freedom depends upon the outcome of the battles of North Afrika? The Big Shots would want you to believe it does. The freedom of America is not at stake!

We respect the freedom of your country. We are merely fighting those, who succeed time and again to make others die for them.

German troops are fair. They treat you decently. Do not waste your life. Preserve it for your country's and your family's sake.

A very rare *Afrikakorps* propaganda leaflet dropped over the Americans in 1943. This leaflet was picked-up by an American soldier in May 1943 ten miles east of Mateur, Tunisia.

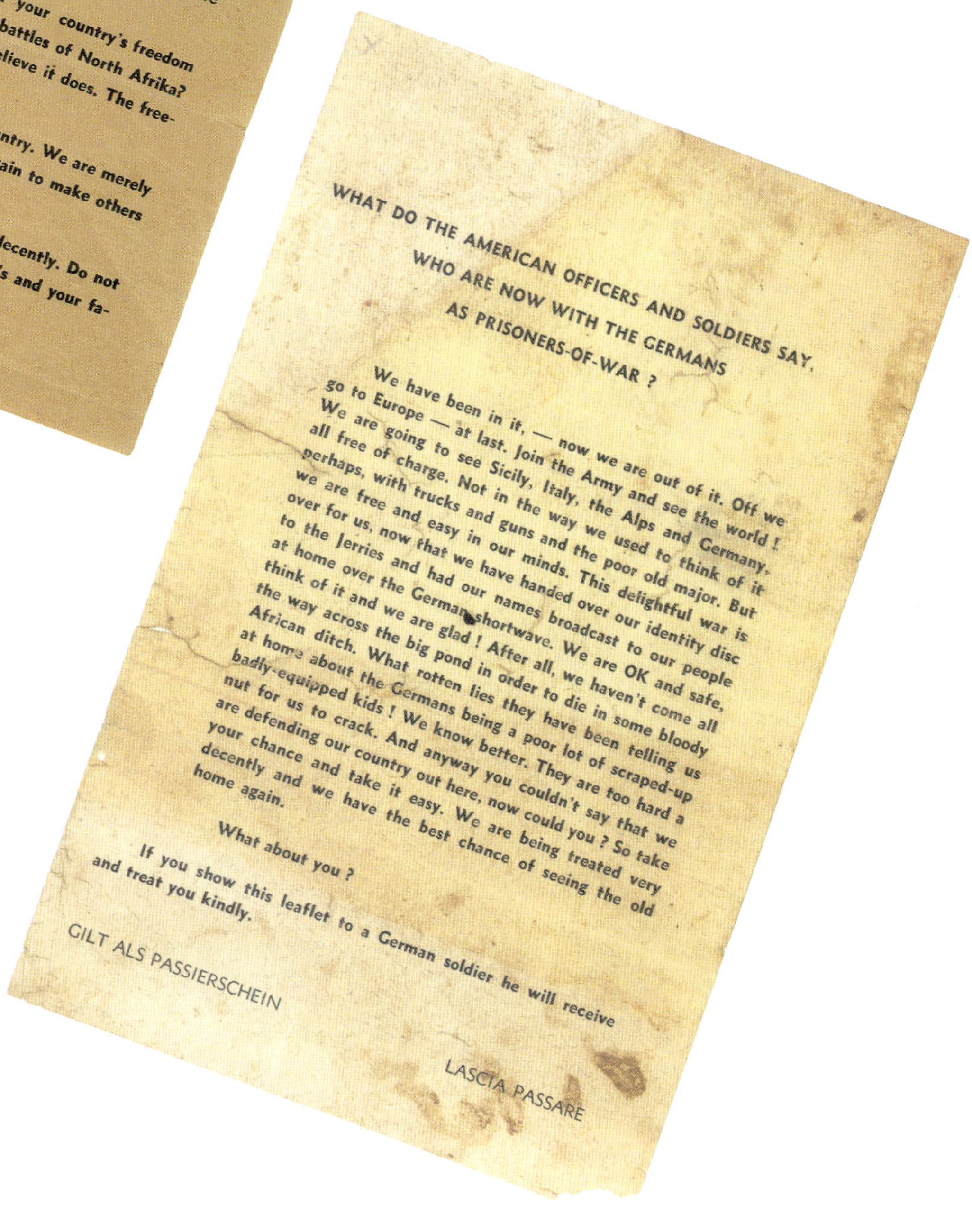

WHAT DO THE AMERICAN OFFICERS AND SOLDIERS SAY, WHO ARE NOW WITH THE GERMANS AS PRISONERS-OF-WAR ?

We have been in it, — now we are out of it. Off we go to Europe — at last. Join the Army and see the world ! We are going to see Sicily, Italy, the Alps and Germany, all free of charge. Not in the way we used to think of it perhaps, with trucks and guns and the poor old major. But we are free and easy in our minds. This delightful war is over for us, now that we have handed over our identity disc to the Jerries and had our names broadcast to our people at home over the German shortwave. We are OK and safe, think of it and we are glad ! After all, we haven't come all the way across the big pond in order to die in some bloody African ditch. What rotten lies they have been telling us at home about the Germans being a poor lot of scraped-up badly-equipped kids ! We know better. They are too hard a nut for us to crack. And anyway you couldn't say that we are defending our country out here, now could you ? So take your chance and take it easy. We are being treated very decently and we have the best chance of seeing the old home again.

What about you ?

If you show this leaflet to a German soldier he will receive and treat you kindly.

GILT ALS PASSIERSCHEIN

LASCIA PASSARE

...other rare *Afrikakorps* propaganda leaflet directed ...rds the Americans in 1943.

Afrikakorps propaganda leaflet aimed at the New Zealanders in 1942 to promote anti-British sentiment of the war.

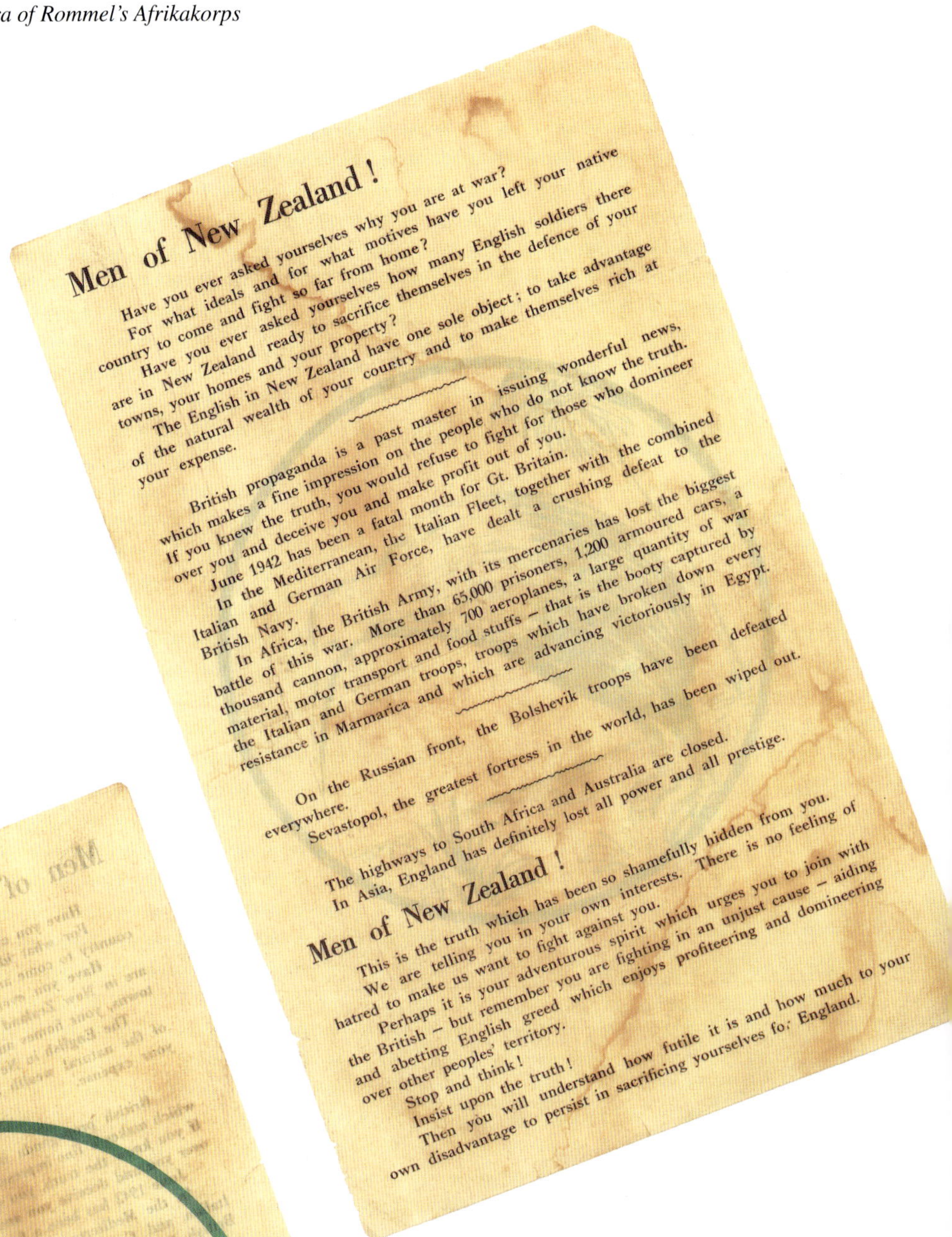

Men of New Zealand !

Have you ever asked yourselves why you are at war? For what ideals and for what motives have you left your native country to come and fight so far from home?

Have you ever asked yourselves how many English soldiers there are in New Zealand ready to sacrifice themselves in the defence of your towns, your homes and your property?

The English in New Zealand have one sole object; to take advantage of the natural wealth of your country and to make themselves rich at your expense.

British propaganda is a past master in issuing wonderful news, which makes a fine impression on the people who do not know the truth. If you knew the truth, you would refuse to fight for those who domineer over you and deceive you and make profit out of you.

June 1942 has been a fatal month for Gt. Britain.

In the Mediterranean, the Italian Fleet, together with the combined Italian and German Air Force, have dealt a crushing defeat to the British Navy.

In Africa, the British Army, with its mercenaries has lost the biggest battle of this war. More than 65,000 prisoners, 1,200 armoured cars, a thousand cannon, approximately 700 aeroplanes, a large quantity of war material, motor transport and food stuffs – that is the booty captured by the Italian and German troops, troops which have broken down every resistance in Marmarica and which are advancing victoriously in Egypt.

On the Russian front, the Bolshevik troops have been defeated everywhere.

Sevastopol, the greatest fortress in the world, has been wiped out.

The highways to South Africa and Australia are closed.

In Asia, England has definitely lost all power and all prestige.

Men of New Zealand !

This is the truth which has been so shamefully hidden from you.

We are telling you in your own interests. There is no feeling of hatred to make us want to fight against you.

Perhaps it is your adventurous spirit which urges you to join with the British – but remember you are fighting in an unjust cause – aiding and abetting English greed which enjoys profiteering and domineering over other peoples' territory.

Stop and think!

Insist upon the truth!

Then you will understand how futile it is and how much to your own disadvantage to persist in sacrificing yourselves fo: England.

The reverse side of the German leaflet directed towa the New Zealanders with a Kiwi bird.

A very rare English one-pound "bank note" dropped by the Germans over Egypt in 1942. It is a photographically reproduced note with a message in Arabic on the back aiming to undermine Arab faith in the British Empire and its currency.

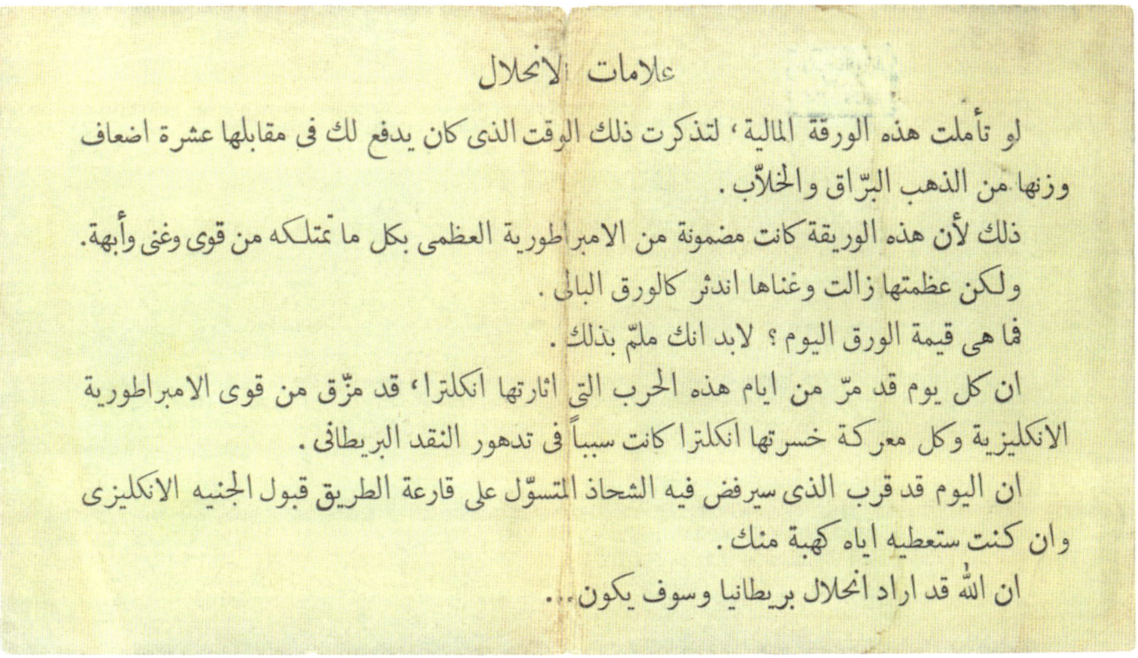

On the back of this reproduced British pound note is the following German propaganda in Arabic:

The Bank Note

If you consider this paper money you will remember the time when you could have given in its place ten small pieces of attractive shining gold.

That was because the note was guaranteed by the greatest Empire, which possessed power, riches and splendor. But her greatness has disappeared and her riches effaced like decayed leaves.

What is the value of this note today? You must be completely familiar with that.

Every day that has passed in this war that England chose, the power of the British Empire has been torn to pieces and each battle lost by England is the reason for the fate of British money.

Today we have nearly come to the time when the beggar at the side of the road will refuse an English guinea (or Pound Sterling) if you give him one. God wills the decay of Britain and so it will be.

CHAPTER SIX

Magazines, Books, Misc.

Signal was the most widely circulated German magazine in Europe during the war and was distributed in twenty languages. Dated June 1941, this issue is in French and depicts a German soldier well protected from the blowing sand in Africa. (David Bunch)

German *Signal* magazine in French with a front-page photograph of Rommel in Africa. (David Bunch)

...over of the Munich Illustrated Press. The caption reads: "On the ...ting front of the German Africa Corps. Orders are issued at a ...mand post." (David Bunch)

Cover of the Berlin Illustrated News. The caption reads: "Watchers on the palm tree." (David Bunch)

...over of the Berlin Illustrated News. The caption ...ds: "The African sun fries eggs." (David Bunch)

Cover of *Die Wehrmacht* dated December 16, 1942. The caption reads: "*The dash to Tunis.*" (David Bunch)

Cover of *Die Wehrmacht*, a weekly newspaper issued by the Armed Forces High Command. The caption reads: "*They were supposed to hold Tobruk!*" (David Bunch)

This October 21, 1942 issue of *Die Wehrmacht* had on its cover the much-celebrated *Luftwaffe* fighter ace *Hauptmann* Hans-Joachim Marseille getting ready to fly in his Me 109. The caption denotes his 158 victories. Before this issue went to press, Marseille was killed near El Alamein on September 30, 1942. (David Bunch)

over of another weekly German magazine with a photo of an *Afrikakorps* opaganda Company officer drawing a sketch in the field. (David Bunch)

Cover of the official *Luftwaffe* magazine *Der Adler*. The caption reads: "*African Interlude*." (David Bunch)

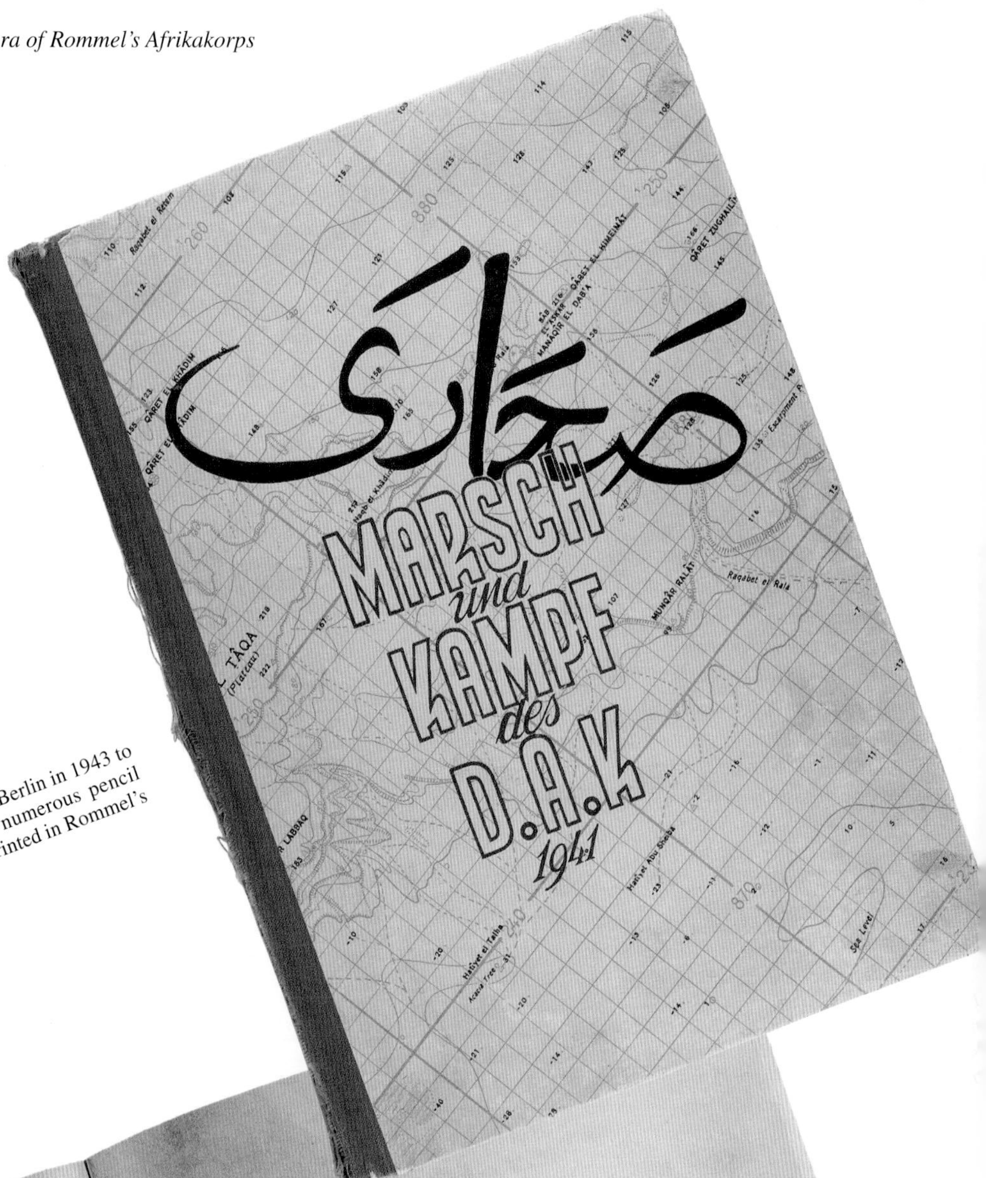

March and Battle - the D.A.K. 1941 was a book published in Berlin in 1943 to tout the early success of the *Afrikakorps*. The book has numerous pencil sketchings of various scenes in Africa. The foreword was printed in Rommel's own handwriting. (David Bunch)

A commemorative book on *Luftwaffe Jagdgeschwader 27* in Africa during 941-1942. Produced in Berlin, all the photographs were matted to the pages d presented in full color with captions. The foreword is dated Christmas, 2 with a printed signature of *Major* Neumann, the unit commander. (David ch)

Balkan Cross Over Desert Sands – a work of color photos of the Afrikakorps. Printed in Germany in 1943, this book honored the brave men of the Afrikakorps with an ending tribute to Hans-Joachim Marseille. (David Bunch)

Heroes of the Desert was another book published in Germany in 1943 to pay tribute to the German forces fighting in North Africa. The introduction was written by Erwin Rommel and has many color photos! (David Bunch)

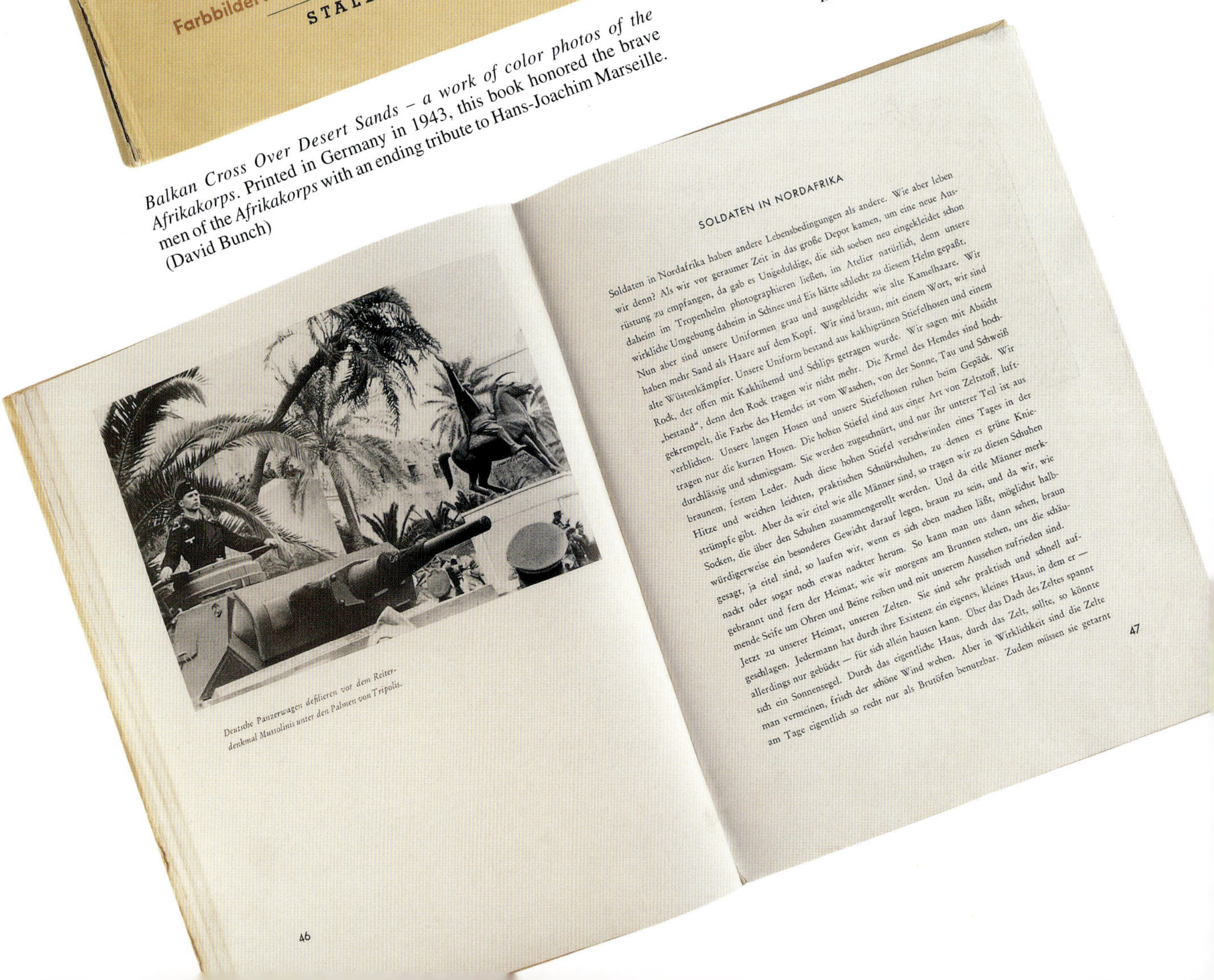

Deutsche Panzerwagen defilieren vor dem Reiterdenkmal Mussolinis unter den Palmen von Tripolis.

46

SOLDATEN IN NORDAFRIKA

Soldaten in Nordafrika haben andere Lebensbedingungen als andere. Wie aber leben wir denn? Als wir vor geraumer Zeit in das große Depot kamen, um eine neue Ausrüstung zu empfangen, da gab es Ungeduldige, die sich soeben neu eingekleidet schon daheim im Tropenhelm photographieren ließen, im Atelier natürlich, denn unsere wirkliche Umgebung daheim in Schnee und Eis hätte schlecht zu diesem Helm gepaßt. Nun aber sind unsere Uniformen grau und ausgebleicht wie alte Kamelhaare. Wir haben mehr Sand als Haare auf dem Kopf. Wir sind braun, mit einem Wort, wir sind alte Wüstenkämpfer. Unsere Uniform bestand aus kakhigrünen Stiefelhosen und einem Rock, der offen mit Kakhihemd und Schlips getragen wurde. Wir sagen mit Absicht „bestand", denn den Rock tragen wir nicht mehr. Die Ärmel des Hemdes sind hochgekrempelt, die Farbe des Hemdes ist vom Waschen, von der Sonne, Tau und Schweiß verblichen. Unsere langen Hosen und unsere Stiefelhosen ruhen beim Gepäck. Wir tragen nur die kurzen Hosen. Die hohen Stiefel sind aus einer Art von Zeltstoff, luftdurchlässig und schmiegsam. Sie werden zugeschnürt, und nur ihr unterer Teil ist aus braunem, festem Leder. Auch diese hohen Stiefel verschwinden eines Tages in der Hitze und weichen leichten, praktischen Schnürschuhen, zu denen es grüne Kniestrümpfe gibt. Aber da wir eitel wie alle Männer sind, so tragen wir zu diesen Schuhen Socken, die über den Schuhen zusammengerollt werden. Und da eitle Männer merkwürdigerweise ein besonderes Gewicht darauf legen, braun zu sein, und da wir, wie gesagt, ja eitel sind, so laufen wir, wenn es sich eben machen läßt, möglichst halbnackt oder sogar noch etwas nackter herum. So kann man uns dann sehen, braungebrannt und fern der Heimat, wie wir morgens am Brunnen stehen, uns die schäumende Seife um Ohren und Beine reiben und mit unserem Aussehen zufrieden sind. Jetzt zu unserer Heimat, unseren Zelten. Sie sind sehr praktisch und schnell aufgeschlagen. Jedermann hat durch ihre Existenz ein eigenes, kleines Haus, in dem er — allerdings nur gebückt — für sich allein hausen kann. Über das Dach des Zeltes spannt sich ein Sonnensegel. Durch das eigentliche Haus, durch das Zelt, sollte, so könnte man vermeinen, frisch der schöne Wind wehen. Aber in Wirklichkeit sind die Zelte am Tage eigentlich so recht nur als Brutöfen benutzbar. Zudem müssen sie getarnt

47

rikanisches Skizzenbuch" (African Sketchbook), this book entails a collection of rcolor sketches depicting various scenes and natives in North Africa. (David Bunch)

Rommel's famous book, *Infantry Attack*. First published in 1937, Rommel wrote of his lessons learned during the First World War. It was upon reading this book that Adolf Hitler (an infantry private in the German Army in World War I) took special note of Rommel's expertise and value. Even today, this book is widely acclaimed as a classic and is considered one of the best infantry manuals ever written. This edition was printed in 1943 and reflects Erwin Rommel's rank as *General-feldmarschall*. The inside front cover of this book was personally signed by Rommel. (David Bunch)

A small, illustrated publication printed in Munich in 1941 by NSDAP publisher Franz Eher. "Against England in North Africa", this small twenty-four page picture booklet was typical of most German propaganda inside the Reich during this period. (David Bunch)

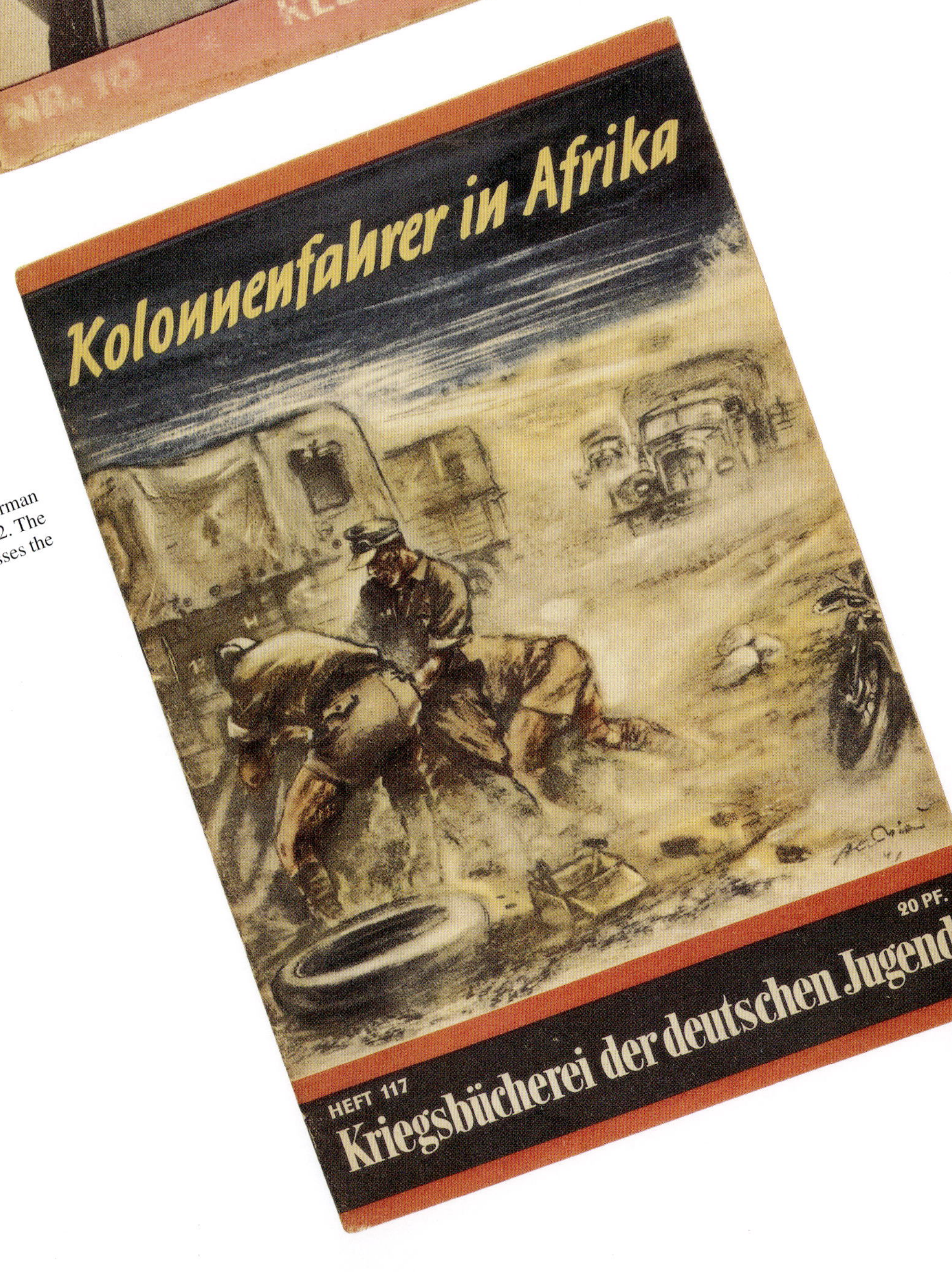

Issue number 117 of a series titled "War Library of the German Youth." They appeared weekly from 1939 through 1942. The subject title is "Column Leader in Africa" and it discusses the African campaign. (David Bunch)

Various watercolor postcards printed in Germany depicting fighting scenes in Africa. (David Bunch)

Opposite
This large propaganda poster was found in the back of an old Hamburg bookstore in the early 1960s. Designed to instill patriotism in the Reich, this poster depicts a Luftwaffe soldier in his tropical uniform with a paratroop standard. This photo image was also printed on postcards. (David Bunch)

The poster reads:

We stand firm, and where we stand
not one foot of ground will be yielded
without a struggle.
Adolf Hitler on 10 January 1933

A classic postcard of an *Afrikakorps* soldier with the capti "*Africa fighter.*" (David Bunch)

Published in 1941, a rare large songbook for piano and accordion of the famous military march, "*Panzer Rollen in Afrika vor.*" (David Bunch)

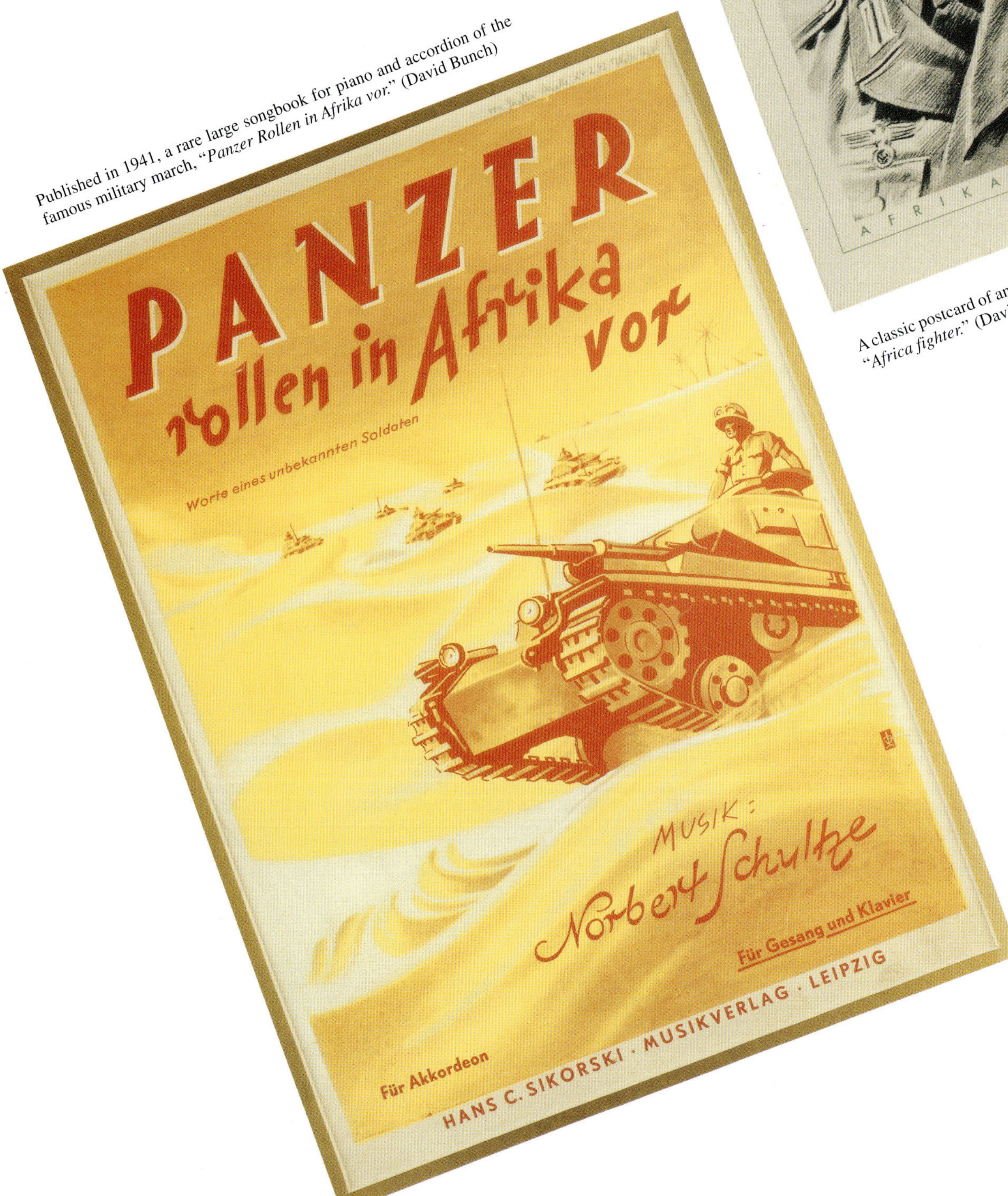

WIR STEHEN FEST UND WO WIR STEHEN
WIRD KEIN FUSS BREIT BODEN OHNE
KAMPF AUFGEGEBEN
ADOLF HITLER
AM 30. JANUAR 1933

ROMMEL

Na západ valí se nepřehledné davy do
Jsou to Britové a především Jihoafričan
nastavovati svou kůži za umírající Empire

Dne 25. června sdělila zpráva vrchního velitelství branné moci, že vojska Osy v severní Africe nastoupila k útoku. Tento útok předešel nepřítele, připraveného ke skoku. Boje byly těžké a rozhořčené. Dne 11. června je dobyto Bir Hacheimu, jižního pilíře v rohu britské fronty a tím se dosahuje rozhodné výhody. Pancéře a motorisované jednotky mocností Osy odbočí na sever, odříznou Brity a Jihoafričany v posici Gazala, překročí Via Balbia a dosáhnou u Acromy moře. Osmá armáda generála Ritchieho je rozlomena, část jí proudí do tobrucké pevnosti, část prchá k egyptské hranici. Již 21. června dobudou německé a italské svazy zteči Tobruku, fanalu britského odporu. 33 000 zajatců, nepřehledný válečný materiál a ohromné zásoby padnou do rukou vítězů. Z dřívějších bojů známé pevnosti Capuzzo, Sollum, Halfaya a britské zásobiště Sidi Barani na egyptské půdě jsou zdolány v bouřlivém

pronásledování a velké části prchajících Britů jsou
vaného střediska odporu Marsa Matruku. Ani tato
vati útočnému zápalu Osy, pročež kapituluje 29.
armády, jejíž velitel Ritchie je zbaven svého místa
sehnaných reserv generála Auchinlecka schytány v
slední to ochranné posici před deltou řeky Nilu, p
Vojska Osy stojí hluboko na egyptské půdě. Osmá
je zbaven svého místa, na „stratéga" Churchilla s
janů, pancéře, jež poslal na pomoc Roosevelt, neb
větši části zničeny. Suezský průplav, životně důležit
ohrožen.

Vítězný vojevůdce, generál polní maršálek Rommel, na svém velitelském voze v bitvě.

Protiletadlové dělo, opatřené kroužky na znamení většího počtu sestřelů, bojuje proti britským pancéřům přímou palbou.

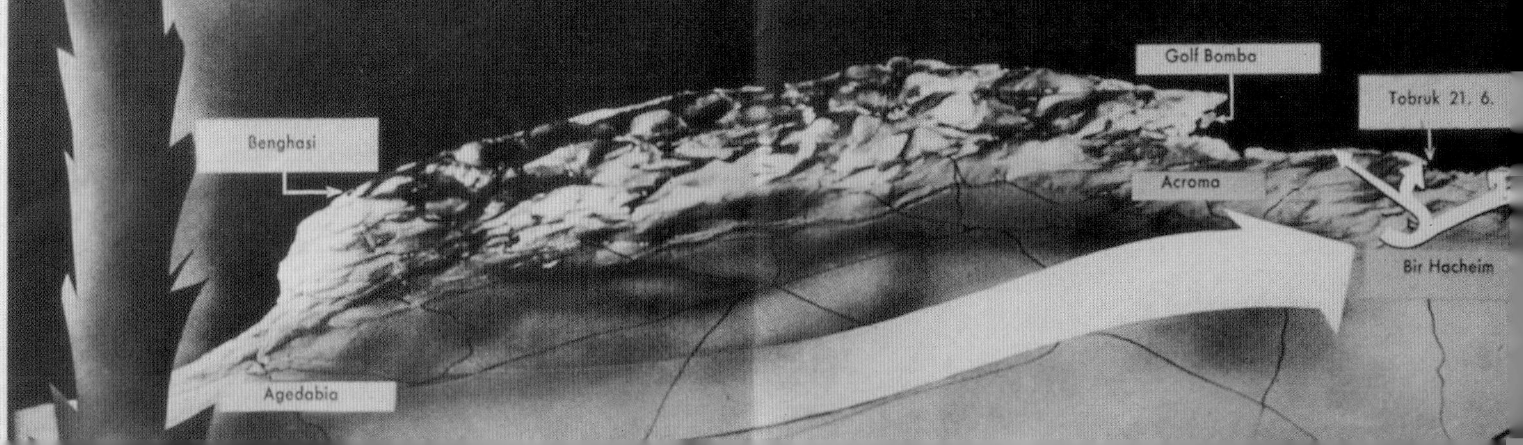

NE BRITY V EGYPTĚ

Na východ však, vpřed do egyptského prostoru, ženou se po tobruckém vítězství pancéře Osy k Marsa Matruk a El Alameinu, poslednímu obrannému postavení Auchinleckově před Káhirou a Alexandrií.

Letadla ke střemhlavému letu startují na letišti v poušti.

Pancéře a letadla, zničená leteckou zbraní a dělostřelectvem. V pozadí hořící Tobruk.

Italské protiletadlové dělostřelectvo bojuje proti útočícím anglickým letadlům.

Německý stíhací letec zaútočil svými palubními zbraněmi na pancéř a zapálil jej střelbou. Letci závodí s děly protiletadlového dělostřelectva a protipancéřové obrany vojska v ničení nepřátelských pancéřů.

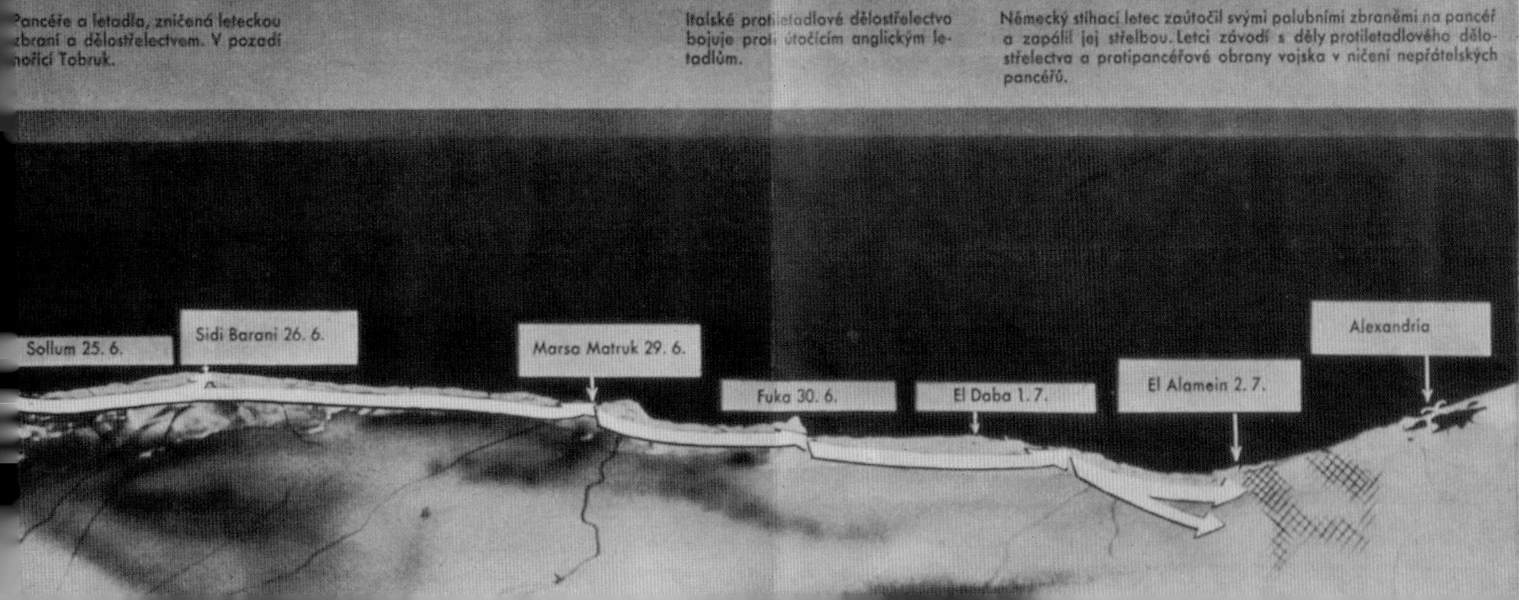

Pages 134-135
A very rare German propaganda poster printed in Europe and directed towards the Czechs in celebration of Rommel's success in Egypt. *General* Rommel was very popular in the Arab world and regarded as a "liberator" from British rule. Joseph Goebbels used his popularity among soldiers and civilians alike to create an image of an invincible *Volksgeneral.* These posters were printed in several languages to promote the news of British defeats in North Africa. (David Bunch)

Afrikakorps rings. A favorite souvenir to reflect a German soldier's time in Africa, these rings were custom made by local merchants and often displayed a variety of African scenes on each side while inscribing the famous *Afrikakorps* symbol on its top. (David Bunch)

Beer stein custom made for *Afrikakorps* veterans during the later part of the war. This stein ha
Nazi DAF maker stamp on its base and was made to honor those soldiers that had fought i
ny of the eleven campaigns listed on the stein. (David Bunch)

***Afrikakorps* Field Art**. This brass plate has been hammered and engraved into a simple tropical motif. The plate has a stylized *Afrikakorps* tactical symbol atop a North African Arab village. Below this is engraved "D-A-K 1942." The plate has lots of hand-chased ornamentation while the crevices have remnants of an old polishing paste. Small items such as these were often made by local Arabs looking to sell their wares. German POWs also made these trinkets to barter and trade with their captors. (David Bunch)

Extremely rare *Sonderverband 288* plaque hand-carved in Africa in early 1943. This unique plaque came from an *Oberfeldwebel* in a *Nachrichten-Abteilungen* (Signals Unit) of the infamous *Sonderverband 288* unit! (Helmut Weitze)

NOTES

NOTES

NOTES

Also from the Publisher

The Private AFRIKAKORPS Photograph Collection
of Rommel's
Chief-of-Staff
Generalleutnant
Fritz Bayerlein
P. A. Spayd & Fritz Dittmar-Bayerlein
A SCHIFFER MILITARY HISTORY BOOK